Celibacies

Duke University Press   Durham and London   2013

Celibacies

American Modernism & Sexual Life

BENJAMIN KAHAN

© 2013 Duke University Press
All rights reserved
Printed in the United States of America on acid-free paper ∞
Designed by Courtney Baker
Typeset in Whitman by Copperline Book Services, Inc.

Library of Congress Cataloging-in-Publication Data
Kahan, Benjamin.
Celibacies : American modernism and sexual life /
Benjamin Kahan.
pages cm
Includes bibliographical references and index.
ISBN 978-0-8223-5554-0 (cloth : alk. paper)
ISBN 978-0-8223-5568-7 (pbk. : alk. paper)
1. Sexual abstinence—Political aspects—United States.
2. Celibacy—Political aspects—United States.
3. Arts—Political aspects—United States—
History—20th century.   I. Title.
HQ800.15K34 2013
613.9—dc23   2013020977

To Mom and Dad | with all my love

Many people have their richest mental/emotional involvement with sexual acts that they don't do, or even don't *want* to do.

—EVE SEDGWICK, *Epistemology of the Closet*

Contents

Acknowledgments

This project's theoretical concern with the sociability of celibacy has more than translated into practice as writing this book "alone" has meant warm exchanges, intense debate, explosive laughter, and friends who keep intellectual curiosity from flagging. This vibrant introduction into academic life began when I was an undergraduate at Northwestern. I wanted to write a senior thesis that would combine my interests in American literature, poetry, and the early modern so that I could work with Jay Grossman, Mary Kinzie, Jeff Masten, Julia Stern, and Wendy Wall. An investigation into Auden's rewriting of *The Tempest* to engage questions of his American citizenship proved just the thing. Though the thesis knew nothing of the questions of gender, sexuality, or celibacy that would come to be at its heart, this project has never stopped receiving support and attention from my wonderful advisers and friends at Northwestern.

Like so many other people, I came to graduate school at Penn to work with Jean-Michel Rabaté and have never been disappointed. His support and guidance have always helped me to map the territory of this project, drawing its boundaries and finding its shape. I am grateful for one conversation in particular in which an offhanded suggestion saved me months of work. I am also deeply indebted to the other members of my committee, Charles Bernstein and Heather Love. Charles's unmatched facility with difficult poetry, help when it counts, and humor have been of inestimable value to this project. Heather has always given this project exactly what it needed: enthusiasm, encouragement, advice, and the deepest kind of engagement. Her inspiring example as a scholar has broadened my horizon of the possible, and her unparalleled mentorship has meant more to my life and work than I can ever express. *what's his work?*

Penn also blessed me with an unusually brilliant and wonderful group of friends and fellow graduate students: GerShun Avilez, David Copenhafer, Sarah Dowling, Jeehyun Lim, Mara Taylor, Cedric Tolliver, and Brandon Woods. Graduate school certainly would not have been as much fun or as absorbing without Rebecca Sheehan's endless good cheer and creativity. I am grateful for the kindness of Ian Cornelius's friendship and the tenacity of his grasp on this project's theoretical concerns. Joe Drury's wit has brought many smiles, and his sharp editing has smoothed many a transition. Greta LaFleur and Melanie Micir helped make Penn a rich forum for asking questions about sexuality. Josh Schuster has instructed me in the art of the manifesto—declaiming, proclaiming; I am ever his poetic coconspirator. His passion has touched many parts of this project.

I am tremendously grateful to many members of Penn's faculty (whose inclusion in an unenumerated list does disservice to the profound appreciation that I feel): Rita Barnard, Herman Beavers, Karen Beckman, Nancy Bentley, Margreta de Grazia, David Eng, Jim English, Jed Esty, Michael Gamer, Amy Kaplan, Suvir Kaul, David Kazanjian, Zach Lesser, Ania Loomba, Vicki Mahaffey, Jo Park, Kathy Peiss, Bob Perelman, Phyllis Rackin, Melissa Sanchez, Peter Stallybrass, and Emily Steiner. I especially want to thank Max Cavitch and Paul Saint-Amour. Max's surgical precision has improved the texture and thought of this project at the level of the word and sentence and brought the project's intellectual throughlines into sharper focus. The most difficult part of leaving Penn has certainly been knowing that I will have less time to learn from Paul's lively mind, eloquence, and poise. In the short period we've known each other, I have already accrued a tremendous debt.

The presence of two friends from graduate school—Dillon Brown and Jessica Rosenfeld—at Washington University in St. Louis made me feel immediately at home. Their equal parts intellectual energy, conviviality, and generosity are great gifts. Additionally, I am grateful to the other members of the Junior Faculty Writing Group: Lara Bovilsky, Dan Grausam, Marina MacKay, and Anca Parvulescu. During my time in St. Louis, I felt especially fortunate to have counted on the good spirits and friendship of Barbara Baumgartner, Ellen Crowell, Mary Ann Dzuback, Kathleen Finneran,

Andrea Friedman, Melissa Haynes, Bill McKelvy, Mike Murphy, Vincent Sherry, and Rafia Zafar. Certainly this project would be diminished were it not for my exchanges with Adrienne Davis, Bill Maxwell, Steven Meyer, and Julia Walker. Finally, Vivian Pollak's encyclopedic command of American poetry and winning ways really brought parts of this project and St. Louis to life for me.

My chairs when I arrived at Louisiana State University—Anna Nardo and Michelle Massé—believed in this project enough to allow me a sojourn to Emory University's Fox Center for Humanistic Inquiry before showing up at work. My postdoc at Emory enabled me to complete my book and soak in the wise counsel of my fellow fellows: Jennifer Brady, Christina Handhardt, Valérie Loichot, Ranaan Rein, Paul Stephens, Karen Stolley, and Angela Willey. Outside the Center, this project received support from many members of Emory's faculty, including Michael Elliot, Paul Kelleher, Rick Rambuss, and Benjamin Reiss. I am especially grateful to Jonathan Goldberg and Michael Moon for their mentorship and intellectual acuity. Undoubtedly the best part of my time in Atlanta was meeting James Mulholland. Reading and rereading my manuscript, James brought light and air to many of the book's most obscure passages. His keen organizational sense, fine ear, and piercing close reading skills were so essential that this book is scarcely imaginable in its present form without him. More than these prodigious gifts, however, James's passion for delicious food and strong drink made many an Atlanta night revelrous and refreshing.

This project was dramatically improved in its final stages at LSU and during my year at the University of Pittsburgh's Humanities Center. Talented graduate students like Stephanie Alexander, Adam Atkinson, Nathan Erro, Madoka Kishi, and Monica Miller have refined many aspects of this project. I am especially indebted to Jaime Cantrell for her expert research assistance. My indefatigable LSU writing group—Elsie Michie, Dan Novak, and Mike Cohen—and the guidance of Jonathan Arac, Don Pease, and Todd Reeser at Pitt have been valuable beyond measure. Chris Barrett's exhilarating arrival at LSU has been a seismic intellectual event. The energy and support of my colleagues at both institutions have been a dream come true. I am particularly thankful to count Sarah Becker, Dana Berkowitz, Bill Boelhower, Lauren Coats, Brannon Costello, Carl Freedman, Lara Glenum, Josef Horcáček, John Lowe, Rick Moreland, Lisi Oliver, Soli Otero, Pallavi Rastogi, Chris Rovee, Loren Schwerd, Sue Weinstein, and Sharon Weltman among my friends. My new colleague Michael Bibler has revealed himself to be one of my anonymous readers. I very much look forward to working with him. This project was sharpened enormously by his reading and that of my other anonymous reader. I am profoundly grateful to them both.

In addition to the material support of Penn, Washington University in St. Louis, Emory, LSU, and Pitt, this project has been supported by the Sophia Smith Collection. I also want to express my thanks to the staff of the Rosenbach Museum and Library, particularly Elizabeth Fuller, Greg Giuliano, Farrar Fitzgerald, and Mike Bersanti, and the staff at the Berg Collection at New York Public Library. Feedback and advice from a far-flung network of friends and colleagues often distant from my various home institutions have never felt far away; I would like to thank Ruben Borg, Marsha Bryant, Stuart Christie, Michael Cobb, Matt Cohen, Lillian Faderman, Jonathan Flatley, Susannah Gottlieb, Wendy Graham, Elizabeth Gregory, Marah Gubar, Cole Hutchison, Annamarie Jagose, Peter Jaros, Nick Jenkins, Sean Keilen, Michael LeMahieu, Chris Looby, Cristanne Miller, Dan Morgan, Sianne Ngai, Gayle Rogers, Bill Sherman, Valerie Traub, and John Vincent. J. B. Capino raised me from a young pup. Crystal Lake is the kind of true friend we all need and want. Through many academic migrations, it has been a great comfort knowing that Crystal's inventiveness, smile, and wisdom were only a phone call away. I prize Brian Glavey's thoughtfulness and feel lucky to have him as an interlocutor. Katie Kent's generous readings have proved instrumental in helping me to understand my project's largest stakes. I have been the beneficiary of Ann Cvetkovich's and D. A. Miller's legendary assistance and encouragement and know it to be not the least bit overrated. Additionally, I want to thank my editor, Courtney Berger. A great editor can help you see a project anew, pushing the scope of your claims, widening them when you long thought they could not be expanded. Courtney is precisely this ideal editor.

My family and closest friends have nurtured this project in countless ways. My friend Michael trained my ear to hear poetry sing for the first time, and I hope never to stop listening to that tune. Leslie is one of my greatest friends: fun, witty, and the most sensitive observer of people that I know; she has sustained me at many points during this project. Andy Gaedtke's friendship is the one indispensable thing that I hope never to have to do without. His dazzling intellect, dark humor, and general good nature have made virtually every aspect of my life and this project better. My parents, brothers, sisters-in-laws, and nieces have showered me with love. I cannot imagine a life made more full of generosity, patience, kindness, and warmth. In particular, I want to thank my mom for enthusiastically and carefully proofreading the entire manuscript. This book's pages are colored by her love.

CHAPTER 2 WAS FIRST published as "'The Viper's Traffic-Knot': Celibacy and Queerness in the 'Late' Marianne Moore," GLQ 14, no. 4 (2008): 509–35.

Chapter 3 was first published as "The Other Harlem Renaissance: Father Divine, Celibate Economics, and the Making of Black Sexuality," *Arizona Quarterly* 65, no. 4 (winter 2009): 37–61. Reprinted with permission from Arizona Quarterly.

Sign & signifier
- what is the constitutive antipode/binary for celibacy (linguistic theory)
- Can the subaltern speak? In what ways does celibacy occupy a certain subaltern status within discourse but those prominent celibates are anything but subaltern. (particularly from a class perspective)
- most compelling part was economic — like status & marriages of Father Divine. But how is locum identity instantiate or

Introduction | The Expressive Hypothesis

Let's talk about Love?.

The time has come to think about celibacy. There is a slipperiness to celibacy that we can't wrap our minds around. We always take it for a phantom or imagine it as something else. My invocation and rewriting of Gayle Rubin's famous call to "think about sex" is meant to draw attention to the ways in which celibacy is nominally positioned as the identical twin of sex. I will claim that celibacy is neither straightforwardly sex's opposite nor is it given an equal valuation. Celibacy is a sexual formation that even champions of sex and advocates of sexual diversity like Alfred Kinsey feel free to denigrate: "The great distortions of sex are the cultural perversions of celibacy, delayed marriage, and asceticism."[1] This project revalues celibacy as possessing special purchase on its putative counterpart "the sexual" (as all binary terms illuminate their opposites), arguing that in revisiting the meanings of the allegedly "nonsexual," *Celibacies* reorganizes, complicates, and expands our current theorizations of what counts as "sex" and what signifies as "sexual."[2] This project historicizes celibacy as a sexuality in addition to exploring celibacy's impact on and intersection with other sexual formations. *Celibacies* argues that attending to the diacritical specificities, meanings, and significations of celibacy enriches and recasts the histories of homosexuality, the women's movement, and modernism.

While this project is rooted in the modernist period, its efforts to pluralize the realm of the nonsexual respond to what I perceive to be an urgent demand in the present: namely, it acts as a riposte to the radical Right's

body? In particular what is the challenge of Madelon Moore and Andy Warhol + their bedroom working the shift toward performative/ public but are always unable to speak

Just discourses?

mobilization of discourses of abstinence to control the meanings of sex. By exploring celibacy's relation to sex, I argue that an abiding public discourse of and around celibacy was a powerful tool of the political Left at the turn of the century and can continue to be so today. My project retrieves this discourse, which has been disavowed by the Right and forgotten by the Left, in order to steal its potent abilities to think and define sexuality back from the political Right. Precisely because celibacy occupies and exceeds discourses of conservative and progressive politics by working between sexuality and asexuality, and between gender ideal and gender failure, the figure of the celibate articulates a new kind of sexual history in the United States that unsettles the familiar repression/liberation and normal/queer binaries.

The elusiveness of celibacy is partially accounted for by its definitional instability; its meanings are as variable and myriad as those of sex. Instead of creating a taxonomy of celibacies with separate and conceptually distinct entries, this project understands the meanings of celibacy to exist simultaneously and concurrently, operating under several epistemological regimes at the same time. These meanings share a family resemblance but are understood to carry different valences for different historical actors. This book charts a genealogy in which celibacy carries the following interrelated and historically coexistent but not coextensive range of meanings:

- Celibacy as a sexuality in its own right
- Celibacy as a synonym for unmarried
- Celibacy as a choice, performative, vow
- Celibacy as a political self-identification
- Celibacy as a resistance to compulsory sexuality
- Celibacy as a period in between sexual activity

As this list makes evident, several senses of the noun "celibacy" intermix and overlap, while other senses contradict and contest each other. I attempt to keep all of these historical differences, tensions, imbrications, and usages in view in mapping celibacy's theoretical terrain.

This project understands celibacy primarily as a coherent sexual identity rather than as a "closeting" screen for another identity. Queer theory tends to read "celibacy" as repression—referring to the celibate as a "latent," "closeted," or "unconscious" homosexual who has detrimentally internalized homophobia. Understanding celibacy as an act of self-censorship, displacement, insincerity, or failed homosexuality continues to construct the closet as an essentially private relation rather than one that, as Michael Warner argues, is publicly "produced by the heteronormative assumptions of everyday talk."[3]

Silence is performative, or at least identity forming

The Expressive Hypothesis

"There is not one but many silences," declares Michel Foucault in an oft-quoted assertion. Despite its frequent citation, this pronouncement usually remains unheeded as queer studies reads silence in only one way: reading the "absence" of sex as itself a sign of homosexuality. Queer readings tend to interpret "absence" (preterition, silence, the closet, the love that dare not speak its name, the "impossibility" of lesbian sex) as "evidence" of same-sex eroticism, covering over our ability to read actual absences of sex. By thinking of celibacy as a sexuality rather than as an internalized homophobia or as a fig leaf for homosexuality, my project reconfigures the epistemology of the closet, understanding celibacy not as an absence or as a stigmatized identity but in positive terms as an attractive identity with its own desires and pleasures. While the epistemology of the closet is an epistemology of the open secret, celibacy offers an epistemology of the empty secret.[5] While we ought to think of celibacy within the confines of Sedgwick's epistemology of the closet (as she does in her reading of Thackeray), this project charts a historicized celibacy which occupies a position that is neither in nor out of the closet.[6] Rather than understanding celibacy as primarily a practice of the closet, *Celibacies* sees it intersecting closetedness on a separate axis of meaning. The very real tension between celibate and queer ways of reading is indicative of more than a hermeneutic question—this divergence maps competing and overlapping sexual ideologies and cultures. The gravitational force of LGBT identity politics has led to the privileging of queer reading over celibate reading because celibacy has no constituency (the celibate is no longer a recognizable identity).[7] This political configuration points us toward the *least* queer aspect of queer theory: its tendency to turn other sexualities into same-sex alloeroticism.

Despite Foucault's pervasive influence, we still have not fully grappled with the immense challenge that the repressive hypothesis poses—namely, how can sexuality studies avoid positioning itself opposite silence, repression, and power? Foucault describes this problem as that of the "speaker's benefit": "What sustains our eagerness to speak of sex in terms of repression is doubtless this opportunity to speak out against the powers that be, to utter truths and promise bliss, to link together enlightenment, liberation and manifold pleasures."[8] Celibacy's unique position on the margins of sexual expression and its implication in regimes of censorship do not promise the bliss or liberation of defying power but rather take up Foucault's challenge to speak within power and censorship. Like Foucault, who resists seeing "defenses, censorships, [and] denials" in merely negative terms, I understand celibacy as an organization of pleasure rather than a failure, renunciation, or even ascesis of pleasure (though I also read it in these terms).[9]

I believe that this understanding of celibacy not only will help us to rethink how we do queer work now but also will alter how we understand the history of the field—particularly the testing of the "repressive hypothesis" by the "sex wars" and the ongoing AIDS crisis. The sex wars divided feminists, staging a battle over the significance of pornography between antipornography feminists and pro-sex feminists. The antipornography feminists aligned themselves with conservative activists and understood pornographic depictions of women to be the primary cause of female oppression. As Lisa Duggan's essay "Censorship in the Name of Feminism" (1984) helpfully explains, "given these views" that "pornography is at the root of virtually every form of exploitation and discrimination known to women," "it is not surprising that they would turn eventually to censorship."[10] As Duggan suggests, pro-sex feminists understood pornographic representations of women to be superstructural issues, peripheral to the core reasons for female subjugation. The debates establish a dichotomy (which queer theory inherits) between censorship and conservative politics on the one hand, and expression and oppositional liberal politics on the other.[11]

In the United States, AIDS activism similarly valorizes expression over censorship, heightening the stakes of the sex wars by seeing expression not merely as the alternative to censorship but as the alternative to death. For example, Leo Bersani writes in *Homos* (1995): "It is as if AIDS, the devastating depletor of the body's energies, had energized the survivors. Look at us: We're still alive. We won't be made to feel guilty, we're having sex—lots of it—again."[12] Here, Bersani and the survivors create an equation whereby not engaging in sex is a capitulation to homophobic forces. Sex becomes not just desirable (energizing) but also a communitarian necessity. The AIDS survivors' articulation through sex, and the sex wars' coupling of expression with radical politics, stand as two key moments that attempt to resist the long history of censorship and silence around queer subjects and knowledges.

Unfortunately, this struggle has created a reaction formation that I call "the expressive hypothesis." The expressive hypothesis posits that the regimes of censorship (the closet, antipornography feminists, etc.) create not only a proliferation of sexual discourse (as Foucault's discussion of "the repressive hypothesis" suggests) but also a proliferation of perceived sexual expression.[13] That is, employing a paranoid hermeneutic that "reads through" censorship to recover sexual expression—in order to make sure that one's sexual identities, desires, and pleasures never fall victim to suppression—inadvertently reduces possible connotations into a single denotative reality. The expressive hypothesis's crusade against censorship leaves no room for sexuality that does not aspire to normative sexual acts. Sex and sexuality have become conflated. Following Wendy Brown's reading of Foucault, we might see the expressive hypothesis as exemplary of a discourse that simultaneously binds and emancipates us.[14]

Along these lines, Sedgwick's essay "Paranoid Reading and Reparative Reading, or, You're So Paranoid, You Probably Think This Essay Is about You" (1997) states: "Paranoia thus became by the mid-1980s a privileged *object* of antihomophobic theory."[15] If we read Sedgwick's turn away from paranoia as implying that queer theory has become a (too) "strong theory," or at least as calling for a strong theory with a different, less negative affect, then we might attempt, as Sedgwick does, to locate places in queer theory that read differently. John Shoptaw's reading of John Ashbery, which does not attempt to "finally crack or unlock" because "Ashbery's poetry contains no secret," provides one such example of what I am calling a "depthless hermeneutic."[16] In opposition to symptomatic reading, depthless reading does not try to decode queer content. This hermeneutic practice leaves the knottedness of coding and difficulty intact, reading the blockage not as an impediment obstructing a flow elsewhere but as an elegant formation in and of itself.[17] *Celibacies* reads with such a depthless lens alongside the symptomatic modes of reading that have defined the field of queer studies. In particular, this project has been influenced by lesbian studies' attempts to materialize the apparitional, invisible, insignificant, unlikely, impossible, and spectral lesbian who haunts lesbian historiography.[18] My work builds on these scholars' efforts to read sexuality and desire where they are made most invisible by cultural norms that foreclose the possibility of visibility.

This reading practice of depth and depthlessness is crucial to capturing celibacy's play along the edge of the intelligible. Etymologically, celibacy does not distinguish between someone who is single and someone

Célibataire vs. so Hero

who abstains from sexual acts. This indeterminacy is precisely what makes celibacy such a suspect sexual identity—outside of ecclesiastical institutions (themselves seen as old-fashioned), celibacy fails to fit into modern frameworks of determined and determinate sexuality. In the rare instance when celibacy is understood as an identity (as opposed to being seen as an absence of sexuality), scholars usually understand it as a placeholder that does not have a particular content or a particular character the way that other sexualities do. Rather than affirm it as an identity, celibacy is understood to be entirely potential; its future is unwritten. Bachelors need to be "confirmed," but even such a confirmation is only partial in its containment of the threat of indeterminacy.[19] Thus, the celibate is uncommitted; he or she can take on any kind of sexual identity because celibacy *can be read* as accommodating multiple identities. This multiplicity often takes the form of socially objectionable desires—pedophilia, impotence, masturbation, and especially homosexuality—for which celibacy functions as a deflecting shield. While I will discuss this model of celibacy, which I call "the potentiality model," more fully in chapter 2, for now, I will say that this model often camouflages the history of celibacy.[20]

Celibate Modernism

The advent of the new modernist studies over the past fifteen years has redefined modernism not as a strictly literary system but rather as a mode of representation whose revolutions cut across political, cultural, philosophical, social, and literary landscapes. One of modernism's hallmarks is a profound capaciousness—open to aesthetics, subject matters, politics, and sexual cultures that fall outside mainstream semiotic systems. Literary modernism in its explicit interrogation of older models of representations provides a particularly sensitive barometer for staging the cultural encounter with, and structuring by, the sexual, helping us to chart period fluctuations between sex, gender, and sexuality. Additionally, literary texts provide a crucial site through which to focalize the theorization of celibacy because, as Heather Love has eloquently written, "literature accounts for experience at the juncture of the psychic and the social."[21]

Celibacy troubles one of our most familiar narratives of twentieth-century modernism. Narrating the well-known story of modernist sexuality, Joseph Boone claims that "libidinal currents," or what he calls "the general modernist rebellion against sexual censorship," have a "bracing impact" on modernist cultural production.[22] In Boone's narrative, sexual transgression is naturalized and fetishized as the quintessential modernist modality. For example, Stephen Spender's *The Temple* (written in 1929) describes the ultramodern Berlin as "a city with no virgins," one where "not even the kittens and puppies are virgins."[23] For many modernists, there is something about celibacy that is not conducive to the modern; George Bernard Shaw sees "celibacy [as] a worse failure than marriage," Friedrich Nietzsche understands "sexual abstinence" to be "dangerous," Remy de Gourmont sees "chastity [as] the most unnatural of the sexual perversions," and Mina Loy calls for "the unconditional surgical destruction of virginity."[24] *celibacy* ✓

While undoubtedly Spender, Shaw, Nietzsche, de Gourmont, and Loy have different relationships to celibacy, I want to focus on Loy because her *marriage* vociferous objection to celibacy foregrounds its then current circulation as a feminist strategy and because no modernist oeuvre that I know is as electrified by the concerns of sexuality, femininity, and maternity. In a letter to Mabel Dodge, Loy proudly refers to the eugenic removal of virginity as "*so daring*," foregrounding the central project of her "Feminist Manifesto" (1914): namely, the destruction of the restraints of purity and virtue. This letter makes the manifesto's Anglo-American audience clear (despite its composition in Italy)—referring to America as "the home of middle class hypocrisy" and drawing inspiration from Havelock Ellis.[25] For Loy, the "fictitious value" of "physical purity" renders women "lethargic in the acquisition of intrinsic merits of character."[26] The constraints of virginity are further underlined in two contemporary Loy texts: "Virgin Plus Curtains Minus Dots" (1914) and "The Black Virginity" (1915). In "Virgin Plus Curtains Minus Dots," for example, celibacy imprisons women ("Houses hold virgins"), preventing their movement and freedom, while men are mobile and free ("See the men pass / They are going somewhere").[27] Similarly, "The Black Virginity" depicts novitiate priests as "Ebony statues training for immobility."[28] In both of these poems, Loy's objection to celibacy revolves around stasis—it is wanting in the face of the movement, fluidity, and vitality of modern life.[29]

Motherhood is one avenue for Loy of gaining this vitality; she disparages celibate suffragettes who seek parity rather than maternity. Loy's derision helps us to bring celibacy's own history into focus: "Professional & commercial careers are opening up for you—Is that all you want?" While she claims that "the feminist movement as at present instituted is inadequate," the opening of careers points to the utility of celibate feminism even as

Loy finds it insufficient. In a way that I will discuss more fully later in this introduction, Margaret Fuller called celibacy "the great fact of the time" in "The Great Lawsuit" (1843) because celibacy was *the* necessary condition for middle- and upper-class white women's legal and financial independence. I do not want to cede modernist celibacy (or the celibacy of our own time) to conservative politics or what Loy calls "the rubbish heap of tradition." Rather, as Christabel Pankhurst's militant promotion of celibacy as a political response to male power makes clear, Loy's celibate enemy effected a revolution of its own, one that is far more foreign to our sense of modernism than Loy's valorization of "daring" sexual transgression. Despite Loy's diminishing remarks, celibacy emerges from her manifesto as a tool of female economic independence.[30]

Celibacies traces the emergence of celibacy as a crucial social identity in the 1840s and charts the evolution of this social identity into a sexual identity, narrating the transformation of chastity from a traditional gender requirement to a sexual practice that is itself the site of modernist innovation. This radical revision of gender scripts is particularly advantageous for disenfranchised subjects like white women and blacks.[31] My project recasts this hypersexualized modernism, focusing on a countercurrent of celibate modernism that draws its power not from revolutionary opposition to bourgeois sexuality but from appearing to follow the rules of normative sexual life exactly. Celibacy distorts the intention of codes of respectability, subverting them from the inside in order to launch a full-scale assault on a deeply inequitable sex/gender system. In short, celibacy forges respectability as revolution.

Even in those instantiations of celibate modernism that do not motivate a revolutionary or even progressive politics, like T. S. Eliot's essay "The Idea of a Christian Society" (1939), celibacy still has a central role to play in modern social life: "But so far has our notion of what is natural become distorted, that people who consider it 'unnatural' and therefore repugnant, that a person of either sex should elect a life of celibacy, consider it perfectly 'natural' that families should be limited to one or two children. It would be perhaps more natural, as well as in better conformity with the Will of God, if there were more celibates and if those who were married had larger families."[32] Here, Eliot attempts to normalize the celibate, mitigating gender and sexual failure as well as domesticating the celibate's revolution in these spheres by suggesting that married people reproduce on the celi-

(margin annotations, handwritten): non performative sex celibacy — what was celibacy? — mind and body? priest?

bate's behalf. Against the grain of Eliot's sex phobia and reactionary politics, his essay locates celibacy as crucial to solving modern problems and managing new anxieties of modernity.

It is my hope that the theories of celibacy and the celibate moderns described in my chapters bring a much larger concept map of celibacy into focus. Despite its allergy to celibacy, modernist scholarship has always charted figures who were sexually recalcitrant, indifferent, alienated, unattached, lonely, and lifelong or periodic celibates—a partial list of whom might include Gustave Flaubert, Emily Dickinson, Baron Corvo, George Santayana, Marcel Proust, Alfred Jarry, Rainer Maria Rilke, E. M. Forster, Franz Kafka, Edna Ferber, Edith Sitwell, T. E. Lawrence, Henry Darger, Josef Sudek, J. R. Ackerley, Jorge Luis Borges, Langston Hughes, Joseph Cornell, Eudora Welty, and May Sarton. Such a list could be further supplemented by writers like Comte de Lautréamont, George Moore, Pauline Hopkins, Willa Cather, Sherwood Anderson, James Joyce, Mina Loy, Marcel Duchamp, Henry de Montherlant, and William Faulkner who take celibacy as an explicit subject matter.[33] Given the strong association between "free verse" and "free love" as analogous enemies of propriety and convention, the prevalence of this international celibate modernism begs the question of form.[34]

Building on the work of Leslie Fiedler and René Girard, *Celibacies* maps what I call "celibate plots" alongside the more familiar courtship and marriage plot. Although there is no one formal feature that defines or signifies celibacy, I chart a family resemblance between this novelistic structure and celibate poetic forms in chapters 1 and 2. In addition to exploring celibacy's literary and social forms in modern America, this book examines celibacy as a central model for literary production within modernism. Taking a cue from Baudelaire's assertion that "the more a man cultivates the arts, the less often he gets an erection," *Celibacies* traces a long genealogy that understands celibacy as deeply ingrained in the history of authorship.[35] The sentiment of Baudelaire's claim is captured in psychoanalysis, where sexuality must escape in religious ecstasy or violence, or must take shape in art or be sublimated into sport. However, where Freud's ideal subject is the nonrevolutionary sublimated subject (the basis for charges of quietism against psychoanalysis), the celibate poses a threat, entailing a more radical withdrawal and reshaping of the social order than is the case with the recognized and validated sublimated subject.

Defining Celibacy

By refusing to understand celibacy as only an alibi or "beard" for homo-sexuality, I am attempting to nuance the important work of scholars like Chauncey and Sedgwick that effaces the bachelor qua bachelor by charting only his figuration in the history of homosexuality.[36] The massive influence of Adrienne Rich's "lesbian continuum"—which posits any relationship of "primary intensity between and among women" as lesbian—has meant both a greater melding of single women and lesbian identity than is the case with single men and a greater attention to "marriage resisters" and the non-sexual aspects of spinster identity.[37] I seek to reimagine this scholarship on singleness that has up until now misrecognized the proximity of the history of representations of same-sex eroticism and the history of representations of celibacy as identity.

I have for the most part chosen to use the word "celibacy" instead of "single" or "singleton" because the word "single" might encompass widow-ers and divorcees. In distinguishing between what Amy Froide calls "ever-married" and "never-married," I hope to chart the political motivations and social position of celibacy.[38] I use the term "celibacy" to mean both "abstain-ing from sexual acts," as it is more commonly used now, and "unmarried," as it was commonly used throughout the nineteenth and mid-twentieth cen-turies in order to disarticulate celibacy and queerness. Because of the taboo on premarital sex during this period—for white middle- and upper-class men and especially for women—celibacy, as the state of being unmarried, culturally registered as abstinence.[39]

Additionally, the term "single" as a marital status embeds an emphasis on marriageability, population, and heterosexuality.[40] This valence is not entirely absent from the word "celibate," as Simone de Beauvoir makes clear: "The celibate woman is to be explained and defined with reference to marriage, whether she is frustrated, rebellious, or even indifferent in regard to that institution."[41] While this project disputes Beauvoir's claim, it also seeks to understand her version of celibacy as a life stage preced-ing marriage. Similarly, the terms "bachelor" and "spinster" suggest the marriage market and the desirability of marriage. In relation to marriage, bachelors and spinsters are figures of gender nonnormativity. For example, Katherine V. Snyder's *Bachelors, Manhood, and the Novel, 1850–1925* (1999) argues that "bachelor trouble was, fundamentally, gender trouble. While they were often seen as violating gendered norms, bachelors were some-times contradictorily thought to incarnate the desires and identifications of hegemonic bourgeois manhood."[42] Here, the bachelor's dissident gender identity demarcates, defines, and critiques the limits of marriage, while at the same time embodying matrimonial ideals of happiness and domesticity.[43] The bachelor and spinster become the historical precursors *par excellence*—appropriated as feminist foremothers, queers *avant la lettre*, or marital exemplars—but seem never to have their own history, never being their own precursors. While both figures have been championed in these roles (even as their own contemporaries have charged them with "gender failure"), *Celibacies* tells their story for the first time.[44]

I have also generally avoided using the words "chastity" and "virginity" because, as Arnold Davidson has argued, "chastity and virginity are moral categories, denoting a relation between the will and the flesh; they are not categories of sexuality."[45] As a category, virginity has the additional problem of being strongly, though not exclusively, associated with women.[46] Occasionally, I use the word "chastity" to describe what Valerie Traub calls "the ideology of bodily integrity that secures the meaning and viability of reproduction for the heterosexual order."[47] While Traub's incisive gloss of early modern "chastity" as a conservative patriarchal tool employed to control women and their sexuality resonates with contemporary chastity movements, this project excavates less familiar, feminist versions of celibacy.[48]

One advantage and pitfall of the term "celibacy," as I use it here, is that it refers to both men and women. This project takes its cue from Herman Melville's short story "The Paradise of Bachelors and the Tartarus of Maids" (1855) by mapping the inequalities and disparities of the lived experience of celibacy between the sexes even as it brings them together.[49] *Celibacies*, thus, enriches the scholarly conversation about bachelors and spinsters (which has hitherto charted sexed singleness independently) by bringing them together without losing the specificity of these sexed histories and asymmetries.[50] The ubiquity of essays in the nineteenth century entitled "Married or Celibate?" begins to suggest that celibacy was conceptualized as a cross-sex category; this point is more colorfully illustrated by the title of Israel Zangwill's book *The Celibates' Club: Being the United Stories of The Bachelors' Club and The Old Maids' Club* (1898).[51] Such cross-pollination between bachelor and spinster identities is evident in the male identifications of Frank Norris's bachelor girl Blix, Emily Dickinson's imagined identification with that most famous of nineteenth-century bachelors, Ik Marvel, and Marianne Moore's appropriation of a "blameless bachelor" identity.[52]

While suffrage supporters are often masculinized in unflattering ways, male celibates are frequently effeminized. Quentin Compson in William Faulkner's *The Sound and the Fury* (1929), for example, says, "In the South you are ashamed of being a virgin. Boys. Men. They lie about it."[53] Here, virginity imperils southern virility. As Eric J. Sundquist has noted, Quentin defends his promiscuous sister Caddy's virginity in an effort to restore and revivify southern honor (a code that Quentin's father continually disparages) after such "rapes" as Sherman's march and Dalton Ames's liaisons.[54] Without success, Quentin attempts to remove himself from sexual economies *tout court*—"It's not not having them [genitals], It's never to have had them."[55] Quentin wonders why he cannot change places with Caddy—"Why couldn't it have been me and not her who is unvirgin?"[56] Here, Faulkner figures Quentin's virginity not as a force but an ineffectuality. Quentin's father tells him, "Women are never virgins"; this is literally an unlivable proposition for Quentin, contributing to his suicide.[57] Not all depictions of effeminate male celibacy are so castigating, as Marcel Duchamp's *Tonsure* (1919 or 1921) makes clear. As Giovanna Zapperi compellingly argues, Duchamp occupies the effeminized position of the priest (the flowing robes of which are associated with female dress) and reclining bachelor in order to protest wartime masculinity.[58] This gender-bending is even more pronounced in Duchamp's *Wedge of Chastity* (1954), suggesting that celibacy itself is a crucial modality of gender-bending.

Because the copious scholarship on nineteenth-century American bachelors and spinsters focuses almost exclusively on gender, this project will chart the content of and associated discourse around something like alloerotic "genital chastity."[59] As Bruce Burgett points out, the history of sexuality is often conflated with the history of genitality.[60] While my genealogy of celibacy as a nongenital sexuality intersects with familiar social and sexological organizations like voyeurism, exhibitionism, sadism, masochism, asceticism, and masturbation, it is not reducible to them.[61] For example, masturbation seems to have more to do with purity or chastity than with celibacy. While masturbation might be incompatible with these former two categories, celibates can masturbate (or not) with little impact on their identity as celibates. Additionally, I refrain from recuperating childhood as the site of celibate modernism (even as Joseph Cornell, Andy Warhol, and Marianne Moore are frequently described as "childlike"), in part, because, as Kathryn Bond Stockton suggests, we tend "to treat all children as straight while we culturally consider them asexual."[62] Asexuality, here, suggests a nonexperience or nonknowledge of sexuality that does not accord with the renunciations of desire and celibate desires that *Celibacies* charts. Rather, in decoupling sex and sexuality, I recover modernist sexual practices in order to offer an immanent critique of queer theory. At the same time, *Celibacies* deploys models of queer reading in order to challenge the traditional notion that sexual demonstrativeness and rebellion are essential components of modernism, enabling me to track celibate modernism to such surprising locales as Andy Warhol's marriage to his tape recorder and the wild dancing of Father Divine's followers.

Catholicism and the Roots of Celibate Reform

Celibacies begins in the 1880s—a decade that witnesses what I will argue is the demographic emergence of a celibate identity, the publication of Henry James's novel *The Bostonians*, and the advent of the White Cross Society in America—and ends with the Stonewall riots and transformations in feminist politics in 1969. While these temporal parameters enable me to explore celibate modernism, without replicating the already heavy emphasis on nineteenth-century America in the scholarship on bachelors and spinsters, celibacy gathers steam a bit earlier. Beginning in the 1840s, celibacy takes shape as a political identity for men and for women; nearly all the first-generation American leaders of the suffrage movement—including Margaret Fuller, Susan B. Anthony, Lucy Stone, and Antoinette Brown—took lifelong vows of celibacy.[63] While only Anthony would ultimately keep her vow, the long-term eschewal of marriage by Fuller, Stone, and Brown suggests the deep connections between celibacy and the culture of reform.[64]

Celibacy's emergence is coextensive with the explosion of virulently anti-Catholic literature in the antebellum period. Writing about this literature, Marie Anne Pagliarini argues that the independence of Catholic nuns (through their rejection of marriage and motherhood) contradicted Protestant ideas of feminine weakness and "signified a dangerous challenge to the ideals of True Womanhood."[65] Moreover, she suggests that the popularity of this anti-Catholic literature "should be understood as a response to this threat" and that the literature strove to undermine this empowering Catholic celibacy by depicting it as "the most flagrant sexual perversion."[66] Maureen Fitzgerald concurs with and enlarges this assessment, arguing that all Irish women, rather than just nuns, challenge Protestant femininity: "Their [Irish womens'] refusal to accept and emulate the gender system of the dominant culture constituted active and deliberate cultural resistance to the value system of the Anglo-Protestant middle class. . . . That challenge inspired the vitriolic surge of anti-convent and anti-nun literature in antebellum America."[67] Additionally, Fitzgerald argues that these attacks "distracted attention" from Protestant middle-class women's assault on the imprisoning "Cult of Domesticity." This assault took the form of Protestant women's increasing entrance into the public sphere through the women's movement, abolition, and other philanthropic organizations.[68] Pushing Fitzgerald's insight that Catholicism aided the progress of the women's movement, I will argue that Protestant women borrowed on and learned from the strategies of Catholic celibacy in order to create a culture of celibate reform, encompassing Protestant men and women, Catholic men and women, as well as individuals operating outside the aegis of religious institutions.

This culture of celibacy is tied to reform because marriage legally and economically disenfranchises women. To put this differently, white middle- and upper-class women's legal and economic independence is contingent upon their being unmarried.[69] Laura Hanft Korobkin's summary of period coverture laws begins to elucidate the relationship between female celibacy and politics: "Through coverture, a wife's legal existence was merged into that of her husband at the moment of marriage; a symbolic 'death' at the altar that extinguished her separate existence as a legal subject and created the fiction that husband and wife were one person. For the duration of the marriage, she was covered by her husband; all the property and legal capacities she formerly enjoyed as a *feme sole* passed automatically to him, and whatever rights, obligations, and entitlements might once have belonged to either now were his alone."[70] Here, Korobkin explicitly points to the much wider legal and economic freedoms enjoyed by the *"feme sole."* Because this connection between celibacy and nascent political identities depends upon coverture, might the erosion of coverture unhinge the two? In order to answer this question, we must turn to the laws largely responsible for the demise of coverture: the Married Women's Property Acts.

In 1839, Mississippi became the first American state that allowed women "to own the property they brought to marriage or acquired afterward by gift or bequest."[71] Spurred by the unprecedented inflation between 1832 and 1837, as well as by the financial panics of 1837 and 1839, this law began to disrupt the legal fiction of coverture, enabling a woman to own property in her own name.[72] By 1865, twenty-nine states out of thirty-six had passed a women's property law (though the specifics varied greatly by state).[73] And yet, the passage of the acts was not particularly revolutionary and might have kept the essential structure of coverture in place longer: "Though feminists had certainly worked for their passage, the acts won legislative approval by garnering the support of conservative businessmen who wanted to remove obstacles to continued commercial growth. Some scholars [Norma Basch and Elizabeth Warbasse] have suggested that in significant ways the gains from the acts were illusory; indeed, by seeming to guarantee equality and change while acting primarily to retain patriarchal economic and social power structures, the acts may have delayed more fundamental substantive progress for women."[74] That is, despite the ambivalent effects of these laws, the unmarried woman, the *feme sole,* would continue to subtend the formation of American female political identity well into the twentieth century.

This necessity for celibacy extends beyond legal theory into the practical difficulties of working. At the end of the nineteenth century, "marriage bars" required the dismissal of female employees upon marriage (called a white "retain bar") or the prohibition of the employment of a married woman (called a "hire bar").[75] These codes regulating the behavior of employees were strictest in the teaching profession but also posed significant problems for women seeking office work.[76] That is, the marriage bars mandated the incompatibility of female marriage and middle-class work. In order for a woman to work, she had to remain unmarried or to hide her marriage. Thus, celibacy is a dynamic feature of the middle class, not just a desirable attribute that the adjective "middle-class" describes but rather a force that constructs the middle class as such. These marriage bars began to ease by 1930; 20 percent of all office workers were married at this time. In 1928, the year of the earliest national survey, 52 percent of school districts had a retain bar and 61 percent had a hire bar.[77] While there is no previous figure with which to compare this, these figures (while still formidable) represent what is undoubtedly a relaxation of the marriage bars. Even in nursing—a profession that began to take on a more middle-class character with the opening of training schools in 1873—women were essentially required to be single.[78] In Susan Reverby's sampling of Boston nursing from the beginning of the twentieth century, she finds that 96.7 percent of nurses were unmarried.[79] This requirement for singleness is borne out in the imperative tone of the closing argument of Florence Nightingale's *Notes on Nursing* (1859), which cautions against the fantasies of "popular novelists" who depict "ladies disappointed in love" as the motive for entering the nursing profession.[80] She then underlines this requirement of singleness (while refusing failed relation) by comparing nurses to nuns. Because women needed to be celibate to access any kind of middle-class work, celibacy is at the very heart of the history of the American workplace.

And yet, this celibacy requirement paradoxically positioned women as unproductive. In Theodore Roosevelt's "On American Motherhood" (1905), he argues that volitionally childless people are not worthy citizens: "But the man or woman who deliberately foregoes these blessings [having children], whether from viciousness, coldness, shallow-heartedness, self-indulgence, or mere failure to appreciate aright the difference between the all-important and the unimportant,—why, such a creature merits contempt as hearty as any visited upon the soldier who runs away in battle, or upon the man who refuses to work for the support of those dependent upon him, and who tho able-bodied is yet content to eat in idleness the bread which others provide."[81] Part of what makes modernism's celibacy as dangerous to the status quo as sexual lawlessness is the threat of "race suicide" that preoccupied Roosevelt and many others. Race suicide is not merely the fear of species extinction but a particularly eugenic fear that inferiors (people of color, immigrants, poor people, social misfits, etc.) will continue to reproduce while Americans (implicitly white and of Anglo-Saxon stock) will die off or their numbers will be greatly diminished. I will discuss the relationship between race and celibacy more fully in chapter 3, but for now it is crucial to note that what Dagmar Herzog calls "the roots of the Religious Right . . . in antiblack racism" are still very much with us.[82] Herzog chronicles the New Right's emergence not in relation to *Roe v. Wade* (1973), as the Right prefers to remember, but in support of the tax-exempt status of a university that forbade interracial dating in *Bob Jones University v. United States* (1983). This eugenic mission continued as the Right coupled abstinence with welfare reform in order to keep unwed women of color (so-called welfare mothers) from having children.[83]

For Roosevelt, the spinster epitomizes, and in fact is the defining feature of, what Kathryn Kent calls "gender failure."[84] In addition to reading the Reconstruction-era spinster's failure to mother as signaling gender failure, Kent sees her as the embodiment of "emergent, queer, protoidentity."[85] And yet, where Kent refuses to read the spinster as occupying "unambivalently, or at all, . . . spinsterhood as an empowering identity category," I see the spinster as activating precisely this "radical feminist ideal."[86] Thus, celibacy has a particular content; it is a particular way of being in the world—a being toward independence, a being toward reform.

Lee Virginia Chambers-Schiller's important study *Liberty, a Better Husband: Single Women in America: The Generations of 1780–1840* (1984) marks the post-Revolutionary era as the moment when the "conjugal imperative" of mandatory marriage begins to subside.[87] She argues that a "Cult of Single Blessedness" emerges alongside the more frequently cited "Cult of Domesticity"; the demise of the conjugal imperative opens a space for a celibate identity within the symbolic order. Where the "Cult of Domesticity" constitutes women as morally centering family and home life through their own spiritual purity, Single Blessedness similarly posits unmarried women as moral centers, having the integrity not to marry for social or economic gain. That is, an unmarried woman was assumed to be able to marry but to have made a principled choice not to wed unless she found true love.

Reinflecting Chambers-Schiller's work, Zsuzsa Berend suggests that rather than rejecting marriage for personal autonomy or self-knowledge— as *Liberty, a Better Husband* suggests—women at the beginning of the nineteenth century did not marry because they idealized the institution of marriage.[88] In other words, their faith in the sanctity of marriage paradoxically prevented them from finding men who adequately met the criterion of true love and mutuality of soul. Berend claims that early nineteenth-century American women followed an ethos of usefulness, attempting to find the place—be it in matrimony or in a vocation—where they could be of the most service. Remaining single is better than marrying the wrong man; spinsterhood is better than fulfilling a conjugal imperative that is not supported by true love.

While the debate between Chambers-Schiller's protofeminist autonomy and independence of the self on the one hand, and Berend's autonomy through service to God on the other, remains unresolved by historians of the first three decades of the nineteenth century, these historians agree that through the 1830s marriage was valued over celibacy: "It [the didactic literature of this period] contained both a carefully constructed criticism of marriage (with the hope of institutional change) and a recognition of the potential richness of single life (without an unqualified affirmation of singlehood)."[89] Despite its nominal emphasis in Chambers-Schiller's account, this characterization is tremendously important for the historicization of the emergence of celibacy as a social and political identity. Chambers-Schiller helps us to hear the profound difference between Sarah

Grimké's *Letter on the Equality of the Sexes* (1837), which criticizes marriage in "the hope of institutional change," and the "unqualified affirmation of singlehood" in Margaret Fuller's "The Great Lawsuit" (1843): "We shall not decline celibacy as the great fact of the time. It is one from which no vow, no arrangement, can at present save a thinking mind."[90] In other words, any mind, of either sex, possessing independence is both celibate and interested in reform.

I have been suggesting that this assertion is remarkable for the way that it privileges celibacy over marriage (even as Fuller also values marriage), but it also astoundingly borrows on a Catholic model of independence.[91] Such borrowing from Catholic models is evident in another text from 1843 written by Catherine Beecher, one of the chief proponents of the Cult of Domesticity:

> I mused whether a time might not come when *Protestant* communities would not take some means to employ the piety, education and wealth among American females that now is all but wasted for want of some such resources as the Catholic church provides for women of talents, enterprize and piety.—In the Catholic church there is a notch for every one—the poor girl can find her post as a working nun or teacher—The rich and noble have places provided as heads of great establishments where in fact they have a power and station and influence which even ambition might seek.[92]

Here, Beecher is envious of this "wasted" Catholic independence, wishing, later in the same letter, for "some future train of operations" that would bring "*Protestant* women the means of extensive influence and activity."[93] This "time" that Beecher imagines will arrive does in fact occur in the 1890s when, in a usurpation of Catholicism, Francis Willard often referred to her supporters as "Protestant nuns."[94] While Beecher and other Protestant women's advocates might here draw on the strategies of Catholic independence, there is a marked difference between Beecher and the Catholic women religious she seeks to emulate: Beecher seizes independence for public life in a way that period Catholic women religious never did.[95] As Kimberly VanEsveld Adams's work makes clear, Fuller, like Beecher, consciously appropriated Catholic, particularly Irish Catholic, strategies of independence and valuations of celibacy over marriage.[96] This borrowing is not limited to these two women but is indicative of a much larger trend of Protestant women learning from a Catholic vanguard. American-Irish

Catholics' sex/gender system placed a much greater value on celibacy than on marriage and endowed celibacy with much more value than its Protestant counterparts.[97]

Celibacy was increasingly connected to the public life of reform and reformers. Whereas most sexual formations are associated with private interests (even as they have public elements), celibacy is associated with the public good. This disinterestedness suggests that celibacy is not just a public identity, but one that motivates (rather than merely instrumentalizes) styles of and performances of publicness. For example, a female speaker's avowed celibacy internalizes the period gender requirement that she be chaperoned (instrumentalizing celibacy) but also acts as an antidote to the negative image of women as licentious or untrustworthy or weak that partially underpins this decorum (motivating future performances of publicness). This association between celibacy and reform increased throughout the nineteenth century: unmarried women—a demarcation that encompassed both those who were single and those who lived in "Boston marriages"—led period social and political movements (suffrage, temperance, and social purity) and composed much of the rank and file.[98] Moreover, the association between spinsters and social movements was even stronger than their numbers indicated, both because they carried far more of the organizational workload than their married counterparts and because, as Laura L. Behling has expertly charted, women who tried to obtain political rights, particularly the right to vote, shared the spinster's association with gender trouble.[99] These intertwined social movements centered around suffrage because women believed that the vote would effect a total transformation of their lives.[100]

This emphasis on enfranchisement appears, then, to create a homology between the politics of celibacy and the politics of liberalism. However, celibacy is not, ultimately, a liberal strategy. As Arthur Riss points out, "Liberalism inaugurates the belief that if certain groups or individuals are refused civil and political rights, they can still appeal for such rights on the basis of their inherent status as 'persons.'"[101] Rather than appealing to the state, the celibates in this book either work to exploit the gaps in the state's regulatory apparatus to seize rights (rather than get recognized for them, as I discuss in chapter 4), or they establish alternative states (as I discuss in chapters 3 and 5)—a strategy that is also dependent on the state's regulatory blindness. Thus, celibacy sidesteps a problem diagnosed by a large body of recent work in feminist and queer theory: namely, that liberalism's protection of privacy and the home has obstructed from view the operations of domination that structure the so-called private institutions of family, household, intimacy, gender, and sexuality by writing them out of public discourse.[102]

While some celibates do draw on liberalism's strategies (I discuss one such exception in chapter 1), celibacy largely eschews liberalism's aspirations to privacy, instead garnering enfranchisement through the modes of publicness and embodiment that Michael Warner associates with the counterpublic. For Warner, a counterpublic is subordinate to and defined by its "tension with a larger public."[103] Its discourse "is not merely a different or alternative idiom but one that in other contexts would be regarded with hostility or a sense of indecorousness."[104] The celibates that I explore in this book desire more than enfranchisement, seeking to transform "not just policy but the space of public life itself."[105] In particular, they reshape the contours of sexual openness and transgression, the relationship between sex and race, citizenship, and a host of other public institutions and discourses.

These counterpublic strategies precipitated a crisis in conjugality, effecting a massive drop in the marriage rate that must be read as a concerted feminist protest against existing social relations and a demand for a new sexual order.[106] Between 1880 and 1920, the rate of unmarried single men and women grew by approximately 150 percent.[107] Women born between 1860 and 1880 marked the highest proportion of women who never married during the period between 1835 and 1980.[108] In cities this explosion of singleness was even more pronounced—approximately 40 percent of men over the age of fifteen were unmarried at any given time between the mid-nineteenth century and the mid-twentieth.[109]

While evidence of the historical occurrence of sex is notoriously difficult to obtain, the existing evidence suggests a strong relationship between the marriage rate and the occurrence of sex. The earliest known American sex survey, the Mosher Survey, features forty-five women, of whom 70 percent were born before 1870. The only question that attends to sexual knowledge before marriage—"What knowledge of sexual physiology had you before marriage?"—elicits answers ranging from "none" to knowledge from textbooks, friends, relatives, and animal observation. Not one of the surveyed women professes to have had any premarital sexual relations.[110] Similarly, John D'Emilio and Estelle Freedman argue that of the roughly 1,000 women who were of marriageable age before World War I in Katharine B. Davis's important 1929 sexual survey *Factors in the Sex Life of Twenty-Two Hundred Women*, only 7 percent had had premarital intercourse, and 80 percent thought such intercourse "was never justified for men or women."[111] These two surveys suggest a strong correlation between being never married and genital chastity. Without overemphasizing the usefulness or accuracy of these numbers (problems in reporting, possible undercounting of homosexuality, etc.), I want to suggest that they paint a broad picture of a relative synonymy between marriage and genital activity until at least the 1920s.

Thus, while celibacy seems to have encompassed men and women across the class spectrum, educated and more affluent individuals were more likely to be celibate. This is especially true of educated women, who formed a vanguard of celibate reform: "An extraordinarily high proportion of women [college] graduates never married. Of women educated at Bryn Mawr between 1889 and 1908, for instance, fifty-three percent remained unwed. For Wellesley and the University of Michigan, the figures were forty-three percent and forty-seven percent. The proportion among those who went on for advanced degrees was even more lopsided: three quarters of the women who received Ph.D.s between 1877 and 1924 remained single. Even among those who did marry, a significant percentage never had children."[112] Borrowing Raymond Williams's four-part structure of cultural change, I see celibate political identity as preemergent before the 1840s, emergent in the 1840s, becoming dominant in the 1880s, and residual by the late 1920s. This time line charts relatively affluent northeastern and Mid-Atlantic white Protestant men and women. Perhaps one reason that many of the texts considered in *Celibacies* are drawn from or set in New England and the Mid-Atlantic is that these regions have rates of celibacy that are double the national rate.[113] This number is increased when considering well-to-do white people.[114] My discussion in chapter 3 draws attention to the uneven production of celibacy, charting a different time line for poor black men and women. While historians and demographers debate the cause of this massive demographic shift, undoubtedly the lack of available men resulting from Civil War deaths played an important role. But what I am suggesting here is that celibacy's connection to reform made it desirable in a way that cannot be accounted for by mere statistics.

The popularity and prominence of celibacy are quelled, in part, by the economic concerns of the 1930s. Marriage provides greater economic security than celibacy. Additionally, as John D'Emilio has argued, the 1920s mark a key moment in the history of companionate marriage in which family becomes the locus "of satisfying, mutually enhancing relationships," making it increasingly attractive.[115] By the late 1920s, sexual happiness rather than just spiritual union was an expectation for married life, and celibacy was vilified as unhealthy and unnatural. As one popular marriage manual put it, "Celibacy . . . warps the soul and twists the inner nature."[116] Even the eminent left-wing critic Floyd Dell attacked the "inwardly compulsive careers of celibacy" in his *Love in the Machine Age* (1930) as "overcompensatory in their zeal" to transform the patriarchal family (which Dell felt could just be reformed).[117] In addition to changing economic and social landscapes, the political transformation of the successful passage of the Nineteenth Amendment in 1920 dealt a further blow to celibacy. So much energy was aimed at suffrage that its enactment left the women's movement disorganized and without a clear sense of purpose, leading to the dissolution of celibacy as a political identity. Additionally, as Margot Canaday has argued, unattached people were increasingly associated with homosexuality.[118] All these factors contribute to the demise of celibacy as a political and social identity throughout the 1920s and 1930s.

[handwritten marginal note: But Canaday proposes unattached might form ? new family AND this book controversial but visible celibate "marriage"]

The Emergence of Modern Celibate Political Identity

I have been arguing that more than any other text from the 1840s, Fuller's "The Great Lawsuit" theorizes the emergence of celibacy as a social practice that proposes to actualize sex/gender equality. Additionally, it contains the beginnings of the evolution of celibacy from a social identity to the sexual identity that it will become by the 1880s. Christina Zwarg importantly begins to examine Fuller's method when she suggests celibacy as "a site of feminist resistance."[119] Celibacy is the only solution for Fuller because the celibate is closest to God; this special relationship between celibacy and divinity builds on a long Pauline tradition: "The [unmarried] person *may gain*, undistracted by other relationships, a closer communion with the One."[120] Here, we must attend to the rarity in Fuller's "may gain": "How many old maids take this high stand [of closer communion with the One], we cannot say; it is an unhappy fact that too many of those who come before the eye are gossips rather, and not always good-natured gossips. But, if these abuse, and none make the best of their vocation, yet, it has not failed to produce some good fruit."[121] Here, Fuller suggests that celibacy is a largely unactualized potential, which, although it has "produce[d] some good fruit," has the power to transform the relationship between men and women. Seeing the celibate woman as more self-sufficient than her dependent married counterpart, Fuller argues that the celibate woman does not bear the supervision of her husband or the time-consuming burden of child rearing. These freedoms allow a greater independence and participation in public life, enabling celibate women to lead the way toward greater equality.

While Fuller is largely concerned with the transformative power of female celibacy, her emphasis on the non-sex-specific character of any "thinking mind" suggests that celibacy is a strategy for men as well. As I map bachelorhood's relation to reform, I understand this content to be far less marked by being toward reform than female celibacy, since male legal and economic independence does not depend on celibacy in the same way. We might follow historians like George Chauncey, Peter Laipson, and Howard Chudacoff in seeing bachelorhood possessing a content of leisure and enjoyment, rather than the promise of cultural and social well-being that female celibacy holds.[122] This tradition of the bachelor as a figure of lavishness, of obscene pleasure (exemplified by the homosocial utopia of Herman Melville's "Paradise of Bachelors and Tartarus of Maids") is always in danger of shading into homosexuality (as in Melville's "Billy Budd"), masturbation (as in Ik Marvel's *Reveries of a Bachelor*), whoremongering, and other excesses (associated with "bachelor's disease" or spermatorrhea).[123]

In charting the bachelor's relation to reform, in order to focus on the shared content of male and female celibacy, I want to bracket this better-known connection between the bachelor and excess to highlight another kind of bachelorhood, one committed not to selfishness but to the public good. Henry David Thoreau's persona in *Walden* (1854) exemplifies this position: "The generative energy, which, when we are loose, dissipates and makes us unclean, when we are continent invigorates and inspires us. Chastity is the flowering of man; and what are called Genius, Heroism, Holiness, and the like, are but various fruits which succeed it. Man flows at once to God when the channel of purity is open."[124] In contrast to his fellow bachelor who is part flaneur, part gourmand, and interested in a life of absolute pleasure, this figure articulates an "inspir[ing]" celibacy that buoys up his fellow man. While the extraordinary work of Michael Warner and Henry Abelove makes clear that Thoreau's renunciation is as queer as the leisured bachelor's vice, this passage illuminates two crucial aspects of the history of celibacy: First, celibacy's relation to autoeroticism is as variable as celibacy itself.[125] While some versions of celibacy incorporate or extol the autoerotic, others—like Thoreau's—clearly resist masturbatory practices as "unclean."[126] Autoeroticism is compatible with celibacy without being essential to it. Second, the "enterprise of self-vigilance intended to discover sinful inclinations within the soul" that Leo Bersani sees as characteristic of Christian self-examination is extended by Thoreau and the variety of bachelors he exemplifies from the self to fashion the common good.[127] Thus, celibacy's purity politics point us to a male content of celibate reform.

This shared connection between male and female celibacy gained national prominence as Republican reformers (known as the Mugwumps) supported and led Democratic presidential candidate and bachelor Grover Cleveland to victory in 1884. Kevin Murphy's *Political Manhood* (2008) contends that the Mugwumps were associated with effeminacy and homosexuality. Members of neither party, they were considered inadequately "manly" for the rough-and-tumble world of party politics. The Mugwumps' political rivals (most prominently Theodore Roosevelt) slurred them with sexologically inflected defamations—associating them with a "third sex" (being of neither party) and "political hermaphroditism."[128] Where party politicians were associated with practicality, the Mugwumps positioned themselves as "pure"—not beholden to the corrupting influence of party politics. The core Mugwump institution—the City Reform Club—established a "chastity clause," which mandated that its members were independent of party and were not running for political office. The chastity clause equated an individual's self-governance with the corruption-free governance of the state. The Mugwumps' political opponents seized on this lack of political strength and organization (because the Mugwumps feared the taint of party) to characterize them as ineffectual eunuchs and neuters who were "undesiring" because they did not want to accomplish anything "practical." In contrast, the Mugwumps saw celibacy and chastity as the foundation of a powerful strategy; for Henry Adams, a prominent Mugwump, celibacy had as much "force" as the dynamo: "The Virgin had acted as the greatest force the western world ever felt, and had drawn man's activities to herself more strongly than any other power, natural or supernatural, had ever done."[129] Celibacy for Adams and many others was the key to reform.

Along these lines, Transcendentalist thought appealed to many prominent Mugwumps like Adams and Thomas Wentworth Higginson (Emily Dickinson's mentor and posthumous publisher). Transcendentalist bastions of reform like Boston and New York also became Mugwump strongholds. For example, the unmarried reformer and wit Thomas Gold Appleton's most famous essay, "The New England Conscience" (1875), describes a fervent spirit of New England reform that is drafting "all human forces to action and thought."[130] This spirit's strong association with celibacy is also causing the "unpeopling [of] our nurseries," suggesting that by the 1880s, celibacy has arisen not just as an important, massively available progressive political identity for women but as one for men too.[131] It is no surprise, then, that this period would see the election of America's second bachelor president—Grover Cleveland.[132] *who was first (Buchanan)*

Celibacies begins, then, in the period of celibacy's dominance of political life in America. Dr. Benjamin Franklin DeCosta brought the White Cross Society to America; it immediately became an enormously popular social movement in which men (there was a sister organization for women, the White Shield) wore white crosses to mark their commitment to "the white life" (which encompassed virginity before marriage and chastity within it). The external marking of the body with white crosses and white shields is an inaugural moment for *Celibacies* because it flags a widely available celibate identity.

While exact membership figures are unavailable because the societies were highly decentralized and did not keep detailed institutional records, tens of thousands are thought to have enrolled by 1886, and by 1887 DeCosta could assert: "During these three years branches have been established in every state in the Union and in churches of every denomination, including the Catholic."[133] This final and somewhat reluctant inclusion, "including the Catholic," raises the specter of other exclusions—particularly of black members. Such "purity" in both the White Cross and the Women's Christian Temperance Union, which was a major advocate for celibacy, was rooted in whiteness and constructed against the impossibility of nonwhite celibacies. Francis Willard—the leader of the Women's Christian Temperance Union—characteristically asserted: "The grogshop is the Negro's center of power. Better whiskey and more of it is the rallying cry of great dark faced mobs."[134] Willard would also refer to "the infidel foreign population of our country" and "the scum of the Old World" to suggest that only white Protestants were capable of sexual and social virtue.[135]

The White Cross specifically sought to make "the law of purity as equally binding upon men and women."[136] Thus, this organization not only attempted and achieved the prescription of celibate sexual practice but also imbued this practice with wide-ranging political implications for reforming and transforming gender behavior ("to treat all women with respect, and endeavor to protect them from wrong and degradation").[137] In addition to thinking of celibacy as transformative of sex/gender relations, DeCosta's *The White Cross: Its Origin and Progress* (1887) explicitly links this (male) religious identity to other reform movements: "Of this movement it may truly be said that it has no ambitions and is animated by no spirit of rivalry. It is co-operative in its principles and policy, being ready to work with or operate independently of other organizations."[138] While many of these other reform organizations have a similarly religious bent, over the course of the twentieth century, celibacy as a political identity becomes untied from both religion and reform.

For example, Frederic Milton Thrasher's landmark study *The Gang* (1927) details the deep dependence of machine politics upon gangs while at the same time suggesting that the central reason for the dissipation of a gang was marriage: "Ultimately the biological function of sex serves, perhaps, as the chief disintegrating force in the gang. . . . Consequently it [marriage] represents the ultimate undoing of most gangs."[139] Thrasher argues that in order for a gang to be a gang (in the case of political gangs, in order for it to do its political work), the members needed to be celibate. In his chapter "The Gang in Politics," Thrasher details the constitutive importance of these gangs to machine politics in Chicago, while simultaneously suggesting homologous situations in "Boston, New York, Philadelphia, St. Louis, and other cities."[140] In other words, Thrasher suggests the widespread existence of an urban bachelor political identity that is associated with reform.

This study ends in 1969 in part because gay liberation and women's liberation dramatically reconfigured the meanings of gender, sex, and sexuality during this period. The "gay-in" created a new politics of demonstrative sex that made celibacy unfashionable. But rather than further reifying Stonewall as a historical break by suggesting that gay liberation replaces celibacy, *Celibacies* is more interested in tracing the energies with which celibacy continues to fuel gay politics. For example, the Mattachine Society, one of the largest early homophile organizations, had several prior instantiations in which it was called "Bachelors for Wallace," "Bachelors Anonymous," and "International Fraternal Order of Bachelors." The word "Mattachine" in its nomination of "unmarried townspeople" is also associated with celibacy. Similarly, another homophile organization in Los Angeles carried the monastic name the Cloistered Order of Conclaved Knights of Sophisticracy.[141] This book charts an alternative genealogy of sexual liberation through modernism. Rather than seeing Mina Loy and the free love movement as the ancestors of the 1960s, I posit Marianne Moore and the White Cross as its forebears.

Feminism was also drawing new power from celibacy—particularly more militant second-wave feminisms like Valerie Solanas's scum *Mani-*

festo (1968), Ti-Grace Atkinson's The Feminists, Women Against Sex (WAS), and Roxanne Dunbar-Ortiz's Boston-based group, Cell 16.[142] Second-wave feminism's emphasis on "having it all" (defined as balancing "marriage, motherhood, and work") has resulted in a shift away from celibacy and single women.[143] Emphasizing the centrality of celibacy for first-wave feminism as well as recovering a history of celibacy within the radical second wave both creates a greater continuity between the first and second waves and enriches the history of the feminist second wave. Additionally, such continuity draws out the implications of a larger culture of celibacy for the constructions of the nineteenth- and twentieth-century polity.

By technologically delinking phallo-vaginal penetration from reproduction, oral contraceptives transformed the meaning of heterosexual sex and abstention from it. The latter half of *Celibacies* will understand episodic celibacy in two ways—on the one hand, the senseless background against which sexual acts and practices take on their sense ("no one is having sex all the time," "everyone has dry spells," etc.), and on the other as an intentional lifestyle instituted by a felicitous performative (the vow of celibacy). While it is not examined here, timing sexual activity to periods of low fertility in a menstrual cycle might constitute a third modality of celibacy—an embodied and habitual practice that anticipates or gambles on an uncertain future. It is structured by one's body and its possibilities, and structuring of the uses one makes of one's body at a given moment. It is a habitual practice rather than either a vow or senseless facticity. Before the Pill, heterosexual intercourse was not so much repressed or inhibited as episodically celibate, suggesting that celibacy provided a practice that is continued by the Pill and its narrative of sexual liberation.

Fashioning a celibate reading practice, each of the chapters of *Celibacies* uses a different theoretical lever to shift sexuality studies, considering celibacy's relation to Boston marriage, temporality, racialization, queer citizenship, and sociality. This project's recovery of celibacy as a pathologized and idealized identity as well as a nonidentarian practice pushes the boundaries and rubrics of sexuality studies. I attempt to think sexuality without sex and to find the sexiness of no sex, taking what is usually understood as the shabbiness of spinsterhood and trying to imagine its sex appeal.[144]

Chapter 1, "The Longue Durée of Celibacy," attempts to break the deadlocked debate about whether or not the institution of Boston marriage is sexual. This chapter uncovers a letter which contains a usage of the term "Boston marriage" that predates the previous earliest known citation by more than a decade. This letter's emphasis on work informs my reading of James's novel and its Boston marriage of the "so essentially celibate" Olive and her "friend" Verena.[145] Olive's purchase of Verena's labor from Verena's father suggests that the business contract rather than the marriage contract underwrites Boston marriage. The business contract affords fewer privacy protections and a lesser degree of public recognition than the marriage contract. These mutually reinforcing impediments to their relationship leave open the opportunity for intrusion on the privacy of Olive and Verena's tie. This claim extends my examination of marriage bars because these prohibitions imply that women must be married to their work. Celibacy helps Olive (almost) attain the full legal personhood that would provide her Boston marriage with the same contractual protections of marriage. This reading of the novel opens out a theorization of what I call the "celibacy plot," redrawing two influential narratological models: René Girard's "'triangular' desire" and Leslie Fiedler's "innocent homosexuality" thesis. The celibacy plot understands the triangular relation of the novel's three principal characters as a structure of desire rather than modeling its repression. This chapter closes by considering the commonalities between Olive's celibacy and James's own, and the impact of his celibacy on his theory of the novel. Exemplifying his frequent references to his bachelorhood and understanding of himself as "hopelessly celibate," James writes, "An amiable bachelor here and there doesn't strike me as at all amiss, and I think he too may forward the cause of civilization."[146] James's valuation of the ordinarily stigmatized bachelor and his emphasis on moving "the cause of civilization" "forward" inaugurate a genealogy that understands celibacy as a mode of engagement. This Jamesian genealogy of celibate authorship runs throughout my project, suturing celibacy's politics of reform with what I will call a celibate aesthetic practice.

Chapter 2, "Celibate Time," elaborates a definition of celibate temporality in relation to recent work on queer temporality. Under both these rubrics, time is an ideological force that regulates sex: for example, the "old maid" is "late" according to a trajectory of normal sexual maturation that must pass through marriage. *Tell Me, Tell Me* (1966), Marianne Moore's last single volume of original work, offers a depathologized temporal model of celibacy by unfolding a life narrative that does not punish the "old maid" for being developmentally "late." Rather than seeing celibates as lacking desire or as failing to achieve their desire, Moore's volume posits a nonteleological desire, one where the desirer does not attempt to transform desire into an act. Instead, Moore's volume theorizes celibate desire as the reiterative practice of celibacy over time. I argue that *Tell Me, Tell Me* is "a told-backward biography," organized in reverse chronological order—rather than following a Freudian telos—that forges celibacy as a livable, nonstigmatized identity. Moore reanimates Progressive Era celibacy as a political identity in the 1950s and 1960s, when it no longer seems viable, in order to rejuvenate socially, sexually, and temporally abject spinsters. Rather than understanding Moore as a boring spinster, I see her unaffiliated status as a fascinating self-depiction that promises to indicate the inadequacy of the lonely spinster model on the one hand, and romantic friendship models and more pro-sex models of female-female relations on the other.

Chapter 3, "The Other Harlem Renaissance," revisits the "whiteness" of celibacy through an examination of the religious leader Father Divine. Where previous scholarship has understood celibacy as foreclosed to blacks, I argue that Father Divine authorizes black celibacy at a time when lynching hypersexualized the black male body and when black female bodies were widely understood as unclean and lacking in virtue. This new, "virtuous" black body is undifferentiated from white bodies and begins to explain Divine's near-total exclusion from the scholarship and historiography of the Harlem Renaissance. In spite of his appearances in a vast array of texts by Harlem Renaissance writers and artists, Father Divine is excluded from Renaissance historiography because he offers a different narrative of the period: one that is religious and celibate and that eschews the New Negro. He is also excluded from more class-inflected narratives of the Red 1930s despite the tremendous economic success of what I call Divine's "celibate economics." Reading Claude McKay's economic history *Harlem: Negro Metropolis* (1940), I argue that Divine's business acumen stems from his alternative cross-racial social structure rooted in the infinite attachability of celibacy (as opposed to the numeric restrictions of the nuclear family) and its concomitant economies of scale. In addition to pooling their resources, these celibate black-white conglomerates enable blacks to circumvent racist rental policies by having white members negotiate on behalf of the group. This living arrangement is only possible because celibacy greatly lessens the risk of violence that would ordinarily ensue from black and white cohabitation.

Chapter 4, "The Celibate American," begins with Auden's little-known vow of lifelong celibacy. I chart how this vow—which Auden takes and then renounces prematurely in 1928—initially offered an escape from his

[handwritten annotations] If christ an place what does that do to space. Privilege the verbal a refusal a vowel. linguists understa experiential as proofs of signs?

homosexuality. Reading Auden's *The Sea and the Mirror* (1944), American citizenship laws, and the controversy around Auden's citizenship, I argue for the continuing importance of celibacy to Auden long after he has ceased practicing it. Rather than seeing homosexuality and celibacy as mutually exclusive as he does in the 1920s and 1930s, Auden deploys celibacy as an instrumental disguise for homosexuality in order to gain access to American citizenship at a historical moment when homosexuals were not allowed by law to become citizens. Thus, I argue that Auden's changing relationship to celibacy is integral to his relationship to his homosexuality and national identity. While all the chapters in *Celibacies* take what Sedgwick calls a "universalizing" view of celibacy, arguing that celibacy impacts "the lives of people across the spectrum of sexualities," chapter 4 marks a shift in methodological emphasis.[147] This chapter still imagines celibacy in this "universalizing" way, understanding it as a part of and crucial to many modern sexual identities and orientations, but it moves away from the immutability of an identarian framework of sexuality. While the first three chapters understand celibacy as an identity-defining practice of lifelong celibates that dramatically reconfigures the American public sphere, chapters 4 and 5 examine figures who are marked, guided, and transformed by periods of celibacy. Because virtually everyone is volitionally celibate sometime (making a decision to "not date anyone right now" or to be "off the market"), chapters 4 and 5 promise to clarify celibacy's impact across a range of sexualities.

Chapter 5, "Philosophical Bachelorhood, Philosophical Spinsterhood, and Celibate Modernity," locates Andy Warhol and his attempted assassin, Valerie Solanas, within a tradition of what John Guillory calls "philosophical bachelorhood" in order to theorize an alloerotic celibacy.[148] This chapter zooms out from the modernist work that I focus on in my larger project to encompass a longer view of celibate modernity. Guillory understands bachelorhood as the dominant underpinning of philosophy, arguing that the choice not to marry is indicative of a willingness to think outside existing social structures and thus is associated with freedom of thought. Philosophical bachelorhood resists stagnant social institutions and imagines alternative modes of governance in their place (exemplified by the "philosopher-king"). While Guillory sees philosophical bachelorhood as a largely early modern phenomenon, I read Warhol's *The Philosophy of Andy Warhol (From A to B and Back Again)* (1975) and Solanas's scum *Manifesto* as self-consciously updating this tradition and offering philosophies of governance for the Factory and scum, respectively. In particular, I read

Warhol's 1964 marriage to his tape recorder and Solanas's becoming SCUM as turns toward the contemplative life. This chapter closes by theorizing group celibacy from the models of government practiced in the celibate socialities of the Factory and SCUM. While we are familiar with groups of religious celibates (as in the monastic life described by Thomas Merton or in Father Divine's kingdoms discussed in chapter 3), this chapter maps a secular group celibacy and the particular Eros native to it. I argue that this erotics of celibacy does not just involve one person (as we typically imagine celibacy) but is alloerotic and interpersonal like hetero- and homosexuality.

In my conclusion, "Asexuality/Neutrality/Relationality," I argue that the Asexuality Movement, or A-Pride, is the most important heir to the Leftist progressive impulses pioneered by celibacy. I historicize this emergent orientation in relation to Roland Barthes's concept of the Neutral, theorizing *Read* its ability to arrest (at least momentarily) the hegemonic operation of the homo/hetero binary. In the process, I revisit the introduction's "expressive hypothesis," arguing that asexuality's potential to unthread the tie between modern sexuality and its underpinning in the psychoanalytic drives provides new insight into the narrativity of sexuality. From the vantage of the twenty-first century, the politics of celibacy have returned with renewed vigor. Gay marriage, as Heather Love points out, has meant a married future is available for all, leading to a foreclosure of celibacy.[149] At the same time, asexuality is becoming an increasingly prominent political category. Mapping the contours of asexuality enables us to see celibacy anew. Asexuality is frequently distinguished from celibacy as being an orientation or describing a set of desires rather than being a choice, practice, or behavior. My theorization of celibate desire and understanding of celibacy as a sexuality sharpen the differences between celibacy and asexuality.

Celibacy is part of the closet's repressive history, but it also exceeds this repression as a mode of activism and of authorship. Celibacy is part of a phase prior to marriage, but it is also an alternative to marriage, constituting a powerful feminist critique of inequitable gender relations. Celibacy is both railed against by modernists seeking sexual expression and taken up as a revolutionary sexual expression on its own terms. Celibate reading is not designed to replace queer or feminist reading but instead enhances the resolution of these reading practices. Mapping celibacy across sexuality studies' major conceptual grids (homo/hetero, active/passive, acts/identities, fantasy/practice, autoeroticism/alloeroticism, normal/queer, friendship/homosexuality), my project argues that celibacy forces us to reconceive our sexual categories as well as to reconceptualize the period polity in which "sex" was vehemently negotiated. The photograph by the celibate Czech photographer Josef Sudek that appears on this book's cover offers a visual analogue for celibacy.[150] Creating a stunning range of gray tones, the light from the window falls on Sudek's acquaintance Jan Sampalik.[151] It is an image of celibacy's ghostliness and loneliness, but also its opportunity. The open door with its triangulation of man, shadow, and reflection seems to offer a glimpse of celibacy's variety: it is a sexuality that is individual and collective, in the foreground and in the background, haunting and promising. The celibacy of this photograph and in the book as a whole helps us to see how the separations between modernist, feminist, queer, and celibate histories, as well as their commonalities, narrate the history of sexuality in all its richness.

Chapter One

The Longue Durée of Celibacy

Boston Marriage, Female Friendship, and
the Invention of Homosexuality

In the introduction I sought to make a double gesture: carving out celibacy's particular history separate from that of homosexuality and marking celibacy's imbrication with homosexuality. By clarifying the nature of the specific entwinement between celibacy and homosexuality across a longue durée, this chapter attempts to alleviate the busyness of the sex / no sex debate that plagues sexuality studies. The title chapter of David Halperin's *How to Do the History of Homosexuality* (2002) lays out an ambitious project that will help us to achieve this goal: "I shall try to describe very tentatively, very speculatively, some important pre-homosexual discourses, practices, categories, patterns, or models (I am really not sure what to call them) and to sketch their similarities with and differences from what goes by the name of homosexuality nowadays."[1] Halperin explores four prehomosexual discourses—effeminacy, "active" sodomy, friendship, and inversion—in order to construct a genealogy of homosexuality that contains transhistorical elements and accounts for its current historical shape and functions. One of the strengths of Halperin's approach is the way it disarticulates these discourses from homosexuality at the same time that it binds them to homosexuality. This chapter takes Halperin's incitement to "correct and complete" his project as an occasion to build on his work, arguing that we must understand celibacy as an additional pattern or model that striates the long history of homosexuality before its emergence as such.[2] Celibacy, then, does not just paper over homosexuality but is woven into its very fabric. Like Halperin, I hope to describe this new prehomosexual discourse with as much "positivity and . . . specificity as possible," while confessing that my examples are more theoretical and historiographical than properly historical or narrating a history of celibacy over the longue durée.[3] My charting of celibacy seeks to clarify the relationship between Halperin's practices of homosexuality and friendship, as well as allowing us to speculate about how homosexuality develops into an "orientation." In particular, this latter hypothesis will surmise that celibacy's long association with vocation endows homosexuality with its vocabulary of "career," suggesting that "career" provides an inchoate language of "sexual orientation."[4]

Kathryn Ringrose's study of Byzantine eunuchs provides evidence that celibacy as a prehomosexual discourse dates at least back to the first millennium. The involuntary celibacy of eunuchs enabled them to hold the office of "perfect servants," as late antiquity Christianity increasingly valorized celibacy as a religious ideal. Byzantine culture ascribed to eunuchs what Ringrose calls a "third gender," seeing them as "'unnatural' (in the sense that they were artificially, culturally created); they existed outside of what was perceived to be the natural order of the biological world."[5] When this formulation of a third gender is placed alongside Ringrose's contention that "eunuchs by nature" is a phrase that connotes "castrated men who actively seek out sexual relations with other men," we can begin to see how celibacy functions as a transhistorical prehomosexual discourse in the same manner as Halperin's four other patterns.[6] The phrase "eunuchs by nature" implies that the Byzantine perception of the "natural" occurrence of homosexuality is embodied in the cultural process of surgical castration. Because this castration allegedly made one incapable of sex, the expression "eunuchs by nature" suggests that the language of celibacy (and of the eunuch in particular) was a language of homosexuality before its invention.

This network between celibacy and homosexuality is also evident in a poem titled "I Am Already Changing My Mind" (likely dating from the twelfth century) in which one cleric tells his male lover that he will become a monk if God will grant his beloved (who is ill) health again. Here, celibacy is figured as a performance of homosexual love.[7] While similar examples of this transhistorical relay between celibacy and homosexuality might be found in figures like Leonardo da Vinci, Washington Irving, and Hans Christian Anderson, the eighteenth-century British poet Thomas Gray provides a particularly rich example. While scholarship by George

Haggerty, Robert Gleckner, and others has pointed out the erotic nature of Gray's friendships with Horace Walpole, Richard West, and later Charles Victor de Bonstetten, the standard Gray biography describes these relationships in the context of Gray's celibacy: "We possess no evidence—no proof of overt behavior—to suggest that Gray ever (either as a child or as an adult) engaged in intimate, sexual relations of any kind."[8] The simultaneity of homosexuality and celibacy (and career) comes through very clearly in a letter to Bonstetten. Gray quotes "another Greek writer" who describes one of the qualifications for a career in philosophy as "be[ing] little inclined to sensual pleasures, and consequently temperate," but then takes issue with this assertion, complicating it by saying that "extraordinary vices and extraordinary virtues are equally the produce of a vigorous mind: little souls are alike incapable of the one and the other."[9] The entwinement of homosexuality ("extraordinary vices") and celibacy ("extraordinary virtues") in the context of career is only enhanced by the fact that Gray quotes a Greek writer (with its associations of homosexuality) to a man with whom he is in a "platonic" friendship, but one that is fueled (at least for Gray) by a "volatile erotic fire."[10]

Turning back to the historical period on which this study centers, we find similar examples of this configuration in four more modern figures: Baron Corvo, Ralph Werther, Henry Lehr, and Quentin Crisp. Like the office of the eunuch, the vocation of the monk, and the calling of the philosopher, these figures triangulate celibacy, career, and homosexuality. A. J. A. Symons's experimental biography *The Quest for Corvo* (1934), for example, writes of its subject: "Set among those who had voluntarily embraced celibacy, his [Corvo's] abnormality [homosexuality] became, not a possible vice, but a sign of Vocation."[11] Here, celibacy cloaks homosexuality but also celebrates, harnesses, and embraces it to open a career.

During this period, the practice of homosexuality was regularly understood as a "career"; Ralph Werther uses the locution "my open career as a fairie" or "my career as a fairie" more than a dozen times in his autobiography.[12] While this association certainly arises partly out of the incompatibility of homosexuality with any other career (what the queer Samuel Steward laments as the choice "between love and a career"), celibacy's history as a calling or vocation underwrites the trope of the homosexual career.[13] This is nowhere clearer than in *"King Lehr" and the Gilded Age* (1935), where the queer Lehr is described as "completely sexless"; he credits celibacy as "the secret of [his] success": "Love affairs are fatal to ambition."[14] This nexus is also evident in Quentin Crisp's *The Naked Civil Servant* (1968), where the title imagines Crisp's sex life through the language of occupation. Crisp's text describes him "living without sexual encounters at all" "for many years" in 1920s England and nominates him "Miss Arc's only rival."[15] Crisp teasingly sprinkles his celibacy with Eros by referring to his erotic "rivalry" with Joan of Arc. Moreover, we might take Crisp's cue that celibacy (and the trope of Joan of Arc in particular) is part of a prelesbian as well as a prehomosexual discourse.[16]

Such an exploration is of vital importance both because the debate between sex and no sex forces is most pronounced in relation to lesbian sexuality and because celibacy is even more closely tied to career for women. Understanding celibacy as a prelesbian pattern will clarify not only the historical forces that enable and constitute the invention of homosexuality (broadly conceived) but also the specific collision between friendship and lesbianism. The imbrication between celibacy and lesbianism goes at least back to Desiderius Erasmus's "The Girl with No Interest in Marriage" (1523). Here, Erasmus's representative, Eubulus, attempts to dissuade Catharine from entering a convent:

> EUBULUS: What's more, not everything's virginal among those virgins in other respects, either.
> CATHARINE: No? Why not, if you please?
> EUBULUS: Because there are more who copy Sappho's behaviour than share her talent.[17]

Here, in the context of a discussion about the choice of vocation, Eubulus equates virgins and the virginal with Sapphic behavior, suggesting the importance of reading practices that interpret celibacy as homosexuality.

Recent work by Valerie Traub, Theodora Jankowski, and Kathleen Coyne Kelly and Marina Leslie also tells another story, positing a queer virginity that looks less like the same-sex acts of the Erasmus text and more like a discourse or pattern that is unexpectedly (to borrow Kelly and Leslie's term) "menacing."[18] Traub, for example, not only asks whether Queen Elizabeth's chastity is queer or whether it stands "*against* heterosexuality or is . . . an alternative form *of* heterosexuality," but explores "the erotic license that the paradigm of chastity enables."[19] Traub helps us to see "how the cultural fetishization of the hymen obscures the array of erotic activities open to, and deemed pleasurable by, women."[20] Here, Traub argues that chastity is working in concert with and laying out the conditions of possibility for homosexuality, even as it also queers patriarchy and heterosexuality. I would add that while we must be careful not to assign Queen Elizabeth's sexual practices to the realm of the sovereign exception, there can be little doubt that celibacy is crucial to her role as queen. Therefore, we must mark the deviance of celibacy (emphasized by Jankowski and Kelly and Leslie), as well as its simultaneous normativity (emphasized by Traub), which enables lesbianism to go unnoticed. Thus, while celibacy is not an orientation and does not involve genital acts as homosexuality (usually) does, it does share some of homosexuality's relation to gender and sexual deviance. We might see these medieval and early modern queer virginities as connected to the celibate deviance in the American and British nineteenth century that I discussed in the introduction.

This long tradition of deviance differs markedly from what Heather Love describes as friendship's place "at the very top of the hierarchy of intimate relations" "over the long course of Western history."[21] Lillian Faderman's *Surpassing the Love of Men* (1981), for example, argues for the absolute alterity between friendship and homosexuality. In a chapter tellingly entitled "The Last Breath of Innocence," Faderman sees sexology as "outing" idyllic friendship, transmogrifying and demonizing it into a pernicious vice known as lesbianism.[22] Placing this narrative alongside the increasing eroticization of the heterosexual couple that I charted in the introduction, we might see a larger narrative: namely, the increasing eroticization of all dyadic relations at the historical moment when homosexuality is invented. Faderman's much-maligned account of what Love calls "the end of friendship" is not so much wrong as it overstates the rupture between friendship and homosexuality. Charting the ways in which this break is overemphasized, Love reinstalls experimentalism and trouble into the heart of friendship to forge continuities across the friendship-homosexuality divide. Similarly, Martha Vicinus and Alan Bray are interested in thinking about how Eros and carnality (Vicinus) and alliance and publicness (Bray) move across this divide.[23] Following these thinkers, this chapter explores how celibacy organizes both friendship and homosexuality to create continuities between the two, while exploring how celibacy narrates a separate history of vocation and authorship. In particular, I explore how vows of celibacy are ritualistically deployed to forge what Love calls "the relatively unstructured nature of friendship as a mode of intimacy."[24] However, I am interested in how the practice of celibacy is significantly more flexible and less structured than friendship or homosexuality when it does not overlap with, intersect, or provide the condition of possibility for either of these relations. I hope that this longer view will enable us to understand the intersection between celibacy, homosexuality, and friendship at the moment of the invention of homosexuality in a new way. This is of the utmost importance because this nexus of prelesbian (and to a lesser extent prehomosexual) discourses is the most contested site of sex in the history of sexuality. Or, to recast this in slightly different terms, this chapter will consider the most contested site of celibacy in the history of homosexuality: Boston marriage.

The Beginnings of Boston Marriage

The term "Boston marriage" describes a long-term partnership between two women who live together and share their lives with one another. Even as Boston marriage is considered to be a historical precursor to contemporary lesbian relationships, many scholars question whether the women in these relationships engaged in what we would today recognize as lesbian sexual acts. While there is scholarly consensus that the institution dates from the late nineteenth century, the earliest textual instantiation was discovered by Lillian Faderman to date from the early twentieth century.[25] The status of Henry James's *The Bostonians* (1886) as by far the most famous depiction of Boston marriage in American literature and its description by James as "a study of one of those friendships between women which are so common in New England" bestow upon the text a prominent place in the history of Boston marriage.[26] This chapter traces a new origin of the term "Boston marriage," which significantly recasts the history of the institution and James's text, and which will enable us to remap the terrain between celibacy and homosexuality. Additionally, this chapter reconfigures the relationship between Boston marriage and literary production posited by Faderman. While Faderman's posited origin of the term has been the earliest known citation for nearly thirty years, I have found a usage that appears approximately fifteen years earlier, at the beginning of 1893.

The marriage of Boston's most eligible bachelor, Nathan Appleton, to the much younger Jeanette Ovington was hailed in 1887 as the social event of the season. Two years later the couple separated, and after the split, Mrs. Appleton lived with her former maid of honor before moving in with Miss Catherine Parsons in June 1891. Six months later, Miss Parsons's father, the esteemed Colonel Parsons, hired a lawyer and appealed to a local official to help him recover his daughter from Mrs. Appleton. In the press coverage of the scandal, there are strong implications of lesbianism. It was reported, for example, that the women were asked to leave the boardinghouse in which they were staying because "they established a reputation for singularity of behavior."[27] The word "singular," as Susan Lanser has pointed out, has been "used frequently [since the late eighteenth century] . . . to describe women suspected of homoerotic desires."[28] The suspicions of lesbianism are heightened by repeated accusation that Mrs. Appleton hypnotized Miss Parsons. As Pamela Thurschwell has argued in another context, hypnotism and other alternate states function as a "trope and ground" for sexuality.[29] Hypnotism implies not just an unnatural state of mind but also a state of mind counter to Miss Parsons's volition (as if coercion were the only basis for lesbianism). Mrs. Appleton's intimate life provides the basis for what may be the first time that the term "Boston marriage" comes into print.

The earliest usage of the term that I have been able to find relates directly to this social scandal. It appears at the beginning of 1893 in a letter to the editor of *Open Court* protesting Colonel Parsons's intrusion on his daughter and Mrs. Appleton (though it does not refer to them by name). The letter was written by Ednah Dow Littlehale Cheney—a now largely forgotten feminist author, reformer, and biographer. In the scant scholarship on Cheney, she is remembered primarily as the first biographer of Louisa May Alcott and the object of Bronson Alcott's illicit desires and likely unconsummated affections.[30] Her letter to the editor is of tremendous interest not only because it moves the dating of Boston marriage earlier—the text itself refers to even earlier usages—but also because it is a document that prescribes usage, providing insight into how at least one prominent feminist understood the relationship that we call Boston marriage. The most valuable feature of the letter, however, is the way in which it foregrounds the "old maid" as crucial to the production of Boston marriage.

This new emphasis recasts the literary underpinning of Lillian Faderman's narrative of Boston marriage. Additionally, it has important consequences for our understanding of *The Bostonians* and for James's theory of authorship. James's novel and his participation in the *Atlantic Monthly* circle provide a significant origin for Faderman's narrative of Boston marriage: "The term 'Boston Marriage' may have been coined by Mark DeWolfe Howe, editor of the *Atlantic Monthly*, about his good friends Annie Fields and Sarah Orne Jewett."[31] She offers as evidence a passage from *The Gentle Americans* (1965), Helen Howe's biography of her father, Mark:

There were, in my parents' circle of friends in Boston, several households consisting of two ladies, living sweetly and devotedly together. Such an alliance I was brought up to hear called a "Boston marriage." Such a "marriage" existed between Mrs. Fields and Sarah Orne Jewett. Father wrote of it as a "union—there is no truer word for it." What Henry James, whose *The Bostonians* was published in 1888 [*sic*], found to "catch at" in the friendship between the Charles Street ladies we can only guess. All we get is that "their reach together was of the firmest and easiest and I verily remember being struck with the stretch of wings that the spirit of Charles Street could bring off."[32]

I am less interested in the implausibility of Howe's coinage of the term "Boston marriage" than in his suggestion that the institution is associated with collaborative literary production ("'their reach together was of the firmest and easiest'") and fosters the written output of Jewett and Fields, respectively. Cheney's letter, in contrast, highlights the way that James's vision of both Boston marriage and authorship eschews collaboration.

Cheney's letter posits a more monadic understanding of Boston marriage (one associated with a different sense of "singularity") when she comments on the strangeness of a father's decision to take legal action to get his daughter to return home from the house of a woman with whom she lives:

> This [the legal action] seems very strange to one, who for many years has been accustomed to the existence of ties between women so intimate and persistent, that they are fully recognised by their friends, and of late have acquired, if not a local habitation, at least a name, for they have been christened "Boston Marriages." This institution deserves to be recognised as a really valuable one for women in our present state of civilisation. With the great number of women in our state, in excess of the men, and with the present independence of women, which renders marriage, merely for a home, no longer acceptable, the proportion of those who can enter into that relation is diminished, and the "glorious phalanx of old maids" must find some substitute for the joys of family life. These relations so far as I have known, and I have known many of them, are not usually planned for convenience or economy, but grow out of a constantly increasing attachment, favored by circumstances, which make such a marriage the best refuge against the solitude of a growing age.[33]

Here, Cheney suggests that a "'glorious phalanx of old maids'" has emerged, in part, because of an "excess" of women, but that this demographic fact is accentuated by "the present independence of women," which keeps heterosexual marriage from being a desirable choice for many of them. Cheney's account of the independence of these unmarried women helps us to theorize celibacy as a way of being in the world. This celibate way of being entails a being toward independence, toward reform, and makes Boston marriage possible. While Cheney initially suggests that Boston marriage is a "substitute for the joys of family life," her contrast between heterosexual marriage as marriage "merely for a home" and Boston marriage, which does not grow out of "convenience or economy," asserts that Boston marriage is, in her view, better than marriage. Cheney reads celibate independence as a necessary condition of Boston marriage. This is not surprising given that she was a student of Margaret Fuller, who, as I discussed in the introduction, stressed celibacy as the only possible path to female independence.[34] Cheney thus lays the groundwork to move our scholarly conversations about Boston marriage from debating the presence of sex to acknowledging the essential, constitutive role of celibacy in Boston marriage.

This letter points toward the methodological necessity of holding *The Bostonians'* avowed celibacy copresent with its lesbianism without foreclosing either. Thinking of celibacy as the precondition for Boston marriage will help us to understand Olive Chancellor's reception as a lesbian, even as *The Bostonians* nominates her as "so essentially a celibate" (17). While Lillian Faderman and Terry Castle have traded barbs about whether Boston marriage is sexual, Cheney helps us to break this deadlock by arguing that a celibate way of being in the world, a being toward independence, is essential to the production of Boston marriage, whether or not such arrangements encompass lesbian sex acts.[35] That is, while many Boston marriages were celibate, both celibate Boston marriages and what we would recognize as lesbian Boston marriages share a social identity with celibacy.[36]

The Bostonians begins with Olive Chancellor inviting her cousin Basil, whom she has never met, to a suffragist meeting. At the meeting, Olive and Basil encounter and simultaneously become infatuated with Verena Tarrant—a young and beautiful feminist lecturer. From that moment forward, the cousins are romantic rivals. Olive pursues Verena by tutoring her in women's history and inducting her into a "feverish cult of virginity" modeled by Joan of Arc and in the works of Goethe.[37] Basil's competing courtship ultimately wins the day when he carries Verena away moments before her first large-scale public debut. The text ends by forecasting Verena's unhappy marriage to Basil while Olive is left to take the lecture stage. Most scholars have emphasized the novel's marriage plot, but I would like to chart a celibacy plot that parallels and occurs simultaneously to it. I read Olive's courtship of Verena less as a failure than as a spur helping Olive to deploy her celibate independence to become a successful feminist speaker.[38] This narrative marks celibacy's key role in the campaign for suffrage. Furthermore, this celibacy plot is not unique to James's text. It is, in fact, a crucial part of the entire genre of the Boston marriage novel. It serves as a structuring component in Sarah Orne Jewett's *The Country of the Pointed Firs* (1896), Florence Converse's *Diana Victrix* (1897), and Gertrude Stein's *Fernhurst* (1904), all of which are similarly organized by celibacy.[39] This generic convention suggests that rather than choosing between hermeneutic practices, celibacy on the one hand, or queerness on the other, we must read with both lenses simultaneously.

The Business of Marriage

In the previous section, I have charted the independent spirit of celibate life as essential to the cultural production of Boston marriage. In this section, I will elaborate how this celibate mode of being is predicated on a specifically economic motive. Here, I expand my initial claim, arguing that celibacy underwrites Boston marriage because it is the only status available to women at this historical moment that enables their economic self-determination. As I demonstrated in the introduction, throughout the first three decades of the twentieth century, so-called marriage bars legally prohibited the hiring of married women and required female employees' dismissal upon marriage. This made marriage incompatible with middle-class work and implied, as one commentator put it, that work was "a quasi-marriage, demanding duty and devotion in the same way that a marriage [does]."[40] This economic and social situation in which celibacy is *the* necessary condition for white women's social and economic independence gives rise to the linking of unmarried women and professional careers on a massive scale.

This expanding demographic of vocationally oriented women leads Basil to muse: "I don't object to the *old* old maids; they were delightful; they had always plenty to do, and didn't wander about the world crying out for a vocation. It is the new old maid that you have invented from whom I pray to be delivered" (328). Here, Basil describes two kinds of celibate women, preferring those who do not seek to enter the public sphere (women who "don't wander about the world crying out for a vocation"). He wants old maids to be the innocuous handmaidens of men that he imagines they have always been and should be rather than the activists that some new old maids have, in Basil's phrase, "invented" themselves as. The old maid has transformed from a being toward family to the new being toward independence that I have been charting.

Miss Birdseye and Dr. Prance exemplify this new spirit of celibate independence. When Miss Birdseye gives up everything for the work of reform, her "asceticism" (20) reaches parodic heights: "No one had an idea how she lived; whenever money was given her she gave it away to a negro or a refugee" (26). Birdseye gives away her money, her looks, her life, and her love to reform—"She was in love . . . only with causes, and she languished only for emancipations" (26). Everything about Birdseye is collective and public: even her "faded face" bears the "reflection of ugly lecture-lamps" (25). Doctor Prance is also deeply invested in making life for women better, but she is a separatist (perhaps modeled on Dr. Marie Zakrzewska, who along with Cheney cofounded the New England Hospital for Women and Children)—"The time hadn't come when a lady-doctor was sent for by a gentleman, and she hoped it never would, though some people seemed to think that this was what lady-doctors were working for" (41). Thus, Prance does not seek redress for injustice or abstract rights—a condition that by no means guarantees lived equality—but instead advocates hard work and the instrumental use of the freedoms already in her possession: "It was certain that whatever might become of the movement at large, Doctor Prance's own little revolution was a success" (46). Prance is uninterested in the collective and instead is concerned with what Olive calls the "petty questions of physiological science and of her own professional activity" (365). Olive finds these questions "petty" because she believes that they are narrowly professional instead of operating on a logic of social betterment, utility, or collectivity. Rather, Prance structures her actions around her interests, her desires, and her freedom—seeing freedom as its own raison d'être.

Olive's celibacy is more personal than Birdseye's and more collective than Prance's. Olive combines the liberal strategies of Birdseye with the counterpublic ones of Prance: "Miss Chancellor was a signal old maid. That was her quality, her destiny; nothing could be more distinctly written. There are women who are unmarried by accident, and others who are unmarried by option; but Olive Chancellor was unmarried by every implication of her being. She was a spinster as Shelley was a lyric poet, or as the month of August is sultry" (17). This passage generates and positions Olive within a taxonomy of celibacy. Olive's celibacy glows with eroticism, exemplifying a sexuality without a normative aspiration to sexual acts. Olive is constituted by her celibacy, vocationally called to it with a religious zeal.[41] Her status as a signal old maid defines her, making it difficult to understand her simply as a lesbian.

Annamarie Jagose's claim that the structuring binary of *The Bostonians* is not that between the married and the unmarried but between the marriageable and the unmarriageable helps us to clarify the relationship between lesbianism and Olive's celibate way of being:

> Both a mark of her peculiar character ("her quality") and her inevitable fate ("her destiny"), Olive's being unmarried is not a simple declaration of her marital status—married or unmarried—but an indication that she is altogether beyond the institution of marriage, with its organizing of affect and kinship, its authorizations and its dispensations. Unmarried by neither chance ("by accident") nor design ("by option")—these two conditions commonly being understood to explain the circumstances of any event—the narration goes to some lengths to secure that fact which "could [not] be more distinctly written": Olive is a spinster by definition. Against the tolling of the narrative's repeated "unmarried," "unmarried," "unmarried," a harder truth can be heard: Olive is unmarriageable.[42]

For Jagose, unmarriageability describes the "structural effect of the regulatory exclusions of marriage" that disenfranchises lesbians from legal marriage.[43] I understand the division between the marriageable and the unmarriageable to signify differently, to signify a political division between those who support the political underpinnings of the institution of marriage and those for whom the institution of marriage, at this historical moment, is politically oppressive.

That is, Olive is unmarriageable in my sense because marriage is an anathema to her politics. Unmarriageability serves as the basis for feminist public life; thus, Verena's rejection of public life forces her to choose between Olive and Basil (also a culinary choice) at the end of the novel. Olive is constituted by her celibacy. Vocationally called to it with a religious zeal, it is her "destiny" and "being"; she is the inheritor of the special access that Fuller's spinster has to "communion with the One." Moreover, this unmarriageability helps us to see why Olive understands Verena's interest in men—much like her own "phase" "during which she accompanied gentlemen to respectable places of amusement" (114)—as part of a moment prior to full political recognition. And yet, as Verena's pale shop maiden precursors, who care more about young men "than about the ballot" (33), make clear, this phase might, and ultimately does, thwart Olive's plans for Verena. (As I suggested in the introduction, the "paleness" of these shop maidens reinforces that the ballot and associated rights are the property of whiteness.) In spite of this prehistory, Olive imagines this temporary interest in the marital tie will end when Verena reaches full political maturity.

Despite Olive's personal opposition to "the marriage-tie," she does not favor its abolition—"that particular reform" (82)—because she recognizes that it is not a practical mode of action. That is, marriage is too central to the social order. Rather than attacking marriage's centrality like the sex radicals Emma Goldman, Margaret Sanger, and even Verena, or participating in marriage as it is currently constituted (like Mrs. Farrinder and other upholders of the Cult of Domesticity), Olive attempts to widen marriage's scope, to make it more encompassing by making Boston marriage signify in the public sphere. Celibacy's public signification provides the first step in creating female-female friendship as an alternative public relation, one that is institutionally authenticated as marriage is, and is not usually thought to matter in the public sphere.

Olive inherits her understanding of celibacy as a requirement for public friendship from Fuller's Transcendentalism. In addition to being the unit of individual political autonomy for men, and especially for women, celibacy is also the precondition for political organization, association, and collectivity: "For now the rowers are pausing on their oars; they wait a change before they can pull together. All tends to illustrate the thought of a wise contemporary. Union is only possible to those who are units. To be fit for relations in time, souls, whether of man or woman, must be able to do without them in spirit."[44] The prerequisite that Fuller places on celibacy is that each individual must be self-sufficient, must be a unit before participating in society. Here, as Caleb Crain and others have persuasively argued, the "wise contemporary" referred to is Ralph Waldo Emerson (specifically his essay "Friendship").[45] Following Emerson, Fuller points toward the necessarily self-sufficient relations of friendship. That is to say, an individual must be a "unit" unto him- or herself, a fully formed rower, before he or she can row with others.

The tenuousness and power of celibacy as a mode of signification are evident in a story that Elizabeth Barrett Browning tells to her sister Arabel about meeting Charlotte Cushman and Matilda Hays: "I understand that she & Miss Hayes [sic] have made vows of celibacy & eternal attachment to each other—they live together, dress alike . . . it is a female marriage. I happened to say to a friend, 'Well I never heard of such a thing before,' to a friend who answered, 'Oh, it is by no means uncommon.'"[46] Here, the vows of celibacy do not seem to signify for Browning, while her friend is able to recognize them immediately. Her explanatory tone might signal that she fears that her sister may also be unaware of the meaning of the vow. The recognition of Browning's friend, however, suggests not only celibacy's ability to forge voluntary kinship ties between women—operating as a promise and ritual—but also the historical centrality of celibacy to lesbianism over time.

Olive similarly understands that celibacy must underwrite any recognizably public social tie involving women, bemoaning as she does that revolutions must "begin with one's self—with internal convulsions, sacrifices, executions" (109). Here, Olive's belief in the necessity of personal revolution as the driving force behind social revolution underwrites her celibacy as an enfranchising act as well as explains her injunction to Verena—"Promise me not to marry!" (131): "She knew that Olive's injunction ought not to have surprised her; she had already felt it in the air; she would have said at any time, if she had been asked, that she didn't suppose Miss Chancellor would want her to marry. But the idea, uttered as her friend had uttered it, had a new solemnity, and the effect of that quick, violent colloquy was to make her nervous and impatient, as if she had had a sudden glimpse of futurity. That was rather awful, even if it represented the fate one would like" (131). Olive attempts to hasten the public signification of her relationship with Verena by extracting a vow from her. It is precisely because Verena is not a "unit" that she feels the vow as coercive and public signification fails. To put it differently, Verena's singleness has not yet, and will not, shift from the register of the marriageable to that of the unmarriageable and its ensuing implications of independence and usefulness. Olive's insistence ("Promise *me*" [my emphasis]) suggests her personal interest in the vow; Mrs. Luna's claim that getting Verena to join the "single sisterhood" is Olive's way of having Verena "for herself" (252) sharply distinguishes Olive's celibacy from Birdseye's selfless celibacy.

In contrast to married women in this period who had virtually no control over their labor, Olive's celibacy enables her to engage in contracts.[47]

The discourse of contract recognizes Olive and other celibate women as independent parties. Returning again to Cheney's letter as a guide for Boston marriage, we see that Boston marriage may have a more embattled beginning than has hitherto been noted. Cheney's insistence that "privacy especially become[s]" Boston marriage, while considering (and rejecting) the formal adoption of "Boston Marriage into our civil code," highlights the institution's uncertain signification in the public sphere.

And yet, as Cheney's letter suggests, the independence associated with celibacy plays a crucial role in the establishment of Boston marriage. This receives one of its most provocative treatments in James's text when Olive contracts with Verena's father to purchase his assurance that he will not disrupt Olive's private life with Verena:

> She [Olive] notified Tarrant [Verena's father] that she should keep Verena a long time, and Tarrant remarked that it was certainly very pleasant to see her so happily located. But he also intimated that he should like to know what Miss Chancellor laid out to do with her; and the tone of this suggestion made Olive feel how right she had been to foresee that their interview would have the stamp of business. It assumed that complexion very definitely when she crossed over to her desk and wrote Mr. Tarrant a cheque for a very considerable amount. "Leave us alone—entirely alone—for a year, and then I will write you another." (160–161)

Here, Olive's celibacy enables her to participate in the traffic in women to purchase Verena's time, labor, and affection. The text emphasizes the value of Verena's labor by describing both how hard she used to work and the necessity of her replacement. In light of the critical history of the text, which emphasizes a "union of soul" (78) between the pair, this moment radically defamiliarizes our sense of the Olive-Verena relationship.[48]

Though Brook Thomas's insightful chapter on *The Bostonians* does not take up this scene, his discussion illuminates the limitations and possibilities of this contract between Olive and Mr. Tarrant. Thomas chronicles the right to privacy described famously as "the right to be left alone," a phrase that reverberates with and may provide the origins of Olive's demand directed at Tarrant: "'Leave us alone—entirely alone—for a year.'"[49] Thomas argues that marriage contracts are both more public and more private than business contracts.[50] With this in mind, we see that the relationship purchased by or blackmailed out of Olive lacks both the sacrosanct privacy and the full publicness of marriage. These mutually reinforcing impediments to their relationship leave open the opportunity for Basil (if not Verena's parents) to intrude on the privacy of Olive and Verena's tie. Olive uses her unmarried state, her celibacy, to secure the privileges of a business contract. But she also deploys a liberal strategy, announcing her grievance (that female friendship does not register as culturally worthy of privacy) and hoping that the full public recognition of female friendship will garner her the greater privileges afforded heterosexual marriage. Thus, we must read celibacy and Boston marriage as having a life outside of heterosexual marriage, while remembering heterosexual marriage's continuing and powerful ability to mark and influence these alternative identities and institutions. Rather than representing Boston marriage and Olive as either celibate or lesbian, this passage points to the necessary entwinement of celibacy, Boston marriage, and heteronormative marriage.

The Celibacy Plot

This intersection of celibacy, Boston marriage, and heterosexual marriage helps us to rethink the plot of *The Bostonians*. Hugh Stevens reads the novel (and much of James's oeuvre) as privileging "heterosexual bonds over homosexual bonds," thus precipitating tragedy.[51] While Stevens reads *The Bostonians* as unhappily parting Verena and Olive and installing Verena into a tear-filled future marriage with Basil, I want to suggest that we might read a celibate plot, charting celibate sociability alongside the text's homosexual and heterosexual bonds. Two models of plotting seem especially well suited for this task: René Girard's "'triangular' desire" and Leslie Fiedler's "innocent homosexuality" thesis.[52]

Sedgwick helpfully summarizes Girard's argument:

> Through readings of major European fictions, Girard traced a calculus of power that was structured by the relation of rivalry between the two active members of an erotic triangle. What is most interesting for our purposes in his study is its insistence that, in any erotic rivalry, the bond that links the two rivals is as intense and potent as the bond that links either of the rivals to the beloved: that the bonds of "rivalry" and "love," differently as they are experienced, are equally powerful and in many senses equivalent. For instance, Girard finds many examples in which the choice of the beloved is

determined in the first place, not by the qualities of the beloved, but by the beloved's already being the choice of the person who has been chosen as a rival. In fact, Girard seems to see the bond between rivals in an erotic triangle as being even stronger, more heavily determinant of actions and choice, than anything in the bond between either of the lovers and the beloved.[53]

Even though Girard's work refers to a European tradition that reads rivalry between men (rather than between a man and a woman), one could easily imagine mounting a Girardian reading of *The Bostonians*. Such a reading would note that even before Basil and Olive are introduced to Verena, they are figured as rivals; in fact, Olive only invites Basil to Boston to contend with him: "Of all things in the world, contention was most sweet to her . . . and it was very possible Basil Ransom would not care to contend. Nothing could be more displeasing than this indifference when people didn't agree with you. That he should agree she did not in the least expect of him; how could a Mississippian agree? If she had supposed he would agree, she would not have written to him" (13). While Olive initially fears that Basil either will not be a worthy opponent (he will be "too simple—too Mississippian") or will not "care to contend" (13), she changes her mind after the antagonistic carriage ride to see Birdseye: "She had a perception that Ransom would be vigorous" (44). With the rivals on equal footing, they are able to mediate the desire of the other. For Girard, both rivals claim to be the originator rather than the imitator of desire, reversing "the logical and chronological order of desires in order to hide . . . imitation."[54] In *The Bostonians*, it is not immediately apprehensible who the initial mediator of the desire is. While the narrator's earliest mention of Verena describes her as "very pretty," Olive's free indirect discourse first positions Verena in relation to the rivals: "At any rate, if he [Basil] was bored, he could speak to some one. . . . He could speak to that pretty girl who had just come in—the one with red hair—if he liked" (30, 38). Olive's apprehension of Verena's beauty is framed by the conjuration of Basil speaking to Verena. Thus, it is not clear whether Olive incites Basil's desire for Verena (she notices Verena first within the diegesis of the text) or whether it is her fantasy that Basil will like Verena that leads Olive to think that she is "very pretty" in the first place. This play of "logical and chronological order" continues as Basil observes his cousin's interest in Verena, wondering "whether her curiosity [about Verena] had pushed her to boldness" (51).

I could certainly expound a much fuller Girardian reading. This might begin with an exploration of Verena as the perfect Girardian object; because the "qualities of the beloved" are not determinative of Girardian desirability, her status as a contentless cipher on whom the rivals can project their fantasies and inscriptions emphasizes the bonds of rivalry over those of love.[55] Such a reading might continue with the repeated obstructions and abductions that Basil and Olive employ to increase the geographic and spiritual distance between their respective rivals and Verena while examining the constant apprehension of Verena through the mediator's desire. But I cut this reading short in order to return to our focus on celibate plotting. Instead, I want to turn to that aspect of Girard's model which Sedgwick recasts and which *Celibacies* aims to reimagine: what Girard calls "latent homosexuality."

While Girard insists that "the impulse toward the object is ultimately an impulse toward the mediator," he refuses to read it as homosexual. For example, in his reading of Fyodor Dostoyevsky's *The Eternal Husband* (1870), Girard asserts, "Some critics would like to see in Pavel Pavlovitch a 'latent homosexual. . . . ' Nothing is gained by reducing triangular desire to a homosexuality."[56] According to Sedgwick, Girard's model is dependent on "*suppressing* [a] subjective, historically determined account of . . . 'sexuality.'"[57] It is precisely this latent homosexuality that Sedgwick seeks to recover.

Yet neither Girard's interdiction nor Sedgwick's readings of repressed elaborations of homosexual desire provide an adequate description of the celibate plotting in *The Bostonians*. The desire between Olive and Basil is overt; Olive finds Basil "very handsome" before remembering that "she hated men, as a class, anyway" (20). At their first repast, Basil imagines marrying Olive: "It came over him, while he waited for his hostess to reappear, that she was unmarried as well as rich, that she was sociable (her letter answered for that) as well as single; and he had for a moment a whimsical vision of becoming a partner in so flourishing a firm" (16). This "whimsical vision" quickly dissipates as he realizes "nothing would induce him to make love to such a type as that" (16). This refusal of Olive's type directly precedes Basil's description of Olive as a reformer who is "unmarried by every implication of her being" (17). These overt displays of desire are interrupted by ideological considerations—Olive's hatred of men "as a class" and Basil's rejection of Olive as "a type"—suggesting that the straight line of desire to the mediator is blocked on political grounds. This is not the repression of desire in Sedgwick's model but rather the refusal of socially sanctioned consummation (marriage to one's cousin is lauded as a social good), generating a configuration of desire rooted in celibate sociability.[58] This new celibate configuration negates the possibility of marriage to Basil in advance, suggesting that Olive invites Basil to town as a rival "to contend" in order to increase her own desirability. While Olive has been unable to woo the pale shop maidens, she hopes that if she acquires a worthy rival, her own stock will rise and she will be able to win a woman like Verena. Here, the reform politics of celibacy act as a narrative motor that intersects the courtship plot perpendicularly, blocking it and keeping it from progressing. This interruption of heterosexual marriage (between Olive and Basil) occurs either temporarily, only to constitute a different marital coupling (Basil and Verena in the case of *The Bostonians*), or occurs permanently to end in Boston marriage (as in *Diana Victrix*).

Sedgwick's modification of Girard's work and the work of scholars like Richard Kaye and David Kurnick has sought to dislodge "the end of the text as the end of analysis," displacing the heteronormativity of the marriage plot and capturing the queer energies of plot as it unfolds.[59] In contrast, Leslie Fiedler's work has brought the queerness of endings to the forefront of our attention. No thesis in American literature has had a greater impact on queer plotting than Fiedler's claim that the central structure of American literature is the "turn from society to nature or nightmare out of a desperate need to avoid the facts of wooing, marriage, and childbearing."[60] Fiedler describes "the typical male protagonist" as "a man on the run, harried into the forest and out to sea, down the river or into combat—anywhere to avoid 'civilization,' which is to say, the confrontation of a man and a woman which leads to the fall to sex, marriage, and responsibility."[61] The conclusion of *The Bostonians* does not conform to this Fiedlerian pattern—such an ending would figure Olive and Verena departing on a feminist speaking tour, figuring their travels as a version of "light[ing] out for the territory." But while the ending does not follow Fiedler's framework, Olive and Verena's travels throughout the middle of *The Bostonians* might be helpfully read as a fleeing from Fiedlerian "'civilization.'" This reading might figure "civilization" as the conservative forces of tradition that Olive and (to some extent) Verena work to fight against.

Where Fiedler's celibate protagonist eventually finds a wife/mother substitute in the figure of a dark-skinned companion with whom he shares an "innocent homosexuality," my reading suggests that we read "innocent homosexuality" throughout James's text rather than primarily at its conclusion.[62] While Christopher Looby understands Fiedler's "innocent homosexuality" as implying a "guilty homosexuality," I see Fiedler's category having a more positive inflection (not as the opposite of "guilty homosexuality" but opposite something like Blakean "experience").[63] My reading of the imbrications between marriage, Boston marriage, celibacy, and homosexuality in *The Bostonians* has attempted to excavate "innocent homosexuality" obliquely, thematizing and clarifying the "perplex[ing]" and often nebulous territory of homoeroticism.[64]

Because *The Bostonians* does not conform to Fiedler's plotting, many readers would contend that the ending of the novel is heteronormative. But the celibate plot allows us to interpret the conclusion in which Olive painfully loses Verena not only as a failure (the defeat of one rival over another) but also as the decisive beginning of Olive's feminist speaking career.[65] One is preceded and necessitated by the other; Olive's romantic defeat is her political victory and her confirmation of singularity. When Olive takes the stage after Basil has carried Verena away, James writes: "Every sound instantly dropped, the hush was respectful, the great public waited." Verena's departure enables Olive to seize the crowd's respectful hush and to find the confidence to speak in public for the first time. Olive instrumentalizes celibacy as a tool of independence and feminist reform. Where Olive has continually sought a vehicle for her feminist agenda in other women, she realizes as she takes the stage that she is capable of being her own conduit, the messenger for her own message.

Celibate Artistry

In the previous two sections, I have been arguing that without the self-mastery of celibacy, Boston marriage cannot signify in the public sphere. In this section, I will argue that James's own celibacy enables his authorship to signify in the public sphere. A discussion of James's celibacy enhances my earlier consideration of *The Bostonians* by locating Olive's identity as a spinster in relation to constructions of bachelorhood and returns us to the question with which we began: What is celibacy's relation to homosexuality? In Wendy Graham's account of James's sexuality, she argues that his "abstention from full genital contact did not deprive him of a homosexual identity."[66] Graham sees James's "lifelong celibacy" as a characteristic feature of queer life, much as I argued earlier.[67] Unlike other homosexuals he knew

(Gosse, Symonds, Wilde, and Sargent), James never married or fathered children. While Graham sees this as a product of James's fear that he came from weak stock (prone to sickness, anxiety, and other ailments), I see his singleness as an artistic choice that is central to his identity as an author and to his theory of the novel.[68] It is a choice that, as subsequent chapters will show, was repeated throughout the twentieth century by other queer artists like Auden and Warhol.

In one light, this genealogy might look like a story of sublimation. In this story, sexual energy is rechanneled in a socially useful direction such as the creation of art. As Tim Dean has eloquently pointed out, "We are always sublimating to one degree or another."[69] He suggests the capaciousness of the idea of sublimating, going so far as to suggest that "if we take *satisfaction of the drive without repression* as our definition of sublimation—as Freudian metapsychology urges us to do—then we're led to the counterintuitive conclusion that heterosexual copulation itself constitutes a kind of sublimation."[70] With this understanding in mind, I certainly think it is possible to understand James's choice (as well as those of Auden and Warhol) as participating in such a genealogy. However, I will contend that it is more productive to think celibacy outside the logics of sublimation for two reasons (in addition to the overcapaciousness of sublimation itself). First, as I argued in the introduction, sublimation is normative at its heart (even if it does not necessarily entail what Jean Laplanche calls "the value judgements . . . of some conformist consensus") and thus does not capture the queer, revolutionary, and socially disprized aspects of modernist celibacy that this study explores.[71] Second, as the counterintuitive nature of Dean's claim implies, sublimation is a profoundly desexualizing rubric (even as it can encompass sex). My commitment to theorizing celibacy as a sexuality, rather than its absence, suggests a second reason for eschewing sublimation as the primary way of understanding this Jamesian genealogy of authorship.

James's 1881 reflections upon his arrival in London exemplify the profound importance of his singleness to his artistic identity: "London is on the whole the most possible form of life. I take it as an artist and a bachelor; as one who has the passion of observation and whose business is the study of human life."[72] Here, the identities of artist and bachelor are both engaged in observing human life.[73] While this "business" is clearly associated with that of the realist novelist, I want to draw attention to the celibate's association with observation, rather than with the participation that is emblematic of Olive and other feminist activists. In "Irving's Posterity" (2000), Michael

Warner argues that the "deep and resilient moral fantasy . . . that reproduction is essentially generous" alienates those, like the celibate, who are "estranged from reproductive sexuality," and even "from life itself."[74] This alienation "from life itself" is underlined by the long-established trope of the bachelor as observer, which begins in America with Washington Irving and Walt Whitman and is carried into the twentieth century by Marianne Moore, T. S. Eliot, and Joseph Cornell.[75] James highlights his sense of alienation from life, his refuge in observation, when he claims that "London is on the whole the most possible form of life." The monotony and boredom of the celibate life (excluded from the events and rhythms of marriage and child rearing) make the celibate a keen observer. Small changes and what Heather Love describes as "the minor events and details" that characterize "lonely or out-of-the-way lives" are the only consolation that James understands the celibate to possess.[76] London makes available the most a bachelor and an artist can expect from his limited, nonreproductive life.[77]

In "The Art of Fiction" (1884), artist and bachelor fuse, becoming one identity. In addition to sharing the bachelor's powers of observation, the artist, like the bachelor, is fundamentally monadic, apart from spheres of influence: "The guides and philosophers who might have most to say to him must leave him alone when it comes to the application of precepts, as we leave the painter in communion with his palette."[78] The celibacy of James's authorship becomes particularly important insofar as "The Art of Fiction" directly responds to Walter Besant's earlier essay of the same name. Besant and James Rice composed one of the most prolific and professional writing teams of the 1870s and 1880s.[79] While Besant would later denounce this collaboration in his 1902 autobiography, James uses the mediocrity of Besant and Rice's collaborative writing as a backdrop against which to make his argument for the necessity of solitary, celibate authorship.[80] Similarly, James's nearly contemporaneous story, "The Lesson of the Master" (1888), interlaces celibacy with artistic greatness. The story depicts a young novelist, Paul Overt, who isolates himself and forgoes his ladylove at the suggestion of an older novelist (the eponymous master). While scholarly interpretations generally cannot decide whether the master planned to send Overt away in order to steal his beloved, to help him write, or both, a reading of the celibacy plot suggests that whatever the motive of the master, the result of the advice is the production of a great masterpiece forged by the independence of celibacy.

Rather than seeing James's celibacy as only an element of a homosexual identity, I understand it as a crucial component of his novelistic production and, as he will argue in "The Future of the Novel" (1899), a frequent part of its consumption: "The larger part of the great multitude that sustains the teller and the publisher of tales is constituted by boys and girls; by girls in especial, if we apply the term to the later stages of the life of the innumerable women who, under modern arrangements, increasingly fail to marry—fail, apparently, even, largely, to desire to."[81] Novels in both conception and reception are figured by James as celibate. James's theory of the novel here underlines the centrality of celibacy plots. While "The Art of Fiction," "The Lesson of the Master," and "The Future of the Novel" sharply distinguish between the manly intelligent bachelor-producer of the novel and its childlike "irreflective and uncritical" spinster consumer, *The Bostonians* draws a far less distinct line between bachelors and spinsters.[82] With this understanding of James's own celibacy in mind, his description of Olive as celibate reverberates differently: "She was a spinster as Shelley was a lyric poet, or as the month of August is sultry" (17). Here, the suffragist is the artist's kin: the celibate Olive is compared to the poet Shelley, not the "irreflective and uncritical" spinster reader. Thus, we must understand her sacrifice as that of an artistic renunciation akin to Overt's renunciation in "The Lesson of the Master." In James's career-long meditation on singleness, *The Bostonians* anomalously imagines a bachelor-like female celibacy as a mode of and catalyst for action and creativity. Olive's celibacy is put in dialogue with James's own, endowing it with a second content, a second way of being in the world: that of the artist.

| Chapter Two | Celibate Time |

The "Late" Moore

Marianne Moore's appearance in a Braniff airlines commercial with Mickey Spillane, the author of popular, sexually explicit and violent detective novels, illustrates the enormity of her fame in the late 1960s (fig. 2.1).[1] The tremendous financial success of the Braniff advertising campaign and the repetitious play of the commercial make it the most widely circulated image of Moore in her lifetime.[2] The advertisement offers a fascinating site for examining the paradox of Moore's celibate celebrity: Moore's celibacy is forged in modesty, while the publicity of celebrity demands exposure. Moreover, Moore's poetics famously employ the language of advertising, while Braniff traffics in the sale of women's bodies, celebrity bodies, and of course airplanes.[3] Braniff's stewardesses, for example, would take off layers of clothing in flight as part of what was known as the "air strip." I will argue that in spite of and because of this relationship to women's bodies, Moore participated in the Braniff campaign ("When you got it—flaunt it!"). Thus, I see Moore as part of what Kathleen M. Barry calls "the increasing eroticization of airline marketing" in the 1960s, even as Moore transforms the erotic object from that of a young woman to that of an older one.[4] Moore relocates the spinster in an economy of desire and desirability, an economy of style and unavailability that nonetheless avoids a sense of undesirability.

FIGURE 2.1. Publicity still from Braniff Airlines commercial featuring Marianne Moore and Mickey Spillane. TV still shot by director Timothy Galfas. Reprinted by permission of David M. Moore, Esquire, Administrator of the Literary Estate of Marianne Moore, and of George Lois. Image courtesy of The Rosenbach Museum & Library.

This play of desire was extraordinarily effective; legendary ad man George Lois describes the campaign that he created as "a zany, outrageous campaign that featured a smorgasbord of the world's oddest couples, exchanging the screwiest and most sophisticated chatter heard on television. Our juxtaposition of unlikely couples was unprecedented, creating the perception that when you flew Braniff International, you never knew who might be in the seat next to you."[5] But Lois does not explain why Moore and Spillane are an odd couple other than to say that Moore is a "poet" and Spillane a "crime novelist." Lois's statement might be interpreted as locating the oddness of the pairing in the relationship between poetry and prose or between Moore's relatively meager sales and cultural capital in relation to Spillane's astronomical financial success and lack of critical acclaim. While these oppositions no doubt hold, I will argue that Moore's celibacy, particularly the anachronistic celibate temporality that is the subject of this chapter, is juxtaposed with Spillane's highly gendered promiscuous sexuality.

Because the commercial is not publicly available, I reproduce the dialogue here it in its entirety:

MICKEY SPILLANE: Well, I'll tell you frankly.
What I really wanted to be all my life was a poet.
Only I couldn't think of any of the rhymes.
You know what I mean?

MARIANNE MOORE: *I* know what you mean.

ANNOUNCER VOICE-OVER: Tough Mickey Spillane and the great Marianne Moore always fly Braniff. They like our food. They like our girls. They like our style. And they like to be on time. Thanks for flying Braniff, folks.

MM: When you got it—flaunt it!

MS: You know, you got a way with words. (*Marianne giggles.*)[6]

Spillane's opening dialogue functions as a confession as he "frankly" reveals that his life's secret dream was to be a poet. This confession places Moore in a position of power—the confessor listening to the confessant.[7] This power differential between Moore and Spillane is most obvious insofar as the commercial operates at Spillane's expense when he misrecognizes Braniff's slogan ("When you got it—flaunt it!") as Moore's eloquence ("You know, you got a way with words"), pointing at her and causing her to laugh. Moore's emphatic pronunciation of the word "I" as she "sympathetically" responds to and identifies with Spillane further flaunts her style in response to his confession: "*I* know what you mean" (even as she identically rhymes "mean" with "mean"). For the informed viewer familiar with Moore's work and modernist poetry generally, there is an embedded joke—poetry is much more than rhyme (though Spillane does not know this) and, as is the case with much of Moore's work, exists without rhyme. However, for most viewers, the likely result of this line is to dissociate Moore from poetry. Spillane and many viewers think she has trouble rhyming, though as her identical rhyme clearly indicates, she does not.[8]

The most striking way in which the commercial elevates Moore over Spillane, however, is temporally. She occupies his desired future ("a poet"), embodying the path not chosen: an alternative, brighter, more stylish future. The beverages visible in figure 2.1 emphasize this temporal narrative as Spillane's milk positions him as a child in relation to the teasing sophistication of Moore's champagne maturity.[9] While my section title's invocation of "lateness" signifies Moore at the end of her career, this chapter is less preoccupied with a kind of chronological biographical unfolding than a developmental "lateness": the "has-been" Moore who inhabits the past and is developmentally "late," as all "old maids" are according to a trajectory of normal sexual maturation that must pass through marriage. Moore refunctions the Braniff announcer's claim that she "like[s] to be on time" in order to renovate this denigrating logic and to forge her desirability.

This commercial has not been examined in part because literary scholars continue to be uninterested in the late Moore. Her writing career spanned seven decades and began to receive serious attention by the likes of H.D., Ezra Pound, and T. S. Eliot by the late 1910s. In the 1920s, Moore was regarded as one of the greatest women of American letters, known for her wit, her formal innovation, and her lifelong celibacy. While she was revered in the highest terms by a select coterie of readers, only the late Moore would receive widespread fame. This is the period of Moore's public celibacy, which began when she won the Bollingen Prize, the National Book Award, and the Pulitzer Prize in the first six months of 1952 and culminates with the 1969 commercial. This publicity-filled moment acts as a barometer for national attitudes toward celibacy. Moore seizes this moment to fashion herself a celibate celebrity and to recast the social position of celibates more generally. The Braniff commercial exemplifies Moore's use of an acrobatic temporal strategy (Moore as Spillane's desirable future) to reinvent the spinster. Elizabeth Bishop's "Efforts of Affection: A Memoir of Marianne Moore" (1979), the text that more than any other produces Moore's posthumous image, theorizes Moore's relationship to time even more fully and articulates Moore's strong feminism over the objections and criticisms from the feminists of her time (143–144). More recent feminist scholars like Jeanne Heuving have also seen Moore as a strong feminist but only by pathologizing Moore's "maidenly" image.[10]

Rather than interpreting this image as limiting, creating a boring spinster, I see Moore's unaffiliated spinster status as a fascinating self-depiction that promises to indicate the inadequacy of the lonely spinster model on the one hand, and romantic friendship models and more pro-sex models of female-female relations on the other.[11] Thus, I hope that by reading the most famous instantiation of this stereotype, as well as the more ancillary texts of its wide dissemination, we may understand how Moore deployed and managed this image. More important, this image helps us to understand how celibacy, even as it is crucial to the history of homosexuality, is separate from that history in vitally interesting and unexplored ways. Along these lines, I will elaborate the importance of Moore's celibate temporality to her poetics and politics, arguing that she attempts to live celibacy as a depathologized and deinstitutionalized identity, or, in her pithy formulation: "What of chastity? It confers a particular strength."[12] Rather than seeing celibacy as deflectional, hiding another identity, Moore attempts to redeem celibacy on its own terms by anachronistically identifying with its past.

Celibate Temporality

Elizabeth Freeman's meditation on anachronism in her essay "Packing History, Count(er)ing Generations" (2000) begins with a powerful anecdote about bodies that record their temporality (detailing the transformation of "identification into identity"):

> As a graduate student . . . at a moment when "identity" was rapidly morphing into cross-gender identification, I told an anecdote I thought would illustrate this crossing: "I wear this T-shirt that says 'Big Fag' sometimes, because lesbians give potlucks and dykes fix cars. I've never done well at either, so 'Big Fag' feels more appropriate." A student came to see me in office hours, quite upset. She was in her early twenties, a few years younger than I, but she dressed like my feminist teachers had in college. She stood before me in Birkenstocks, wool socks, jeans, and a women's music T-shirt, and declared that she felt dismissed and marginalized by my comment, that lesbians-who-give-potlucks described her exactly, and that I had clearly fashioned a more interesting identity with her own as a foil. I had thought I was telling a story about being inadequate to prevailing lesbian identity-forms, or about allying with gay men, or perhaps even about the lack of representational choices for signaling *femme*. But it turned out that I was telling a story about anachronism, with "lesbian" as the sign of times gone by and her body as an implicit teaching text.[13]

Freeman resists "the rehabilitative gesture" to mobilize temporal crossings like that of her student in the service of "a better future feminism."[14] Rather, Freeman is interested in "amnesiatic gaps" within social movements, charting how identities *surpass* one another (in the progression from, say, lesbian to "'Big Fag'"), foreclosing and disavowing the possibility of "earlier" identities.[15]

As Freeman's theorization suggests, Moore's celibacy is foreclosed not only by queer theory but also by second-wave feminism. As I argued in the introduction, second-wave feminism leaves the single woman behind in favor of her married counterpart.[16] Moore reanimates Progressive Era celibacy as a political identity in the 1950s and 1960s, when it no longer seems viable, in order to rejuvenate socially, sexually, and temporally abject spinsters. It is not just that Moore is old-fashioned, but that celibate temporality is indelibly marked by the past. Celibates like Henry James's Olive Chancellor and George Santayana's Nathaniel Alden are described as being prematurely old, as if they were born in a metaphoric past that preceded their actual birth date. For example, the narrator of *The Bostonians* (1886) says of Olive: "She was so essentially a celibate that Ransom found himself thinking of her as old, though when he came to look at her . . . it was apparent that her years were fewer than his own."[17] Similarly, the abstemious Nathaniel is described as young "but had put on old age in his youth."[18] These celibates feel old-fashioned or out of sync to us, in part, because queer theory's revolutionary force grows out of the sexual revolution, which connects sexual expression and freedom. By attending to Moore's anachronism, we can summon a new genealogy of sexual agency—one that deploys past conventions to rattle the present—for queer theory.

Moore's poetics and politics reject the normative script of life expectations, unwriting belatedness and pastness as problems and rewriting them as guides for the future. The startling transformations that her citational poetics enact upon the luminous details of newspaper accounts and other mundane writing suggest the way in which the plodding pace of the belated—off the fast track to the future or even to the present—can create new futures from past happenings. This celibate temporality does not inhere in celibate identity (though I am arguing that it does inhere in Moore), as Charles Dickens's Miss Havisham and Patrick White's Theodora Goodman make clear; rather, celibate temporality is a tool for critiquing heteronormative and couple-oriented understandings of time. The disruption of celibate temporality's anachronism jars us, as Freeman suggests, to "reimagine our historical categories."[19] While for Freeman these historical categories seem to refer to the histories and temporal orderings of social movements like "feminist 'waves' and queer 'generations,'"[20] I am interested in the ways that Moore's belatedness forces us to reimagine much broader historical categories, asking: What is a sexuality? What is a sex act? What constitutes queerness?

Celibacy's powerful anachronism stems, I would contend, not just from its association with repression but also, as I argued in the introduction, from its failure (outside ecclesiastical institutions) to fit into modern frameworks of determined and determinate sexuality. In this potentiality model of celibacy, celibacy's future is vastly indeterminate, pure becoming. If this potentiality model of celibacy makes clear that celibacy has no easy relation to the future, Robert Payne's birthday encomium for Moore, "On Mariamna De Maura" (1964), suggests that celibacy's relation to its Victorian past is similarly overdetermined. In his tribute, he imagines Mariamna as a fourteenth-century poet, associating her timeless fame with celibacy: locked chests in "monasteries and nunneries," books of "the lives of the saints," and her formal "prun[ing] in excess of desire."[21] Payne's work offers one example of the many pasts with which Moore is associated—Victorian, medieval, and even prehistoric, as in Bryher's metrical nickname "(ptero)dactyl"—creating a complex relationship between Moore and the past.[22] Bishop remarks early in her narrative of Moore: "No matter how early one arrived, Marianne was always there first" (124). While this statement can and must be assimilated to a discussion of influence—Marianne as ever-looming precursor—it also demands our attention because of the sheer number of times Bishop mentions Moore arriving first in the brief memoir: first to the library, the circus, the elevator, the YMHA, and the poetry reading. In this memoir centrally preoccupied by questions of untimeliness—earliness, lateness, and belatedness—the time of celibacy is the past, the prior. Bishop corrects for her temporal anxiety by positing Moore as a relic of the past, while she significantly represents a past that, for Moore, is talismanic, a guide for the future.

What might Bishop's vexed depiction of Moore as a relic of the (talismanic) past help us to understand about the older poet? To begin to answer this question, I turn to the meeting of these poets described by Bishop: "She was forty-seven, an age that seemed old to me then, and her hair was mixed with white to a faint rust pink, and her rust-pink eyebrows were frosted with white. The large flat black hat was as I'd expected it to be. She wore a blue tweed suit that day and, as she usually did then, a man's 'polo shirt,' as they were called, with a black bow at the neck. The effect was quaint, vaguely Bryn Mawr 1909, but stylish at the same time" (124). This passage marks Moore's age as seeming old and dotes on her hair mixed with white and similarly frosted eyebrows. In obsessively referring to Moore (or her practices, possessions, and manners) as "old," "older," "olden," and "old-fashioned," as well as making various other intimations of age without specifically using the word "old," Bishop establishes Moore's "bad timing" in relation to her own New Womanly contemporaneity (drinking, smoking, and wearing silk stockings). But the most revealing detail in the passage is the "vaguely Bryn Mawr 1909" effect at this 1934 meeting. When Bishop describes Moore as "vaguely Bryn Mawr 1909," she associates her with the arrested development and adolescence of college. Because Bishop admits this description's "vague[ness]," we know that this association is not a universal one; perhaps, then, Bishop makes it to carve out her maturity in relation to the college-associated Moore. But when we read Moore described as "vaguely Bryn Mawr 1909," we must also see her dressed in what Elizabeth Freeman calls "temporal drag"—an identification with an earlier historical moment.[23] The citation of Moore's dress is neither "parodic" (the outfit is "stylish") nor "consolidating of authority, in that they leave the very authority they cite visible as a ruin" (the effect is *vaguely* Bryn Mawr—a Bryn Mawr long past).[24]

The "stylish[ness]" of Moore's ensemble begins to suggest the talismanic relation that Moore draws from the past, a relation heightened by Bishop's description of the Moore home:

> The atmosphere of 260 Cumberland Street was of course "old-fashioned," but even more, otherworldly—as if one were living in a diving bell from a different world, let down through the crass atmosphere of the twentieth century. Leaving the diving bell . . . one was apt to have a slight case of mental or moral bends. . . . Yet I never left Cumberland Street without feeling happier: uplifted, even inspired, determined to be good, to work harder, not to worry about what other people thought, never to try to publish anything until I thought I'd done my best with it, no matter how many years it took—or never to publish at all. (137)

While this atmosphere is in part uplifting and in part oppressive for Bishop (giving her "a slight case of mental or moral bends" from the difficult temporal transition, as well as keeping her from publication), she recognizes it as a site of inspiration for Moore. The passage implies that Moore's relationship to temporality is essential to her originality. This correspondence between time and originality receives its clearest articulation in Bishop's "completely unscientific theory" about Moore: "For my own amusement, I had already made up a completely unscientific theory that Marianne was possessed of a unique, involuntary sense of rhythm, therefore of meter, quite unlike anyone else's. She looked like no one else; she talked like no one else; her poems showed a mind not much like anyone else's; and her notion of meter and rhyme were unlike all the conventional notions—so why not believe that . . . Marianne from birth, physically, had been set going to a different rhythm?" (139–140). Here, the deferral of emphasis on the theory, its original purpose as an "amusement" and its status as "completely unscientific," belies its importance. Bishop's protestations about her theory confer the status of a textual key: this passage offers itself diegetically as the secret about Marianne Moore. The secret is that Moore has a different relationship to time, one that helps Bishop recognize "the rarity of [Moore's] true originality" (140).

The words "rarity" and "involuntary" are important, since Bishop needs to ensure that Moore is not unique (or at least not fully the author of her uniqueness). The question then becomes, who is like Marianne Moore? One passage toward the end of the memoir begins to provide some answers: "She once remarked, after a visit to her brother and his family, that the state of being married and having children had one enormous advantage: 'One never has to worry about whether one is doing the right thing or not. There isn't time. One is always having to go to the market or drive the children somewhere. There isn't time to wonder, "Is this *right* or isn't it?"'" (154). Time, here, is the purview of the unmarried and childless. Celibates have the "burden" of time, of pastness and reflection, not possessing the half-sarcastic "advantage" of married parents.[25] Moore expresses a similar antinatal sentiment in a November 1961 letter to Henry Allen Moe, the head of the Guggenheim Foundation, sandbagging a pregnant Sylvia Plath by caustically writing in her "recommendation": "You are not subsidized for having a baby especially in view of a world population explosion. You should look before you leap and examine your world-potentialities of responsibility as a contributory parent."[26] These passages are nothing short of an elaboration of an ethics of celibate temporality; the celibate is the only person not too engrossed in the time-consuming scripts of rote existence to puzzle over ethical questions. Pastness functions as a mode of progression because the contemplative life of celibate reflection is, for Moore, the only ethical way to imagine a future.

In order to demonstrate that Moore is like other celibates, that she is a "rarity" but not unique, Bishop locates her in a celibate literary tradition that encompasses (at least) Gerard Manley Hopkins, Lewis Carroll, and the monastic authors of the concluding paragraph's "illuminated manuscript":

Ninety years or so ago, Gerard Manley Hopkins wrote a letter to Robert Bridges about the ideal of the "gentleman," or the "artist" versus the "gentleman." Today his ideas may sound impossibly Victorian, but I find this letter still applicable and very moving: "As a fact poets and men of art are, I am sorry to say, by no means necessarily or commonly gentlemen. For gentlemen do not pander to lust or other baseness nor . . . give themselves airs and affectations, nor do other things to be found in modern works . . . If an artist or thinker feels that were he to become in those ways ever so great, he would still be essentially lower than a gentleman that was no artist and no thinker. And yet to be a gentleman is but on the brim of morals and rather a thing of manners than morals properly. Then how much more must art and philosophy and manners and breeding and everything else in the world be below the least degree of true virtue. This is that chastity of mind which seems to lie at the very heart and be the parent of all good, the seeing at once what is best, and holding to that, and not allowing anything else whatever to be heard pleading to the contrary . . . I agree then, and vehemently, that a gentleman . . . is in the position to despise the poet, were he Dante or Shakespeare, and the painter, were he Angelo or Apelles, for anything that showed him *not* to be a gentleman. He is in a position to do it, but if he is a gentleman perhaps this is what he will not do." The word "gentleman" makes us uncomfortable now, and its feminine counterparts, whether "lady" or "gentlewoman," embarrass us even more. But I am sure that Marianne would have "vehemently agreed" with Hopkins's strictures: to be a poet was not the be-all, end-all of existence. (155–156, her ellipsis and emphasis)

Here, Bishop establishes Hopkins as the poet whose sensibility is closest to Moore's. While we might see this as another gesture of Bishop's articulation of her own modernity in relation to Moore's pastness—that is, Moore's closest poetic contemporary dates from "ninety years" ago—I think Bishop positions Moore in a more profound way. Bishop's Moore revalues the past in order to change our understanding of it, but also to reorder the present and the future. Moore's "virtue" and "chastity of mind" (and it is important to hear the sexual overtones of these terms), which she borrows from a partial identification with the past, might make us "uncomfortable now," but this is precisely what enables Moore to pose "the interesting threat that the genuine *past*-ness of the past sometimes makes to the political present."[27] The "*past*-ness of the past" destabilizes and denaturalizes the existing order by suggesting that social organizations have taken other shapes at other times. Where Raymond Williams posits emergent formations as having the greatest impact on the dominant social organization, Moore activates the residual as a force for social renovation. Her unusual relationship to temporality preserves the possibility of change and suggests that the past is the key to future transformation.

"A Burning Desire to . . ."

This threatening possibility animates Moore's last single volume of original work, *Tell Me, Tell Me: Granite, Steel, and Other Topics* (1966). The volume contains both poetry and prose and was written at the height of Moore's celebrity. I concentrate on this volume because it frequently represents Moore's celebrity and celibacy (beginning with its very first stanza) and theorizes these in relation to the past.[28] While I read this volume in order to highlight the public celibacy of the late Moore, her celibate identity exists from at least as early as her Bryn Mawr years when she was participating in suffrage campaigns. Linda Leavell has suggested that this celibate identity may date from even earlier, since Moore identifies with the bachelor Uncle George in Jacob Abbot's Rollo books as a child and adopts various bachelor roles throughout her adolescence.[29] An examination of this volume brings into focus Moore's career-long goal of improving the lives of spinsters in works such as "Councell to a Bachelor," "And Shall Life Pass an Old Maid By?," "Marriage," and her essay on Emily Dickinson.

Though this volume has never been treated as a whole, and its individual works have scarcely been examined, Moore scholarship has taken up questions of sexuality from a range of perspectives.[30] For example, Charles Molesworth writes in his biography of Moore: "Moore never, as far as I can tell, had an affair or a lover. Yet, paradoxically, Kenneth Burke called her one of the most sexual women he ever met."[31] Molesworth's assertion of Moore's hypereroticized abstinence seems to stand in tension with the claims of commentators like Kathryn Kent who imagine Moore as a lesbian (while recognizing that she never identified as such) and those of commentators like John Vincent and Ellen Levy who see her occupying a queer nonidentity.[32]

To begin to make sense of these competing readings of Moore's sexuality, I turn to a text from *Tell Me, Tell Me* that explicitly presents itself as being about (at least one kind of) desire—Moore's essay "A Burning Desire to Be Explicit" (1966):

Always, in whatever I wrote—prose or verse—I have had a burning desire to be explicit; beset always, however carefully I had written, by the charge of obscurity. Having entered Bryn Mawr with intensive zeal to write, I examined, for comment, the margin of a paper with which I had taken a great deal of trouble and found, "I presume you had an idea if one could find out what it is."

Again—recently! In a reading of my verse for a women's club, I included these lines from "Tell me, tell me":

I vow, rescued tailor
of Gloucester, I am going
to flee: by engineering strategy—
the viper's traffic-knot—flee
to metaphysical newmown hay,
honeysuckle, or woods fragrance. . . .

After the program, a strikingly well-dressed member of the audience, with equally positive manner, inquired, "*What* is metaphysical newmown hay?"

I said, "Oh, something like a sudden whiff of fragrance in contrast with the doggedly continuous opposition to spontaneous conversation that had gone before."

"Then why don't you *say* so?" the impressive lady rejoined.[33]

When Moore attempts explicitness, her writing always faces "the charge of obscurity." She does not obviate this charge in the case of the Bryn Mawr paper, nor does she explain or define what the lines from "Tell me, tell me" mean. Rather, she says they are "something like . . ." An examination of the word "explicit" (meaning open, clear, definite, unambiguous) suggests that Moore's essay fails to achieve its professed desire in practice. Perhaps this essay is also about a different kind of "explicitness." Though the OED does not cite "explicit" as meaning "sexually explicit" until 1971 (five years after the publication of Moore's essay), I have found the word to have this meaning as early as 1963.[34] A burning desire to be sexually explicit, then. Moore compliments the "positive manner" of the "member of the audience" from the "women's club" and calls her "strikingly well-dressed" and "impressive." This string of three compliments would seem to constitute a desire for this audience member as well as for explicitness. This reading finds support in Moore's mention of "Bryn Mawr," which might code lesbian desire, as well as in the flirty exchange with the woman. In contrast to previously asked questions ("the doggedly continuous opposition to spontaneous conversation"), the woman's forthrightness is a "spontaneous" and delightful surprise. I say flirty because Moore seems to imply that the "impressive lady" is the "sudden whiff of fragrance."[35]

The desires (to be explicit and for the "impressive lady") are homologous in that neither desire is achieved in practice. This dissonance between desire and practice obscures her sexuality, lending it an "oddness" in the Gissing sense (uneven, not in a couple), but also a "queerness." While celibacy falls within the penumbra of the queer, celibate and queer readings overlap without being coextensive. Rather, both kinds of readings, so new to Moore studies, are energizing and important in understanding her life and work.

The closing gesture of "A Burning Desire to be Explicit" might be read along both these axes and might help us to tease out the complex relationship between queerness and celibacy: "Writing is a fascinating business. 'And what should it do?' William Faulkner asked. 'It should help a man endure by lifting up his heart.' (—Admitting that his might not have always done that.) It should."[36] Following our earlier reading of Moore's flirtation with the "impressive lady" and our reading of the sexual charge of explicitness, we might read this passage as one more instance of unachieved queer desire.[37] That is, we might see Faulkner's inability to execute his proposition that writing "should help a man endure by lifting up his heart" as a moment that has a structure of lack—one where desire is not achieved in practice. In this reading, the prescription of Moore's declarative—"It should"—reinforces the reading of celibacy as potentially queer and unable to effect action.

But there is another model of celibacy that Moore is also working out here, one in tension with the first model. In this reading, we might interpret Moore's declaration—"It should"—as a closing gesture of explicitness, of openness. The entire essay culminates in this moment. That is, Moore achieves her burning desire for explicitness in writing the sentence "It should," fulfilling the obligation she describes in the process of describing it. If this statement is an achieved moment of explicitness, a performative utterance, then desire and practice would not be dissonant as they are in the potentiality model. Where the potentiality model is underwritten by a teleological construction of desire—the desirer attempts to transform her desire into an act—this second model would be nonteleological. That is, rather than desiring something lacking and trying to obtain it, in this second model *the celibate desire is the reiteration of celibacy itself.*[38] Here, the incessant performance of celibacy is a process organized by celibate desire rather than a singular choice or lone act. Rather than the patient delay of chastity that moderately dispenses its sexual energies over time in discrete acts, celibacy is constantly unfolding.[39] This model revises psychoanalytic models, since it frames desire outside of lack. In other words, celibacy is only figured as a lack when it is understood as a phase in a movement toward an unknown goal, rather than a reiterative identity. Thus, in Moore's closing sentence— "*It should*"—we might read either the continuation of the interruptive potentiality model or a second model where celibacy is both the desire and the practice. To put this differently, the models have different relationships to practice: the lesbian-inflected first model sees Moore's celibacy as a non-practiced desire; the second model sees celibacy as the practice of the desire.

In this second model, we might understand one instantiation of pleasure to be textual. Moore's "desire for explicitness" appears in "whatever [she] wrote." The inscriptive quality of Moore's desire is further articulated in "Saint Valentine," where she worries whether her assistance (by writing the poem) will supplant the object of her homage (which is also simultaneously love):

If those remembered by you [Saint Valentine]
are to think of you and not me,
it seems to me that the memento
or compliment you bestow
should have a name beginning with "V"[40]

Moore's multiplication of yonic *v*'s (which Bishop might echo in her multiplication of *m*'s) functions as a kind of literal/mimetic textual erotics. The "V" of verse threatens to undo Moore's strategy for remembrance of Saint Valentine and love, particularly because "any valentine that is *written* is as the *vendange* to the vine" (Moore's emphasis). Both from "A Burning Desire to be Explicit" and from "Saint Valentine" and its attendant difficulties of replacing love with writing, we know that it is the difficulty of the writing that is the source of its pleasure. Bonnie Costello describes Moore's term "gusto" as "the feeling of pleasure accompanying bafflement."[41] This pleasure in difficulty, in the celibacy of the "the viper's traffic-knot," accounts for the "gusto" of these works. If this textual erotics is present throughout Moore's oeuvre, then the main stratagem of pleasure that emerges in the late Moore is celibate engagement. That is, Moore reinvents the role of the spinster both as a life practice and more performatively as a celibate celebrity to engage the public sphere.

Before moving on to an analysis of celibate engagement, I want to suggest that the pleasure of this life practice is exemplified by "the viper's traffic-knot." "The viper's traffic-knot" is an image of nonreproduction (simultaneously a knotted phallus, a tied tongue, and tied fallopian tubes) and of nonpassage. The denotations of the word "traffic"—illicit trade, intercourse, prostitution (OED)—highlight the "traffic-knot['s]" function as an impediment to sexual acts (if not desire or pleasure). The "traffic-knot" brings everything to a halt. Michael Warner has suggested that "bachelorhood is a category that only makes sense against a narrative background of life expectations."[42] Here, the "traffic-knot" halts expectations and suggests that the way to the future is (when recontextualized in "Tell me, tell me") neither through the well-worn path of expectation and obligation nor through reproduction. "The viper's traffic-knot" is an image not of repression but rather of an enabling blockage that provides an escape.[43] This modesty, this "viper's traffic-knot," is a figure for Moore's celibacy. Celibacy opens up a utopian space—"metaphysical newmown hay, / honeysuckle, or woods fragrance." Here, the word "or" models the reiterative course, the "strategy" "engineer[ed]" by the "viper's traffic-knot," suggesting the movement and interchangeability between "newmown hay," "honeysuckle," and "woods fragrance." Less metaphorically, then, I want to think about Moore's celibacy as impeding the discourse and reality of compulsory heterosexuality and heteronormativity. The citation of "the viper's traffic-knot" in the context of "A Burning Desire" abjures the obligation inherent in the word "*should*," emphasizing the nonteleological reading of her essay.

Telling It Backward

Since the second nonteleological model of celibacy more closely accords with Moore's project to depathologize and improve the lives of spinsters, and because it more accurately describes her celibate poetics, I will focus on this second model for the remainder of the chapter.[44] Harriet Monroe vilifies Moore's poems for possessing "little curve of growth or climax," precisely the quality for which John Ashbery celebrates Moore.[45] An unpublished paper by Cristanne Miller suggests a lack of climax at the level of the line and stanza in addition to a lack of development within the poem. She argues that radical enjambment keeps phrasal units from coinciding with line or stanza breaks.[46] Moore avoids a progressive narrative of sexuality. This avoidance heightens pleasure by suspending closure and resisting climax. This sexual narrative is essential to the construction of her celibate poetics in *Tell Me, Tell Me*. Along these lines, an unpublished letter from Viking Press regarding *Tell Me, Tell Me* contains a table of contents for the forthcoming book where the texts are arranged in reverse chronological order with their original publication dates beside them.[47] Next to "Sun," dated "1961?," Moore's marginal note says, "If 1960, transpose?" (fig. 2.2). This note suggests that reverse chronology is the governing system of ordering in *Tell Me, Tell Me* and that this ordering is crucial to the collection's composition: the collection ends with the 1957 version of the poem "Sun" and begins with the 1966 poem "Granite and Steel." In this vein, the collection as a whole, to borrow a phrase from the closing stanza of "Tell me, tell me," offers itself as a "told-backward biography" of Moore (44).

Resonating with the ways in which Bishop has taught us to recognize Moore, *the collection then appropriates backwardness as a trajectory*. This backwardness also operates at the level of the poem. For instance, the poem "Blue Bug" directly precedes "Arthur Mitchell," but the lines from "Blue Bug"— "bug brother to an Arthur / Mitchell dragonfly"—only make sense after one has read "Arthur Mitchell," illustrating the necessity of a backward reading practice. Such a reading practice is further underscored within the poems as the dragonfly's movements mimic possible and multiple reading practices: "speeding to left / speeding to right; reversible," suggesting the important connection between backwardness and nonteleological movement.[48] Seeing the collection in this light locates Moore's work (usually aligned with the lone lyric) closer to the long poems, process poetics, and sequences of Pound, Zukofsky, Olson, Spicer, and Williams.[49] Heightening Moore's proximity to these poets, the collection does not posit a straight line to the futurity of the past; rather, the past is a set of Doppler effects, diversions, dispersals, swerves, and forking paths: it is, like my second model of celibacy, nonteleological.[50] For example, the poem "Sun" exists in eight versions, leaving no stable origin to move toward. Stuck at the level of the poem, this gusto, this pleasure in difficulty, keeps the reader moving through the collection.

The conditions for the gusto, as a closer look at "Tell me, tell me" demonstrates, take place within the structure of family:

TELL ME, TELL ME

Granite, Steel and Other Topics

CONTENTS

Granite and Steel (1966)	
A BURNING DESIRE TO BE EXPLICIT (1966)	(Christian Science Monitor, 1/11/66)
In Lieu of the Lyre (1965)	(Harvard Advocate, Fall 1965)
The Mind, Intractable Thing (1965)	(The New Yorker, 11/27/65)
Dream (1965)	(The New Yorker, 10/16/65)
Old Amusement Park (1964)	(The New Yorker, 8/29/65)
An Expedient--Leonardo da Vinci's--and a Query	(The New Yorker, 4/18/64) + AO
W. S. Landor (1964)	(The New Yorker, 2/22/64)
To a Giraffe (1964?)	(Steuben booklet) + AO
Charity Overcoming Envy (1963)	(The New Yorker, 3/30/63)
PROFIT IS A DEAD WEIGHT (1963)	(Seventeen, March 1963)
Blue Bug (1962)	(The New Yorker, 5/26/62) + AO
Arthur Mitchell (1962)	(City Center Souvenir, Jan. 1962) + AO
Baseball and Writing (1961)	(The New Yorker, 12/9/61) + AO
"Sun" (1961?)	(The Mentor Book of Religious Verse) + AO, MMR
MY CROW PLUTO--A FANTASY To Victor Hugo of My Crow Pluto (1961)	(Harper's Bazaar Oct. 1961 + AO, MMR + MMR
Rescue with Yul Brynner (1961)	(The New Yorker, 6/20/61) + AO, MMR
Carnegie Hall: Rescued (1960)	(The New Yorker, 8/13/60) + AO, MMR
Tell Me, Tell Me (1960)	(The New Yorker, 4/30/60) + AO, MMR
St. Valentine (1960)	(The New Yorker, 2/13/60)
SUBJECT, PREDICATE, OBJECT (1958)	(Christian Science Monitor, 12/24/58)

AO=The Arctic Ox, Faber 1964

MMR=A Marianne Moore Reader, Viking 1961

caps=prose

FIGURE 2.2. *Tell Me, Tell Me* page proof with Moore's marginal note: "If 1960, transpose?" Reprinted by permission of David M. Moore, Esquire, Administrator of the Literary Estate of Marianne Moore. Image courtesy of The Rosenbach Museum & Library.

A *précis?*
In this told-backward biography
of how the cat's mice when set free
by the tailor of Gloucester, finished
the Lord Mayor's cerise coat—
the tailor's tale ended captivity
in two senses. Besides having told
of a coat which made the tailor's fortune,
it rescued a reader from being driven mad by a scold. (44)

These lines offer themselves as a précis—an annotation or a synopsis—for reading the rest of the poem (and, as I have suggested, the collection as a whole).[51] In order to interpret these lines, one must go backward, rereading the poem as a gloss. The reader must know that Moore referred to her mother, Mary Warner Moore, in family correspondence as "Mouse" and "Mice" over the course of several decades, and that the eponymous character of Beatrix Potter's tale "The Tailor of Gloucester" (1903) is obligated to make a cerise coat for the Lord Mayor's wedding.[52] While working, he hears peculiar sounds and frees some mice that his cat Simpkin has trapped to eat. Shortly afterward, the tailor becomes too sick to work. In repayment for the tailor's lifesaving gesture, the mice finish the coat and help the tailor to become rich. The tailor is "rescued" because without the aid of the mice, he would have continued to live in destitute poverty and would have suffered the Lord Mayor's ill will. The story suggests the danger of life expectations and the value of help, particularly the help of family, in fulfilling obligations.[53]

This reading of obligation and escape begins to situate the citation of the lines from "Tell me, tell me" in "A Burning Desire to be Explicit" and inflects our earlier reading of that essay in its suggestion of the necessity of family in Moore's celibate intervention. In order to contextualize the lines from "Tell me, tell me," to help make them explicit, I turn briefly to the opening of the poem:

Tell me, tell me
where might there be a refuge for me
from egocentricity
and its propensity to bisect,
mis-state, misunderstand
and obliterate continuity? (43)

The speaker's insistent and impatient plea ("Tell me, tell me") and the strong enjambment of line breaks suggest that the self-interested solitude of "egocentricity" is inadequate to maintain the "continuity" of a community.[54] The sought-after "refuge" will instead come in the form of family and the realm of the aesthetic—"Why, oh why, one ventures to ask, set / flatness on some cindery pinnacle / as if on Lord Nelson's revolving diamond rosette?" (43)[55] Here, value is located in "flatness," in modesty and shyness.[56] This value is first figured as the beautiful object, specifically the Paterian "gem" as it appears in its "burnished rarity" (43). But "the absorbing geometry" of this sexualized aesthetic, this "fantasy," is made possible by the celibate's family (43). That is, "the absorbing geometry" is the family structure that modestly hides the celibate's authorial powers.

The celibacy of the list following "the absorbing geometry of a fantasy" highlights this reading:

a James, Miss Potter, Chinese
"passion for the particular," of a
tired man who yet, at dusk,
cut a masterpiece of cerise— (43)

As Linda Leavell has argued, Moore fashioned her family on the closeness of the James family, even reading and discussing the James family letters and autobiographies with her mother (with whom Moore lived almost continuously until her mother's death). In Moore's important essay "Henry James as a Characteristic American" (1934), she writes of James, "There was in him 'the rapture of observation,' but more unequivocally even than that, affection for family. . . . [H]e recalls his mother as so participatingly unremote that he can say, 'I think we almost contested her being separate enough to be proud of us—it was too like being proud of ourselves.'"[57] This familial structure begins to explain Moore's remark that "the cure for loneliness is solitude."[58] Moore merges with her mother to create a Jamesian family that restructures solitude as a mode of relation. Solitary existence is not the isolating loneliness of the closet but rather a fully contented mode of sociability and a crucial part of her poetics. Thus, for Moore, the James family models a way to be a celibate within a family, reducing the "conjugal imperative" placed on celibate women.[59] The Potter family—which in its strictness resembles at least one facet of Moore's family—likely served a similar function in relation to their daughter's unaffiliated status. One marked difference, however, is that the Potter family twice objected to their daughter's proposed engagement, the second time when Potter was forty-seven.[60] While scholarly work on Potter elides her sexuality, paints her as everyone's aunt, ignores her belated marriage, and figures her innocently as a woman writing about animals (very much like older understandings of Moore), she is a figure of nonnormative sexuality.[61] Family enables the intervention of "the viper's traffic-knot," curing loneliness and reducing the time needed "to cut a masterpiece" in cerise or in verse.

Celibate Engagement

Even as I have been arguing that the collection as a whole is a "told-backward biography" (inasmuch as the poems are printed in the chronologically reversed order of their initial publication), this explanation does not fully capture the radical temporality of the volume.[62] The backward-directed *Tell Me, Tell Me: Granite, Steel, and Other Topics* fittingly begins with the Brooklyn Bridge, the exemplum of progressive history—an iconic image of modernity and American engineering. The opening stanza of "Granite and Steel," the collection's other title poem, sketches this progressive utopian America:

> Enfranchising cable, silvered by the sea,
> of woven wire, grayed by the mist,
> and Liberty dominate the Bay—
> her feet as one on shattered chains,
> once whole links wrought by Tyranny. (3)

This stanza encapsulates the whole project of the volume in microcosm. America achieves all of its ideals of liberty and equality, uniting disparate people—the German Roebling, the French Bartholdi, the Mediterranean "Circe" (3), the queer Whitman and Crane.[63] This is America's possibility—the pleasure of the mind in "Granite and Steel" precedes the pleasure of "actuality": "first seen by the eye of the mind, / then by the eye. O steel! O stone!" The beauty is of the dream of America as well as of the actuality of America, even as both pleasures are tempered by the bridge's darker aspect. The poem's notes describe a man who "was unaccountably drawn to climb one of the cables" and was stranded there until the next morning (53). This is the enchanting danger—"crass love of crass priority"—of progress (3). The danger of this progress is also encoded in one of the volume's many demure self-images: post-1789 France was called "Liberty" by its supporters and "Marianne" or Marie-Anne (combining the name of the Virgin Mary and her mother) by its antagonists.[64] In calling "Marianne" Liberty, the volume's opening stanza celebrates celibacy and Moore as unifying a nation.[65]

The poem's reference to the Statue of Liberty also evokes what Elizabeth Gregory describes as Moore's association with "a generalized sense of patriotism," the most potent example of which is Moore's trademark "Washington crossing the Delaware" outfit.[66] In addition to this patriotism, Gregory locates Moore's fame in her seemingly innocuous eccentricity as a single woman, standing alone like Bartholdi's statue: "Moore's age and status as a single woman also fed her appeal: insofar as she seemed sweet and a bit befuddled, she acted as a reassuring counter to the dread that old women, especially spinsters, sometimes engender as reminders both of death and, in their apparent sexlessness, of the possibility that women may escape the sex-work hierarchy."[67] Gregory's invocation of "dread" gets at the heart of normative cultural assumptions about women's "use"; the spinster is a "dreaded" burden (with lesser access to the bachelor's potentialities) in this register: unattractive, barren, invisible, and untouchable. Moore's inhabitation of "Washington" is crucial to her project of restaging the "dread" of the spinster.[68] Washington is associated in the Moore family with the masculinity and accompanying freedom of the "blameless bachelor,"[69] enabling Moore to rewrite the meaning of female celibacy:

> Washington not only discerned the hour of the Birth of a nation under God; but by his acts disclosed how that nation must live under God if it was to endure. . . . Washington, moreover, translated hope into actuality, and showed us at Valley Forge how one ought always to pray and not to faint. To begin the discharge of any duty, leaving God to finish it, nothing doubting. He was the sort of optimist the world needs now! Finally, he showed what with vision, and hope, a man could do to establish his place and nation by service above self.[70]

In this letter from her brother, John Warner Moore's muscular Christianity—an American Protestant movement that attempted to get men into church and crush sentimentality in order to counter what Ann Douglas has called "the feminization of American culture"—comes across in full force.[71] The letter's focus on masculine "acts" and "duty" is here combined with an anachronistic political strategy (and one that muscular Christianity also promoted), namely, celibacy. Moore summons Washington's masculine access to political power and full ideological weight as the Founding Father—

he has no origins and his conception is immaculate—to enfran
spinster fully in the nation. Like another figure born of famousl
origins, Washington, according to Warner Moore, is a great
Washington's monumentality bestows on him an aura that writ(
of the contact of a sexual economy.[72] Moore inhabits the role of the celibate
and the nation, enfranchising and rewriting both.

While Gregory rightly emphasizes Moore's playful relationship with the
authority of her image, I read Moore's seizure of the public sphere after the
death of her mother and after winning the "triple crown" of literary prizes
in 1952 as effecting a fundamental transformation in her career and in the
history of celibacy. She became a frequent guest on TV talk shows (*The Merv
Griffin Show*, *The Tonight Show*, *The Today Show*), wrote for and was featured
in magazines and newspapers, hobnobbed with celebrities, and threw the
first ball out at the opening day Yankee game in 1968.[73] By inhabiting this
celebrity, she attempts to transform the celibate from an observer of life (as
I discussed in the previous chapter, the celibate's association with observation and nonparticipation has a very long history) to a participant. Here,
Moore attempts not an observational strategy, as in her earlier *Observations*
(1924), but one of participation, of masculine acts, of celibate engagement.
Where the textual economy of Moore's earlier work has not had the desired
effect (Bishop's memoir reports that "feminists" have ignored "Marriage"),
here, Moore supplements the textual erotics and politics of her early work
with a new embodied mode of engagement.[74] *embodied*
This engagement moves the celibate from the position of observing the
public sphere at a distance to being a central actor in it. This participation
shifts celibacy from what Sedgwick calls in a different context the "periperformative" realm to the performative one. Sedgwick defines periper-
formatives as a group of statements that "allude to explicit performative
utterances" that inhabit "the neighborhood of the performative."[75] Even
though Sedgwick does not translate these utterances from speech act theory into the realm of the sexual (as Butler has translated the performative
for gender), it is a small step to see that those who understand celibacy as
grounded in lack would see it in the realm of the periperformative. In this
reading celibacy would point to a performance without itself taking part in
one (this would be the case for those readings that understand celibacy as
repressed homosexuality), or would be tinged by sexuality, in its neighborhood, but not participating in the realm of the sexual (the impure thoughts
of Foucault's "The Battle for Chastity" would exemplify this position).[76]

Leaving the periperformative behind, Moore's celibate intervention is at once shy and flamboyant, grounded in modesty—the quiet but powerfully symbolic resistance of "the viper's traffic-knot." Rather than incorporating the nation, her celebrity is a disruptive force—Marianne as much as Liberty.[77] Moore's celibate engagement, then, marked in part by the Washington outfit, is precisely what enables her to stage her coup to improve the lives of spinsters begun in "Councell to a Bachelor," "And Shall Life Pass an Old Maid By?," and "Marriage."

In thinking about the collection as a whole, I read the colon in the title—*Tell Me, Tell Me: Granite, Steel, and Other Topics*—as a fulcrum, creating a careful balance between the egocentric nightmare of "Tell me, tell me," which demands the "viper's traffic-knot," and the progressive utopia of "Granite and Steel," which hints at a mounting danger. On the one hand, "Granite and Steel" opens the possibility of having queer American writers who not only exist but are enfranchised, welcomed, celebrated—"an actuality." On the other hand, the repetition of "refuge" and "refugee" in "Tell me, tell me" summons the damage that a nation can do to its citizens (a point underlined by other poems in the collection like "Rescue with Yul Brynner") even as these citizens do find refuge in their release from "captivity."

To make sense of these ambivalent prognostications, I turn to the final poem of the collection, one in which Moore explicitly discusses her image—"Sun." She punningly writes of "Moorish gorgeousness," which simultaneously describes her celebrity (since the poem's rewritings span her career, it exemplifies Marianne Moorishness), a racialized figure, and a clock:

> O Sun, you shall stay
> with us . . .
> . . . be wound in a device
> of Moorish gorgeousness (49)

This image tips the balance of the collection toward optimism. While "Granite and Steel" rewrites Whitman's "Crossing Brooklyn Ferry"—which is also known as "Sun-Down Poem"—Moore's "Sun" ends the collection's metaphoric day as a kind of "Sun-Up Poem." This image of a rising sun also alludes to Benjamin Franklin's comment at the end of the Constitutional Convention of 1787, expressing his greatest hopes and fears (the poem was originally titled "Fear Is Hope") that the sun carved into the back of Washington's chair was a rising sun not a setting sun, suggesting the sun as a figure for Moore. The racial component of this "Sun[ny]" image emerges from its "Arab abode" (49) and helps to explicate Langston Hughes's oblique 1967 comment about Moore: "I consider her the most famous Negro woman poet in America!"[78] While Arnold Rampersad calls the remark "manic" and suggests that even Hughes did not understand "exactly what he had meant to convey," Hughes is simply offering a reading of a poem published a year earlier.[79] That is, with the Shakespearean precedent of the noble Moor, Hughes calls Moore a Negro to cement her identification with Moorishness and to expand her radically democratic project.[80] By inscribing Moore in a Negro identity, he paradoxically recognizes her as a fellow traveler in the demolition of racial difference as he marks out such a project as intrinsic to the spirit of the Negro.[81]

The rising sun of this image casts its rays on Moore's celebrity and celibacy as well. This portmanteau identification of timeless beauty and Moore's celebrity suggests that the poem responds to the John Skelton lines with which the poem begins—"'No man may him hyde / From Deth holow-eyed'" (49). Here, Moore posits her fame as a method for overcoming mortality. This image offers us a modernism without an emphasis on "the new" and summons the pasts with which Moore is associated—medieval, Victorian, prehistoric, "vaguely Bryn Mawr 1909"—to engage the future and the threat of imminent "Deth." This is by no means the collection's first image of Moore's monumentality. In addition to the vision of Moore/Liberty in "Granite and Steel," her essay "My Crow, Pluto—a Fantasy" describes the favored perch of her crow as a bronze bust by Gaston Lachaise. What she does not say is that the bust is of her.[82] Thus, when her crow croaks "Evermore" from atop the bust, she voices her immortality and connection to the past ("Evermore" signals continuation), while underlining the wisdom of such a gesture (as the bust in Poe's "Raven" is of Athena).[83] This divine identification, this act of monumentality, suggests the culmination of Moore's attempt to live celibacy as a nonstigmatized identity. "Moorish gorgeousness" can be found in the face of an old spinster as well as in an old watch (49).

Looking backward over Moore's career, the art critic Hilton Kramer writes in a 1981 review: "[Moore] may very well have been the last spinster type created by the communications industry before the women's movement radically altered the terms of media mythmaking."[84] Kramer's feminist objection to the media's portrayal of Moore as "the very archetype of the quaint literary spinster" is accompanied by his own bafflement at Moore's promotion of such an image, which he finds "grotesquely at odds" with her work. Kramer's confusion simultaneously opens a window onto one of the last moments when celibate temporality is connected to progressive politics and suggests that both queer history and feminist history obscure celibacy's progressive politics even as celibacy is a part of both those histories. Celibacy challenges us to understand Gerard Manley Hopkins's religious celibacy, the second-wave feminist group Cell 16's support for celibacy as a strategy of self-actualization, Emily Dickinson's erotics of enclosure, Christabel Pankhurst's promotion of celibacy as a political response to male power, and Moore's celibate engagement as part of the same history.[85] While I have emphasized the incongruities between queerness and celibacy, and writers like Hilton Kramer have emphasized the incompatibility of feminism and celibacy, we must also begin to think about how these histories intersect and produce each other, how they are simultaneously feminist, queer, and celibate.

Chapter Three | **The Other Harlem Renaissance**

Father Divine, Celibate Economics,
and the Making of Black Sexuality

Divine Alternatives

Father Divine may be the most important figure of the Harlem Renaissance that you've never heard of. James Baldwin's description in his foreword to Bobby Seale's *A Lonely Rage* (1978) highlights Divine's importance as he narrates the generational differences between his own youth and that of the younger cofounder of the Black Panthers: "The time of my youth was entirely different and the savage irony of hindsight allows me to suggest that the time of my youth was far less hopeful. . . . Our most visible heroes were Father Divine and Joe Louis—we, in the ghetto then, knew very little about Paul Robeson. We knew very little about anything black, in fact, and this was not our fault."[1] Here, the spiritual leader "Father Divine" is as important as the heavyweight champion "Joe Louis," signifying knowledge about blackness and constituting some of the "little" known "about anything black."[2] Langston Hughes similarly flags the importance of Divine and Louis in his distinctly inclusive "The Heart of Harlem" (1945):

> The buildings in Harlem are brick and stone
> And the streets are long and wide,
> But Harlem's much more than these alone,
> Harlem is what's inside —
>
> It's Joe Louis and Dr. W. E. B.,
> A stevedore, a porter, Marian Anderson, and me.

It's Father Divine and the music of Earl Hines,
Adam Powell in Congress, our drivers on bus lines.[3]

Joe Louis's 1938 defeat of the German Max Schmeling was understood allegorically as an American victory over Nazism. Louis was a national hero and a model for (black) manhood during the fearful time of the Depression and coming war. While much has been written about the importance of Joe Louis in relation to national and international politics, it is far less clear what the much-misunderstood and much-maligned Father Divine signifies for black identity in the 1930s and 1940s.[4]

Father Divine was an intellectual and religious leader who believed he was God. In the 1930s, when his religion, the Peace Mission Movement, was at its apex, he had a large following both nationally and abroad. In Harlem, he is estimated to have had between three and four thousand core followers, though his appearances drew crowds of ten to fifteen thousand, and his newspaper, the *Spoken Word*, had a national circulation of about thirty thousand.[5] The size of his global following in the 1930s is disputed but was (erroneously) estimated to be in the millions.[6] The central ritual of the religion was the banquet table at which Divine lavished abundant and delicious food on thousands of unemployed and hungry people. At the table, Divine impresses the hungry visitors with his overwhelming bounty, quieting their grumbling stomachs long enough to hear his message. An important part of this message was celibacy, which at first glance might seem at odds with this practice of indulgent eating, but both practices have the effect of focusing followers' attention on the materiality of his body.[7] He organized his followers into communal interracial celibate living situations called kingdoms. Members of these celibate kingdoms broke ties with their families, friends, and spouses, creating an environment in which to meditate on Divine and his teachings, minimizing influences outside the Peace Mission Movement. Divine's own abstinent marriage underwrites rather than undermines this emphasis on celibacy because he considered his marriage sacrificial, marrying so that his followers would not have to suffer the burdens of conjugality.

Despite Father Divine's following and mass appeal, many believed he was a charlatan and a swindler. Hughes's own "Projection of a Day" (1946) imagines Father Divine speaking the truth only "when the Savoy / leaps clean over to Seventh Avenue / and starts jitterbugging."[8] Owen Dodson's *Divine Comedy* (1938) presents a similarly unfavorable portrait of Divine, as does Chester Himes's *A Rage in Harlem* (1957), where the protagonist analogizes getting conned and believing in Father Divine: "It [the con] hadn't been too hard for him to believe. Other people in Harlem believed that Father Divine was God."[9] Likewise, a character in Claude McKay's newly discovered *Amiable with Big Teeth: A Novel of the Love Affair between the Communists and the Poor Black Sheep of Harlem* (1941) proclaims: "I hate the idea of our working with Father Divine for I despise his guts. When I listen to him spouting that religious rigmarole and his followers calling him 'God,' I feel not only ashamed of my people, but of the whole world of peoples."[10] Period journalism bolsters these literary depictions, and yet, as Baldwin and Hughes suggest, Father Divine occupied an enormous symbolic importance in the everyday lives of black Americans.[11]

This importance is underwritten by his appearance in a vast array of texts written by figures associated with the Harlem Renaissance. In addition to the previously mentioned texts by Hughes, Dodson, and McKay, Divine also figures in McKay's *Harlem Glory* (begun in 1937, but never completed and published posthumously in 1990); Zora Neale Hurston's *Dust Tracks on the Road* (1942); photographs by James Van Der Zee and Aaron Siskind; and Sterling Brown's plans for "The Portrait of the Negro as American" and his "Sister Cities."[12] Divine also appears in a range of other writing, including Richard Wright's *Lawd Today* (completed in 1937–1938, published posthumously in 1963); Bucklin Moon's *The Darker Brother* (1943); Paule Marshall's *Brown Girl, Brownstones* (1959) and *Triangular Road* (2009); Louise Meriwether's *Daddy Was a Number Runner* (1970); James Baldwin's *Just above My Head* (1979) and "Dark Days" (1980); Audre Lorde's *Zami: A New Spelling of My Name* (1982); Lynn Nottage's *Crumbs from the Table of Joy* (1998); Touré's "The Sad Sweet Story of Sugar Lips Shinehot and the Portable Promised Land" (1998); and Aishah Rahman's *Chewed Water* (2001).[13]

While many of these texts are set during the Harlem Renaissance or are authored by writers associated with the period, most of them—even by the most expansive periodizations—were not written during the Renaissance. Because Divine did not become a sensation until December 1931, when his Rockland Palace lectures continually drew audiences of more than ten thousand, those versions of the Renaissance ending with the 1929 stock market crash, like Houston Baker's *Modernism and the Harlem Renaissance* (1987) and Cary Wintz's *Black Culture and the Harlem Renaissance* (1988), would understandably exclude Divine.[14] And yet, many periodizations of the Renaissance end with Prohibition, the Harlem riot of 1935, or later in the 1940s. With this vast (and no doubt incomplete) archive of Father Divine texts assembled here, it is staggering to learn that Father Divine is entirely absent from the major literary and historical scholarship of the Harlem Renaissance that encompasses these longer periodizations. Divine is not mentioned in Nathan Huggins's *Harlem Renaissance* (1971), Brent Hayes Edwards's *The Practice of Diaspora* (2003), or Michelle Stephens's *Black Empire* (2005). Divine's exclusion from Edwards's and Stephens's work is particularly surprising given the international dissemination of the Peace Mission Movement. Even in those texts in which Divine's interracial politics should demand his inclusion, like George Hutchinson's *The Harlem Renaissance in Black and White* (1996), he remains absent. Perhaps most surprisingly, he is not mentioned in any of the essays in *The Cambridge Companion to the Harlem Renaissance* (2007). David Levering Lewis's *When Harlem Was in Vogue* (1979) furnishes an important exception, devoting several pages to Father Divine and briefly correlating him to Reverend Green in Nella Larsen's *Quicksand* (1928). I take Lewis as a methodological precursor, following him in thinking Father Divine helpfully opens up literary texts for new analysis.[15]

My focus is broader than Lewis's as I seek to ask both why Father Divine is excluded from the literary history of the Harlem Renaissance and how his celibacy might begin to reshape that history and modernism more generally. Perhaps the most obvious reason for his exclusion is that he is dismissed as a fraud. Lewis rather ambivalently sees him as representing one of the "odd religious movements" popular in Harlem at the time, even as he suggests that "there was nothing retrograde or unhealthy" about these movements.[16] Given the enormity of his popularity, his oddness and charlatanry hardly seem adequate reasons for his nearly complete absence. Divine's exclusion is partially explained by a remarkable transformation in the historiography of the Harlem Renaissance in the last fifteen years—namely, the emergence of a populist Renaissance. Earlier commentators like Lewis found the Renaissance to be an elitist affair: "The Harlem Renaissance reveals itself to be an elitist response on the part of a tiny group of mostly second-generation, college-educated, and generally affluent Afro-Americans."[17] For Lewis, the Renaissance is not a grassroots phenomenon, a sentiment that Langston Hughes's *The Big Sea* (1940) echoes: "The ordinary Negroes hadn't heard of the Negro Renaissance. And if they had, it hadn't raised their wages any."[18] Yet scholars like William Maxwell, Barbara Foley, Tony Martin, Winston James, Clare Corbould, James Smethurst, and oth-

 grassy roots

ers, have recast the Renaissance as not just the province of the elite but something that touched a much wider mass of people.[19] The scholarship on this grassroots-Renaissance has taken a variety of shapes, mapping the centrality of Caribbean radicalism, Garveyite aesthetics, and the interchange between proletarian literature and African American letters in the making of the Renaissance. In addition, this work has documented the shaping presence of black bolshevism and working-class culture in the earliest Red Summer incarnations of the New Negro. While some of this work reshapes the contours of the Renaissance, much of it also attempts to establish a separate post-Renaissance moment.

Divine is also omitted from the scholarship of these more "workerist" class-inflected accounts of the 1930s. This exclusion is not terribly surprising given Marxism's aversion to religion. As Robert Weisbrot points out, "The party and the Peace Mission might at first appear 'natural enemies.'"[20] The differences, according to Weisbrot, were vast: "Few could fail to note the incongruities between Divine's pantheism and the Communists' dogmatic atheism, between his advocacy of nonviolence and their eager anticipation of the workers' revolution, and between his wariness of unions and their stress on labor organization. Yet the two sides also shared powerful bonds."[21] The communists and the Peace Mission Movement found common ground in civil rights and populism, holding a series of joint marches between 1934 and 1936.[22] In spite of this interaction, Divine is nowhere to be found in accounts of the Red "New Negro."[23] I use the term "New Negro" in its cultural and historical specificity to mean the promised break with (white) racist stereotypes of blacks as stupid, hypersexual, primitive, and lazy. If these stereotypically negative traits characterize the Old Negro left behind by the new one, Divine's followers are smart, industrious celibates who use the term "dark-complected" in order to move away from what they understand to be the negative thinking and stigma of the word "Negro."[24]

In Kevin Gaines's magisterial history of racial uplift, he describes uplift as an elite black ideology that emphasizes "self-help, racial solidarity, temperance, thrift, chastity, social purity, patriarchal authority, and accumulation of wealth."[25] Gaines characterizes this bourgeois morality as containing "deeply embedded assumptions of racial difference [which] were often invisible to them [black elites]."[26] While Divine similarly stigmatizes Negro identity, replicating racial power structures, he does not use sexual morality to articulate or shore up class differences between blacks as so much uplift ideology does. Rather, Divine's followers extend respectability to all black people, rewriting its contours and linking the middle-class women's club and the black aristocracy to a working-class history of respectability. Locating Divine in the important dialectic that Shane Vogel lays out between uplift and the Renaissance on the one hand and the "Cabaret School" and the Vogue on the other, Divine is certainly a figure of uplift.[27] However, Divine bridges the divide between uplift and cabaret because the charge of charlatanry bears a similar stigma to the cabaret's failure to offer "truthful" depictions of Negro life, but also (and more important) because like the Cabaret School, Divine's nonnormative uplift program expands sexual and class possibilities. Moreover, the wide range of literary representations of Divine suggest that an aesthetics of uplift is less monolithic and more dynamic than previous accounts suggest. Divine's dark-complected Renaissance reroutes the emphasis on transgressive sexuality—promiscuity, homosexuality, lesbianism, and queerness—within the scholarship of the Harlem Renaissance and places celibate communes alongside the more familiar black male / white female heterosexual couples familiar to narratives of the black and red 1930s.[28]

Divine promotes and authorizes celibacy in order to write a new narrative about black bodies: one that does not differentiate black bodies from white bodies. This narrative—secured, in part, through white privilege and its control of access to celibacy—enabled Divine to create an alternative social structure that opened up a new set of economic conditions and forged him as an economic leader. I will elaborate the predication of Divine's economic power on this new virtuous black body. I argue that Father Divine uses celibacy to become a business tycoon, while furnishing his followers with an economic program that provides aid to needy people abandoned by the discriminatory policies of the Social Security Act of 1935.[29] Finally, I will consider Divine's transformational impact on the history of black sexuality, tracing the ways in which Divine authorizes celibacy at a time when lynching eroticized the black male body and black female bodies were widely thought to be unclean and lacking in virtue.[30] Building on Siobhan Somerville's work, which attends to the racial foundations of sex and the sexual foundations of race, I read Divine's refashioning of black sexuality as celibate as enabling him to rewrite the boundaries of race and racialization.[31] To put this differently, Divine attempts to move black subjects from the racist register of animality to that of full humanity by countering dehumanizing depictions of black sexuality with celibacy.

Only Divine speaking?

Celibate Economics

Perhaps no Harlem Renaissance figure understood Divine's significance more than Claude McKay. Both fascinated and repelled by Father Divine, McKay wrote a series of articles for the *New Yorker*, an article for the *Nation*, a poem in his "Cycle" series, and a novel, *Harlem Glory* (1990), all about Divine.[32] While McKay's interest in Divine stems, in part, from Divine's association with the Communist Party, it is the peculiarity of this interest that makes McKay's most important Divine text—*Harlem: Negro Metropolis* (1940)—such an odd one.

The dedication of this text to James Weldon Johnson might lead the reader to assume that he will read a text similar to Johnson's *Black Manhattan* (1930). This assumption is strengthened by the similarity of the opening pages between McKay's text and Johnson's and the purported aim of McKay's text to offer a "picture of Harlem."[33] In spite of this initial impression that McKay's text will, like Johnson's, offer an account of the literary and cultural life of Harlem, *Harlem: Negro Metropolis* is much closer to the sociological texts of *Hull House Maps and Papers* (1895), W. E. B. DuBois's *The Philadelphia Negro* (1899), Charles Booth's *Life and Labour of the People of London* (1902), and William Jones's *Recreation and Amusement among Negroes in Washington, D.C.* (1927). Rather than providing the social picture that McKay purports to offer, his book is chiefly an economic history of Harlem that depicts Divine as a shrewd economic leader and "a captain of industry."[34] A quick glance at some of *Harlem*'s chapter titles demonstrates this heavy economic emphasis: "Harlem Businessman"; "The Business of Numbers"; "The Business of Amusements"; "Sufi Abdul Hamid and Organized Labor." Even those chapters focused on religion, politics, and literary culture are reported from an economic point of view.

Such economic points of view (as Hughes's comment about wages suggests) usually leave the Renaissance coming up short. As George Hutchinson writes: "It is hard to know how to respond to a critique for which the standard of success of an artistic movement is its effectiveness in ending centuries of oppression. This standard, however, seems to be in the background of many disappointed interpretations of the Harlem Renaissance, including, admittedly, those of the participants themselves."[35] While McKay's *Harlem* appears to be following Hutchinson's trajectory of disappointment, his account suggests something far different: "The build-up of a fashionable and artistic Harlem became the newest fad of Manhattanites in the middle nineteen twenties. And the propaganda in favor of it was astoundingly out of proportion to the economic potentiality of a Harlem set and the actual artistic and intellectual achievement. New Yorkers had discovered the existence of a fashionable clique, and an artistic and literary set in Harlem. The big racket which crepitated from this discovery resulted in an enormously abnormal advertisement of bohemian Harlem. And even solid real estate values were affected by the fluid idealistic art values of Harlem."[36] Here, McKay's measurement of the "economic potentiality" of "the actual artistic and intellectual achievement[s]" concludes that the Harlem Renaissance offers an aesthetic solution to an economic problem. In fact, the aesthetic not only falls short of alleviating but exacerbates the dire economic situation, negatively affecting "solid real estate values." Rather than finding Garveyite, leftist, and proletarian impulses within the aesthetic sphere, McKay's account leaves the aesthetic behind, suggesting that what is needed is an economic solution to an economic problem. Rather than offering another disappointed assessment, McKay finds that Father Divine offers precisely this economic solution (if not the aesthetics of solidarity highlighted by the passages from Baldwin and Hughes at the beginning of this chapter). This new evaluation of the Renaissance suggests that Divine and his economic program do not occupy a cultural field apart from that of the writers and artists but rather are its vanguard. As we will see, Divine's celibacy avails economic advantage to blacks of all classes and creates a successful economic Renaissance.

Because there are, to my knowledge, no critical articles about *Harlem: Negro Metropolis* and because the biographies give it scant attention, I will rehearse its argument here.[37] The central contention of McKay's book is that the lack of communal enterprise in Harlem—by which he means businesses owned and operated by members of the community—renders the family unit inadequate to the economic demands of daily life. McKay reluctantly crowns Father Divine the hero of his book because what I will call Divine's celibate economics enable him to forge an alternative kinship based on communal enterprise that not only subsists but thrives in Harlem. While McKay dismisses the Harlem Renaissance as "the hectic pseudo-renaissance period of the Aframerican elite" because it is "not an economic asset," he sees the communal enterprise exemplified by Divine as a true renaissance because it opens paths of opportunity for ordinary Harlemites. Or, to put it in the parlance of Langston Hughes, Divine's alternative Renaissance *does* raise wages.

While describing the geography, value, and character of real estate in Harlem, McKay writes: "The prohibitive rent makes the unit of private family life the rarest thing. Almost all families take in lodgers. All available space must be occupied. Rooms, rooms and more rooms to let. Adequate clothing and even vital food must be sacrificed to meet the high cost of housing."[38] Many times in the course of his book, McKay emphasizes the necessity for families to live together—"doubling up"—or rent to lodgers because they cannot afford housing.[39] This strategy as well as the throwing of "rent parties" and the "hot bed" system in which the same mattress is used "for two or more lodgers on different work shifts" all offered means of navigating the woes and costs of the housing crisis.[40] This passage suggests that the racist control of and limitations on available housing undermined blacks' ability to construct private family life. But even as racism accelerates the inadequacy of the nuclear family as a viable economic unit (whites charge blacks higher rents), McKay sees the lack of black-owned and black-managed businesses as the main reason for this insufficiency.

In the concluding pages of the book, he calls for "the constructive development of Negro communities commercially, politically, and culturally," which would result in the emergence of black "police officers, sheriffs and judges, principals of schools, landlords and businessmen, etc."[41] McKay's belief in communal enterprise underwrites his solution for the economic troubles of Harlem and provides the central organizing principle of his book:

An analysis of the popular movements of Harlem show[s] that they all spring from the simple instinctive urge of the Negro masses to support some form of community enterprise. This urge was put into motion by the churning propeller of the romantic Back-To-Africa movement of Marcus Garvey. When the Garvey organization purchased two trucks the people were exuberantly enthusiastic; when it acquired an old boat and manned it with a Negro crew, they went delirious. It was the same spirit that inspired the Sufi campaign and other campaigns for jobs. Under the shibboleth of peace and prancing it also infuses the Father Divine Mission. It injected that tempo and éclat in the numbers game in Harlem which went out of it as soon as white gangsters took it over.[42]

In this self-summarizing moment, the text argues that the Negro masses support leaders who offer community enterprise. While McKay clearly prefers Marcus Garvey ("There has never been a Negro leader like Garvey")[43] and Sufi Abdul Hamid ("the most picturesque and appealing figure in 125th Street")[44] to Father Divine, Divine is the only leader to model the communal enterprise that McKay elaborates successfully. In an economic register, Sufi's success is short-lived and Garvey's Black Star Line is a failure, even as McKay understands both to be symbolic successes.

McKay considers Father Divine to be a charlatan and a dictator but acknowledges that he nourishes thousands and models McKay's own communal program for the future of Harlemites: "Negro women are celebrated as laundry workers, and 75 per cent of women laundry workers are colored. . . . Yet no Negroes thought of operating their own laundries, like the Chinese and small white proprietors, until Father Divine started to reign as God in Harlem. . . . He taught bewildered middle-aged Negro women to work cooperatively by establishing small laundries in which they work in groups."[45] Here, Divine's businesses serve as a model, enlightening the community of "middle-aged Negro women" and awakening others "to the possibilities of the small business."[46] Whatever McKay's ideological differences with Divine, it is clear that Father Divine is *the* economic leader of the black community and an embodiment of what it means to be black for many others, including Baldwin and Hughes.

This economic power, according to McKay, comes from Divine's celibacy and his deification.[47] The absolute authority of his divinity enables "the abnegation of all individuality, collective servitude and strict discipline in every domain of life with one man as supreme dictator."[48] The self-abnegation and "collective servitude" of the Peace Mission followers enable Divine to respond to the inadequacy of the nuclear family by creating a program of communal living. McKay's reference to "collective servitude," however negative, points out the extent to which Divine's followers already think of themselves as a group.

Celibacy crucially facilitates a group-based identity that takes the form of cooperative housing: "What appears most ridiculous to the outside world is the secret of his success and the source of his strength. By outlawing sex from his kingdom he neutralized the unsavory popular reaction which is the inevitable concomitant of intimate association between colored and white persons."[49] Without the "harsh realit[y]" of sex, Father Divine is able to create an alternative social structure.[50] Unlike the nuclear family that McKay has criticized as inadequate, this celibate structure is not only economically stable but financially beneficial. Divine's celibate kingdoms enable an infinite attachability—unrestricted by number in order to refashion the family as a cooperative economic structure.

Divine was not the first person to realize the economic benefits of group living; for example, Robert Stein's article "Girls' Coöperative Boarding Homes" (1898) imagines and documents more than one hundred instances of women living together to avoid marrying out of economic necessity: "If one thousand unmarried women, instead of living scattered over a large city, could be made to combine their incomes and live together in one house, they could obtain a thousand conveniences of which they are deprived while living apart. They would be in far greater financial security, for only a few of them would at any time be out of work, and the expenses of these could be borne by the rest, till, finding employment, they could pay arrears."[51] Joanne Meyerowitz's work on independent women in Chicago suggests that both black and white women engaged in such resource pooling.[52] While celibate attachability enables the cost-saving efficiency of economies of scale afforded by communal living, race mixing (enabled by celibacy) has an additional economic benefit for the black followers of Father Divine that was not available to many of Meyerowitz's "women adrift."[53] This new kinship structure receives "white" treatment, since Divine almost always had one of his white followers negotiate the terms of leasing, purchasing, and other contracts, negating much of the impact of racism. To put this differently, celibacy facilitates a practice of "fronting" that enables the Peace Mission Movement to circumvent the institutions of racism that keep blacks from economic advancement.[54]

This version of celibate economics marks a tremendous departure in the history of celibacy. Celibacy is usually understood to be either a noncirculating commodity that is saved up or hoarded in nunneries and (to a lesser extent) in monasteries, or an object of exchange in the traffic in women.[55] But Divine shifts celibacy from being a commodity to enabling an economics, from something to be valued and saved to something to be used. This de-emphasis of celibacy as a commodity facilitates Divine's reconfiguration and democratization of access to celibacy's power, extending it to those who are sexually experienced. While Divine does value virginity—the members of his Rosebud (for women) and Crusaders (for men) orders were literal virgins—Divine's Lily-buds (also for women) had been "redeemed from the mortal, carnal life" and were not necessarily celibate before their membership.[56] This plasticity and redefinition of celibacy open Divine's Renaissance and its economic power to many who would not otherwise have access. In a striking reversal of the genealogy charted throughout the previous two chapters, here celibacy is made more available for women than for men. While men's access to celibacy is always constrained by surveillance and scrutiny for homosexuality that calls their celibacy into question, period women face the much more substantial obstacle of compulsory marriage, even though, as Nancy Cott, has pointed out, the gender ideal of passionlessness mitigates this hindrance.[57] While women have more difficulty accessing the mobility and freedoms of celibacy, its political power offers more to them, and the black women of the Peace Mission Movement in particular, than to their male counterparts who began with substantially greater autonomy.

In addition to effecting transformations in the history of celibacy, Father Divine's economic program has massive implications, not merely as an alternative to the nuclear family but as a more inclusive structure. For example, seizing on a dispute between sitting president Franklin Delano Roosevelt and the eccentric millionaire Howland Spencer (who may have been suffering financial troubles), Father Divine inexpensively purchased the Krum Elbow estate across the river from Roosevelt's Hyde Park mansion. The acquisition is usually read as dramatizing interracial harmony as it received front-page national coverage, and Father Divine became known as Roosevelt's neighbor (much to the president's chagrin).[58] However, following McKay, we might read it as symbolic of two incompatible economic visions: "The dictator of the Divine Deal carried his mystic-social experiment to the very boundary of the estate of the New Deal's founder. Father Divine's gesture appeared like a challenge to the New Deal and received national notoriety from that angle."[59] Here, McKay reads Father Divine's so-called mystic-social experiment as being at odds with the New Deal, offering a rival economic plan that requires his followers to trust in him by eschewing insurance and welfare. Expanding McKay's reading, we might see this eschewal serving the practical function of helping his followers to live within their means, by paying for everything in full and in cash. It posits a non-family-based community that is self-sufficient rather than a familial economy that is dependent on the state and private business. In this reading, Divine's purchase of an estate, a home, metaphorically signals his rewriting of the bounds of the nuclear family and its bonds. The "Divine Deal" fundamentally challenges the New Deal by suggesting that the family, as a broken unit, creates the negative thinking of welfare. Divine emphasizes positive thinking and self-empowerment through an alternative kinship network (and faith in Father Divine) that has no use for welfare. This celibate attachability enables the kind of cooperative enterprise that McKay sees as the salve of the economic troubles for Harlem.

While I think McKay's astute reading evokes many of the underlying tensions between Divine's theology and Roosevelt's Social Security Act of 1935, I would characterize the relationship between Divine and Roosevelt more starkly: Divine's economic program aided black people while Roosevelt's did not. In *The Segregated Origins of Social Security: African Americans and the Welfare State* (2006), Mary Poole argues that "the Social Security Act was designed to save not just the economy but also white manhood."[60] This focus on white manhood, coupled with the mistaken belief that the exclusion of domestic and agricultural workers was necessary to secure the bill's passage, created a bill that provided very little aid to blacks.[61] This exclusion disenfranchised "the majority of the country's African American wage earners," since 45 percent of domestics were African American, and "African Americans comprised between 40 percent and 77 percent of waged farm workers in southern states and 51.5 percent of sharecroppers."[62] We might understand the Divine Deal not as an attempt to undermine the New Deal or to stand as the New Deal's rival but rather as an attempt to extend support—albeit in a different manner than the New Deal—to a group of people that the New Deal, in its very design, excluded.

Authorizing Celibacy

How is Father Divine able to deploy his celibate economic strategy when the threat of lynching and the legacies of slavery hypersexualize the black body? Rather than understanding celibacy as dramatizing what had to be forsaken in the pursuit of economic and racial survival (in this reading celibacy is the cost of liberation and a symptom of racial melancholia), I see the characteristic jubilation of Father Divine's followers (exemplified by their dancing) as enriching their lives and typifying their experience of celibacy. That Father Divine is able to make a celibate identity available to black subjects at all is one of his lasting impacts on black sexuality. Charles Chesnutt's story "The Wife of His Youth" (1898) and Pauline Hopkins's "Bro'r Abr'm Jimson's Wedding: A Christmas Story" (1901) suggest the impossibility of black celibacy at the turn of the century.[63] Both stories feature an eligible bachelor whose southern wife finds her husband up North a moment before he is about to marry another woman. The southern wife is explicitly the result of a slave marriage in Chesnutt's story and implicitly so in Hopkins's, highlighting black and white Americans' very different access to celibacy by suggesting that slave marriages make it such that blacks are never unmarried. Pauline Hopkins's essay "Higher Education of Colored Women in White Schools and Colleges" (1902) further elaborates this difference: "Education, with us, does not encourage celibacy but is developing pleasant homes and beautiful families."[64] Even as Hopkins remained unmarried herself, the essay's title signals that Hopkins's "with us" refers to black women as opposed to the exploding celibacy rates of college-educated white women.[65] Here, Hopkins depicts celibacy as undesirable even as she herself is using celibacy as a technique of engagement in the public sphere. The conjugal imperative is so strong, in fact, that Hetty Daniels in Jessie Redmon Fauset's *Plum Bun: A Novel without a Moral* (1929) is the object of satire when she boasts that she has kept her "pearl of great price untarnished."[66] Kathryn Kent's work illuminates the differential valuations of celibacy and marriage for white and blacks:

> Under slavery, the married/nonmarried distinction was denied to most slaves, while in the postbellum period a woman's single status or refusal or avoidance of marriage carried very different connotations for white and African American women. As Hortense Spillers has noted, marriage itself took on racially specific political implications, as it was one of the only possible ways that African American men and women could enter into the public sphere, thereby asserting their rights as citizens. Although white, middle-class women were increasingly "escaping" or being forced to exist outside of marriage and in the process finding ways to enter the public sphere, one could argue that for African American women the opposite was true: through marriage (and through a black man) African American women might attain some semblance of entitlement, including the right to exist within the "private," but their status as members of an oppressed minority also meant that marriage was always already a public, civic duty, a way to sustain the race.[67]

My discussion of Father Divine takes up chronologically here where Kent leaves off; by the 1930s, black men and women were utilizing celibacy as a tool, as their white counterparts had done before them, to enter the public sphere.

While the prevalence of marriage as a strategy for civic engagement kept blacks from authorizing a celibate identity, racist depictions of the black body as eroticized and impure were a much greater obstacle.[68] In attempting to create a symbology of black celibacy, we must, following J. L. Austin, seek to understand the circumstances in which black men and women are able to vow celibacy. We might ask, in what contexts can a black man or woman felicitously sign his or her name as celibate? This question becomes all the more crucial as a "vow" in its nominal form seems to be taken almost exclusively in relation to marriage or celibacy.

The Oblate Sisters of Providence, the first Catholic congregation of women religious of African descent, were the first black women in America endowed with the ability to take vows of celibacy. Organized in 1828, this sisterhood defined itself as "a Religious society of Coloured Women, established in Baltimore with the approbation of the Most Reverend Archbishop, [who] renounce the world to consecrate themselves to God, and to the Christian education of young girls of color."[69] In Diane Batts Morrow's history of the Oblate Sisters, she argues that black women at the time of the order's founding were considered "Women Without Virtue" and that "the concept of chaste black women" was oxymoronic.[70] One symptom of this oxymoron was that Archbishop Whitfield rejected the proposed vow status (held by white women religious like the Sisters of Charity) for the Oblate Sisters, only availing them on June 5, 1829, of the lesser status of the promise.[71] Full vow status was achieved on October 2, 1831, when several white male advocates of the Oblate Sisters wrote to the Pontiff and received his ringing endorsement and full enfranchisement of the Oblate Sisters.[72] Here, the citation of celibacy comes through the validation of white men and foreign authorities. The bold Oblate Sisters, even with the aid of the supportive and self-empowered black Baltimorean community, were unable to secure the recognition of their celibate identity amid the racism and discrimination in the slaveholding antebellum city.

The peculiar intersection of Catholic history and the history of Baltimore is crucial to Father Divine's authorization of his own celibate identity, as well as his ability to confer celibacy upon others in the Peace Mission Movement. Father Divine's relation to both of these histories begins with his mother. Jill Watts's pathbreaking biography of Father Divine, *God, Harlem U.S.A.* (1992), convincingly argues that the man who would become the evangelist Father Divine was born George Baker Jr. to Nancy Baker in Rockville, Maryland. Because she was born into slavery, Nancy Baker's birth date is uncertain. By her own estimation and that of others, she was born sometime between 1842 and 1845. Owned by two devout Catholic masters—Lemuel Clements and Henry B. Waring—Nancy Baker was immersed in Catholicism, prayed in a Catholic church, and was expected to uphold Catholic values.[73] Nancy Baker's immersion in and exposure to Catholicism would undoubtedly shape the religious context of Father Divine's spiritual development.

Father Divine (not yet going by that name) moved to Baltimore in 1899 and began to develop his theology.[74] Watts describes his religious philosophy circa 1902 as having "broad appeal" and as "drawing elements from Methodism, Catholicism, the black church, and storefront traditions."[75] My interest here is in the particularly Catholic strain of this thinking. By 1899, the Oblate Sisters were not the only African American celibates. They were joined by the Sisters of the Holy Family in New Orleans (1842),[76] as well as by the light-skinned Healy brothers between 1854 and 1864 and Augustine Tolton.[77] While the Healy brothers no doubt occupy an important place in the history of sacerdotal celibacy, their "light skin, . . . identification with white society and white ministries, and general silence on race questions," as well as the fact that they were generally unknown outside their communities, suggest that they would have little direct impact on Father Divine's celibacy. Moreover, while Augustine Tolton's 1886 ordination is also an important precedent, he, like the Healy brothers, was ordained outside of the United States. Continuing the tradition of the Oblate Sisters, Baltimore would become the most important site of black celibacy in the nation, as it became the first city in the United States to ordain black priests.[78]

Due in large part to the efforts of John R. Slatterly, Baltimore also became the site of the first American seminary to admit blacks, Saint Joseph's. The seminary opened in 1888 and admitted blacks as well as whites so as to ensure (almost) equal treatment. In addition, in 1889 Baltimore became the home of the first preparatory seminary to admit black students.[79] The first three black priests ordained in the United States were ordained in Baltimore. It was not until 1910, nearly twenty years after the 1891 ordination of Charles Uncles, that a black man was ordained outside of Baltimore.[80] But even within Baltimore, the resistance to black priests was considerable.[81] In his important study of the black priesthood, Stephen J. Ochs presents two central reasons for this opposition: First, the Catholic Church bestows the priest with greater power than that granted to Protestant religious leaders. The Catholic priest mediates between God and humanity and has the power to administer the sacraments. White Catholic racism prevented the acceptance of blacks as having such access.[82] Second, celibacy is a part of the sacral position of the Catholic priest. Period racist thinking posited blacks as less capable of chastity.[83] For this reason, Saint Joseph's Seminary in Baltimore required that blacks be thirty years or older (as opposed to their white counterparts, who could be twenty-five) in the hopes that the lasciviousness of youth had passed.[84]

With these obstacles in mind, I turn to one of Father Divine's meditations on his theology: "I have been coming into contact with the different religions from years back. Personally . . . I find there is something good in all of them. I endeavor to be as a honeybee to get the good out of every seed or flower."[85] The ability of black men to mediate God as well as the ability to occupy a celibate identity constituted two of the "good" parts of Catholicism that Father Divine took and made a part of his own burgeoning religious movement. Later, he would transform his religion from being one of mediation, as it was in Baltimore when he was known as the Messenger, to one of divinity itself when he would rechristen himself Father Divine.[86] Even if Father Divine did not have direct contact with the Oblate Sisters or with any of the ordained black priests in Baltimore, he certainly would have been aware of them as a powerful and symbolic force within both the Baltimore community and the Catholic Church. That is, despite the terrible racism and oppression of the Jim Crow South of the late 1890s and early 1900s, Divine is able to authorize his own celibacy and that of his followers, at least in part, because the black Baltimore Catholic community (with the aid of Rome and other whites) has already authorized such an identity.[87]

Father Divine professed (and his followers believed) that the scars on the back of his head were the result of thirty-two unsuccessful lynching attempts; this unlynchable body is the most potent evidence of his celibate identity.[88] In the 1920s and 1930s, the period that McKay's book describes, miscegenation was illegal in twenty-nine out of forty-eight states. Although it was not illegal in New York and Pennsylvania, the two states in which Divine spent most of his life, he frequently faced mob violence.[89] This violence was the result of the celibate cohabitation of whites and blacks in the kingdoms of the Peace Mission Movement, what McKay calls "the unsavory popular reaction which is the inevitable concomitant of intimate association between colored and white persons."[90] E. J. Daniels, one of Divine's chief detractors, helps clarify the relationship between celibacy and violence: "He [Father Divine] will probably remove the 'no sex' ban just as soon as he has grown strong enough to prevent an uprising when Negro men have 'affairs' with white girls."[91] While Daniels assumes that Divine is just using celibacy as a screen to cover his future "'affairs' with white girls," he echoes McKay's suggestion that celibacy (mostly) prevents violence from erupting over the cohabitation that was abhorrent to whites and blacks alike.[92] Father Divine's celibacy (and that of his followers) insulates them from implication in the lynching narrative, enabling them to intervene in the public sphere (on which lynching acts as a prohibition) by gathering a quarter of a million signatures in support of Divine's federal antilynching bill.[93] Despite his symbolic importance, Father Divine and his program of celibacy did not garner him much material success in electoral politics: his influence in the 1936 local and presidential elections (mistakenly thought to be decisive) proved inconsiderable, and his antilynching bill ultimately did not pass.

Divine's chief political intervention comes not in the sphere of mayoral or national politics but rather in redefining and broadening the possibilities for black sexuality. In this chapter, I have charted how Divine uses celibacy to create economic viability and racial equality within the relatively large lifeworld of his kingdoms. This focus on household sexuality attempts to augment Harlem Renaissance scholarship on individual sexual subjectivity and on what George Chauncey calls the "public styles" and "social worlds . . . of middle- and working-class gay men."[94] That is, Divine suggests that the particularities of group living as a sexual, racial, and economic practice are both more normative and stranger than we have anticipated. Collective living is more normative in that it is a widespread practice encompassing such disparate arrangements as lodgers, "doubling up," the "hot bed" system, and even rent parties. But it is also a queerer practice in the case of Divine, since his celibate sociality partially inoculates against the threat of miscegenation and economic discrimination, making a new black-white social configuration possible. Where the household is usually considered a unit of domesticity or economy, Divine's celibacy suggests that it is also a unit of communal sexuality. While his kingdoms point us to this register of sexual life, the range and variety of nonnormative sex that is depicted as transpiring in shared living space during the Renaissance (the representations of Niggerati Manor in Wallace Thurman's *Infants of the Spring* [1932] and Richard Bruce Nugent's *Gentleman Jigger* [1928–1933] furnish ready examples) suggest that household sexuality might prove a powerful tool for illuminating the organization and racialization of intimacy, desire, and privacy.[95]

Chapter Four

The Celibate American

Closetedness, Emigration, and
Queer Citizenship before Stonewall

José Martinez, a Spanish hermaphrodite, attempted to enter America in 1907 with his manager, who intended to exhibit "him as a curiosity."[1] Despite having made a living for the last sixteen years displaying himself as a "phenomenal" in Europe, Martinez was initially excluded by immigration officials.[2] On appeal, however, Martinez's "neat and gentlemanly" appearance and his assurances that his exhibitions would only be for all-male medical societies allayed the immigration authorities' fears of scandal.[3] Martinez helped by explaining that whereas he had initially planned to exhibit "his entire body," he would be willing to make "his exhibitions . . . only to the waist line, which would be an interesting exhibition as one arm is like a woman's, the other like a man's, and the breasts . . . one being like a woman's, one like a man's."[4] Martinez was later admitted to America after posting a thousand-dollar bond. His categorization as a "gentleman" and the air of respectability bestowed by his "neat" appearance kept him from falling into the class-based category of "public charge," which immigration officials initially used to exclude him. These apparent attributes located Martinez at the opposite end of the economic spectrum and prevented him from appearing to be a taxpayer burden. What is most striking about this case, however, is that Martinez's willingness to (literally) keep his pants on and to present his queer body only for inspection by the professional and asexual medical gaze opens an avenue for queer citizenship. By "queer citizenship" I mean the strategies by which queer individuals negotiate citizenship in the face of the restrictions of the state. Martinez makes choices about exhibiting and closeting that were posed to many queer citizens. Not imperiling or challenging the asexuality of the scientific gaze (by exhibiting himself only to the waist) and keeping himself away from the untrained (and thus sexualizing) eyes of the general populace (what an immigration official calls "the vulgar gaze of the public"), Martinez models how practices and appearances of celibacy could be used to circumvent the regulation of the sexual citizen.[5]

Martinez thus provides a striking point of departure for thinking about the regulation of sexuality in relation to American citizenship. In her pathbreaking work on the legal history of the U.S. government's attempts to regulate homosexuality among immigrants, Margot Canaday explains that the McCarran-Walter Act (1952) significantly changed the contours of queer citizenship because it (almost) explicitly excluded aliens who defied sexual and gender norms. The act contained antihomosexual provisions that discriminated in two ways: (1) based on acts, barring immigrants who had committed unspecified "crimes of moral turpitude" (a category that would certainly include sodomy); and (2) based on identities, excluding homosexuals as persons "afflicted with psychopathic personality." In discussions of the McCarran-Walter Act, the Senate Committee on the Judiciary initially favored the use of more explicitly homophobic language. Originally, the act would have barred immigrants who were "psychopathic personalities" or "homosexuals and sex perverts."[6] However, the Public Health Service assured Congress that the terminology of "psychopathic personalities" was "sufficiently broad" to cover homosexuals. Congress made the change but noted in a report that the "change of nomenclature is not to be construed in any way as modifying the intent to exclude all aliens who are sexual deviates."[7]

While this act amplified queer exclusion, the state had two means for excluding homosexuals prior to its passage: the "likely to become a public charge" clause and the provision barring immigrants who had committed "crimes of moral turpitude." Because "moral turpitude" required a conviction, it was mostly used to bolster the much more important "public charge" clause. The vague public charge clause had a low burden of proof and thus could be wielded against a majority of immigrants (most of whom were poor). However, it also produced the category of homosexuality as one linked to poverty and racial degeneration, making it relatively ineffective against well-to-do immigrants like Martinez. Celibacy furnishes one strategy for the queer citizen prior to the passage of the McCarran-Walter Act.

Before this act, the queer citizen could, according to the letter of the law and according to its general mode of enforcement, belong to America so long as he remained celibate or was not caught in an act of moral turpitude. With the passage of the McCarran-Walter Act, the conditions of production of the queer citizen changed. The possibility for a homosexual to be celibate and be a citizen, at least according to the letter of the law, was voided because such a person, by virtue of his identity as a homosexual, would not be eligible for citizenship. In other words, after 1952, queer citizenship changes radically, since it becomes act-based *as well as* identity-based. Prior to 1952, however, celibacy provides a legal refuge for the queer citizen. The sociologist Laud Humphreys describes a version of this strategy that he calls the "breastplate of righteousness" in a slightly later historical moment.[8] In Humphreys's description, men who engage in homosexual acts project a life of "refulgent respectability"—appearing to be exemplary members of society. The breastplate provides its wearer with "a protective shield of superpropriety"; its "shiny quality . . . blind[s] the audience to certain of his practices."[9] We might understand celibacy as operating as one version of this refulgent righteousness. Rather than the affirmative, identity-based communal strategies of the Stonewall era, here we have a celibacy that is not fully reducible to a closet from which one must escape. Instead, it functions as a tactic of belonging for the pre-Stonewall queer citizen.

While Martinez exemplifies this kind of queer celibate citizenship, Henry Abelove's thought-provoking essay "New York City Gay Liberation and the Queer Commuters" charts an alternative American queer citizenship in which writers commute back to the United States from foreign countries. The term "commuter" is important to me because it implies a connection to the territorially bounded nation-state, even as it opens up the possibilities for a more diasporic open-endedness. Abelove explores how a group of queer writers—James Baldwin, Elizabeth Bishop, Jane Bowles, Paul Bowles, William Burroughs, Allen Ginsberg, Paul Goodman, Frank O'Hara, and Ned Rorem—"left or were driven out of the United States during the post–World War II era" by the chill of Cold War homophobia.[10] Specifically, he argues that "nothing like a reasonably secure life in sex or work was at all possible in the United States from the late forties until the early sixties."[11] For Abelove, the departure of these writers constructs the United States as a kind of celibate geography for queers. Paul Bowles, for example, told his biographer that he never had sex when he returned to America "'because of the disapproval of society, . . . the presence of the police, the possibility of blackmail.'"[12] Similarly, Bishop "concealed her lesbianism assiduously," hiding it "as long as she remained in the United States."[13]

Abelove struggles to find a rationale for understanding these writers as a set, contending that they "weren't united by shared literary purposes as a school, or by mutual regard, or by age as a generation, or by a shared political outlook."[14] These queer commuters "did not, as a whole, share an agenda or a style or an allegiance to a particular literary predecessor or contemporary."[15] I want to suggest, however, that all the writers that Abelove discusses—with the important exception of James Baldwin, who I will discuss later in this chapter—have a deep engagement either personally or stylistically with W. H. Auden.[16] Elizabeth Bishop both knew Auden personally and admired him greatly, saying, "When I was in college, and all through the thirties and forties, I and all my friends who were interested in poetry, read him constantly. We hurried to see his latest poem or book, and either wrote as much like him as possible, or tried hard not to."[17] Jane and Paul Bowles shared a house with Auden between 1940 and 1941, with Jane serving as Auden's secretary for part of the time.[18] Burroughs met Auden in 1939 and found his poetry "almost profound."[19] Ginsberg made a pilgrimage to Ischia in 1956 to seek out Auden. Although the meeting started off very badly, the two became friendly, and Auden's work remained a continuing influence.[20] Paul Goodman and Auden praised each other in the highest terms and read each other frequently. One can hardly imagine a more Audenesque writer than Frank O'Hara, who admired Auden so much that out of nervousness he vomited just before meeting him.[21] While not on Abelove's main list, John Ashbery and James Merrill would also certainly qualify as queer commuters, both spending a long period abroad and writing work that thematizes same-sex eroticism. Geoff Ward writes that Ashbery's verse owes "significant debts to Auden."[22] Similarly, James Merrill's work is very much influenced by Auden, even paying him homage by transforming him into one of the main characters in his epic poem *The Changing Light of Sandover* (1982). Additionally, we must add fellow New York school writer James Schuyler, who lived abroad (albeit for a shorter time) in Auden's house in Ischia as well as in other places and was briefly Auden's secretary. Ned Rorem also consistently praises Auden throughout his writings and comments that his librettos achieve a rare status as "works of art" in and of themselves, without the music that librettos usually require to keep them from being "sill[y]."[23] Additionally, Rorem also composed *The Auden Songs* in 1989. Finally, I want to add one more queer commuter to this list: Harold Norse. Norse was a minor poet and a friend and lover of Auden's life partner, Chester Kallman. When Auden came to America, Norse became Auden's personal secretary, spent a great deal of time with Auden, and admired his work greatly. Norse traveled through Italy, France, and Tangier with many of Abelove's other commuters.

These extremely truncated comments about Auden as a literary precursor are intended to suggest the way in which he functions as a kind of queer laureate for these queer commuters. I mean to summon the connotations of national culture embedded in the word "laureate" to suggest that Auden stands at the confluence of the celibate citizenship of Martinez and the transatlantic queer citizenship of my revised and expanded list of queer commuters. Like his fellow commuters, Auden leaves what George Chauncey calls, in a different context, "the constraints of family life and watchful neighbors" to find a freer sexual culture abroad.[24] And yet, as I will argue, this new sexual culture must be experienced in the context of celibacy. Thus, Auden fuses these two modalities of queer citizenship, forging a third path between Martinez's celibacy and the queer commuters' exile. The close personal contact of many of these writers with Auden (the desire of many of them to seek him out in places near and far, and in the case of many of them to become his secretary) proposes him as a life model as well as a literary model.

One particularly compelling example of Auden as a model for how to live queer life well appears in O'Hara's "Memorial Day 1950." In this poem, O'Hara describes learning from Auden and Rimbaud that "our responsibilities . . . began in bed." Just preceding this, O'Hara writes, "Poetry didn't tell me not to play with toys / but alone I could never have figured out that dolls / meant death." The word "alone" here suggests that without the guiding influence of Auden and the homosexual tradition of poetry, O'Hara would have been unable to discover the meaning of dolls. While the lifelessness of dolls associates them with death, Auden teaches O'Hara the deathly consequences of effeminacy, of a man playing with dolls. For these reasons, O'Hara claims, "Love is first of all / a lesson in utility"; Auden proposes the practical lessons of both celibacy and life abroad. This larger network of queer commuters suggests that Auden's personal struggle to craft his queer citizenship carries implications far beyond his individual case for thinking about how queer life was lived in America at midcentury. While Auden's citizenship has been read as representative in this way for England—his move to America sparked a firestorm in which numerous intellectuals condemned him for abandoning England on the brink of war, leading one member of the House of Commons to attempt to force him to repatriate—this chapter sees Auden's citizenship as zeitgeist-setting in America as well.[25]

Celibate Cheating

While the previous chapters have explored celibacy's critical role in enabling disenfranchised subjects to enter the American public sphere, this chapter expands outward to consider the transatlantic politics of celibacy in its exploration of Auden's American citizenship. We might read Auden's 1935 marriage to Thomas Mann's daughter, the lesbian writer Erika Mann, which granted her British citizenship, as an indicator of Auden's ability (even his propensity) to manipulate citizenship law—a skill he deploys in order to acquire American citizenship for himself. This marriage enabled Auden to bring Mann to England permanently and to shelter her from imminent arrest and possibly worse at the hands of the Nazis. Auden's manipulation of the legal privilege of marriage (specifically its capacity to confer derivative citizenship on the spouse of a British national) suggests his willingness to exploit slippages between the enforcement apparatus of the law and citizenship law itself. Auden is able to extend citizenship to Mann in a way that he is not able to receive citizenship from the love of his life, Chester Kallman. Although Auden exchanged vows with Kallman in a commitment ceremony that Auden called a "marriage," even going on a "honeymoon," he still could not derive American citizenship from him. Kallman is one of the main reasons that Auden sought American citizenship—Auden did not want to face the possibility of separation.[26] In spite of this latter marriage's important role in the scholarly and popular conception of Auden as a poet of romantic love, I will argue that celibacy rather than marriage provided Auden with the opportunity to circumvent the prohibition preventing homosexual immigrants from becoming American citizens.[27] Auden's lifelong vow of celibacy—which he takes and then renounces prematurely in 1928—creates a shifting interplay between homosexuality and celibacy that not only provides a structuring dynamic for his early work but also broadly theorizes the decisive dialectic of queer American citizenship in the 1940s. This dialectic creates a "cheating" celibacy in which the queer citizen renounces access to full citizenship rather than demand equality and parity with heterosexual citizenship. Celibacy is the condition of what Aihwa Ong would call the queer citizen's "flexible citizenship."[28] In particular, I focus on Auden's *The Sea and the Mirror* (1944), which explicitly offers itself as a handbook of celibate queer citizenship to gay writers and artists and which thematizes issues of citizenship and sexual exclusion.

Feeling the legal and cultural restrictions of homosexuality, Auden recognized early on that celibacy would provide him with a way to adapt to these constraints. In a letter to his brother John, Auden explains his decision to choose a life of celibacy and describes the three paths open to a homosexual man:

As a bugger, there are only three courses open to one. . . .

1   middle-aged sentimentalism. The educator of youth. School master etc. The hand on the shoulder. You have the glorious gift of youth.
2   The London bugger. Sucking off police in public lavatories. the doors shut. we're all buggers here.
3   Asceticism. The pursed mouth. I have seen too much of the first two classes to wish to find myself among them. Secondly qua writer, I think celibacy is indicated. Flaubert wrote "you shall paint wine, women and glory on condition my good man that you are neither husband nor lover, drunkard nor cuckold."

This of course does not I expect apply to the heterosexual, yet personally if I discover a heterosexual trait in myself, I shall not marry, as it makes the demand for money so imperative, that one will write anything to get it. . . .

As you may imagine, I shall not enjoy asceticism, even if I achieve it as I have anyway for the last year.[29]

The homophobia and self-loathing evident in the description of the "London bugger" and in the claim that asceticism is unnecessary for "the heterosexual" suggest Auden's shame and disgust toward his homosexuality. Auden's use of the verb "achieve" in the letter's closing—"I shall not enjoy asceticism, even if I achieve it as I have anyway for the last year"—suggests the deliberateness of his yearlong celibacy as well as his desire to continue it as a practice. The sense of Auden's celibacy being lifelong is further implied by his imagining of "middle-aged sentimentalism" and marriage as part of these life "courses," suggesting that Auden is imagining these "courses" not in the short-term but as ways of relating to homosexuality for a long duration. Additionally, Auden understands homosexuality and celibacy to operate concurrently rather than excluding one another; celibacy does not transform the identity of the bugger into that of the celibate.

These life courses are further explored in another letter that Auden sent to his brother John (in approximately June 1927) concerning his sexuality and his engagement to a woman named Sheilah Richardson:

> The person who is worth anything is always I think alone. . . . [R]eal artists are not nice people,—all their best feelings go into their work, and life has the residue. As regards sex, whatever your present conditions, I believe you will be better off in the end. Thanks for the homosexual question, marriage for me would be fatal. It would mean doubling the pressure of an already sufficiently obsessive environment. . . . As Flaubert saw you shall paint wine, women and glory on condition my good man that you are none of these, neither husband nor lover, drunkard nor cuckold. As far as I can see it means a complete negation of all the pleasant material things, and nothing in return but one[']s own somewhat skeptical self-satisfaction. However, I don't really complain; it is my own choice, and I believe the most satisfactory cheating of life bar[ring] perhaps the religious life[.][30]

At the time he composed this letter, Auden's home life was tumultuous; in particular, his relationship with his mother was strained.[31] This relationship is important because the lines from Flaubert that he mentions in his letter are written by Flaubert to his own overly proximate mother (with whom he lived until her death) and because Auden attributes his homosexuality to his mother.[32]

Strikingly, Auden responds to his own sexual circumstances in a manner almost identical to Flaubert. However, there is an important difference between Auden and the Flaubertian template from which he draws: while Flaubert writes, in Auden's view, to the source of his homosexuality, Auden writes to his brother. Auden's correspondence with his brother features an extended and repeated quotation of Gustave Flaubert's December 15, 1850, letter to his mother:

> Le marriage pour moi serait une apostasie qui m'épouvante. . . . Tu peindras le vin, l'amour, les femmes, la gloire, à condition, mon bonhomme, que tu ne seras ni ivrogne, ni amant, ni mari, ni tourlourou. Mêlé à la vie, on la voit mal, on en souffre ou [on] en jouit trop.[33]

For me, marriage would be an apostasy, something quite terrifying. . . .
You can depict wine, love, women, [and] glory, on condition, old
thing, of being neither a drunkard, a lover, a husband, or a fighting-
man. If you participate actively in life, you don't see it clearly: you
suffer from it too much or enjoy it too much.[34]

I press hard on this substitution of brother for mother—both because
Auden was deeply invested in psychoanalysis (he considered a career as
an analyst) and because this marks his second surrogation of brother for
mother in a matter of months. How are we to interpret the strangeness of
Auden describing this writerly celibacy (celibacy here predicates the ability
to "depict wine, love, women, [and] glory") to his brother twice in the same
period in almost identical terms?

Totem and Taboo (1913) expounds the role of the brother more exten-
sively than any other text in Freudian psychoanalysis and is of use here,
especially given the questions of sexual ownership raised by Auden's inser-
tion of the word "cuckold" into the Flaubert passage in both letters to his
brother. In Freud's text, he chronicles a mythological time when a new
technological development enabled a band of brothers to kill and devour
their father, who had hoarded all the women that the brothers wanted.
Because every brother was individually much weaker than the father and
none could occupy his former position of strength, garnering a monopoly
over the women, they agree to a "forced celibacy," which becomes the incest
taboo.[35] That is, the brothers forsake access to any of the women of their
tribe—a situation that is unsatisfactory to all of them—in order to create
peace between them. The figure of the brother, then, is important to Auden
in at least two ways. First, brothers enable the renunciation of at least one
kind of desire—the incest taboo—and thus are figures for at least one kind
of celibacy. Second, the brother is the only figure who, by killing the father,
is able to reorganize the sex/gender system. Along these lines, at least one
story survives of Auden's father chaperoning him to prevent Auden from
having sex (much like *Totem and Taboo*'s patriarch).[36] Moreover, because
Auden's family organization was, in his view, responsible for his homosexuality, Auden turned to his brother both in his letters and in *Paid on
Both Sides* (1928) (which features a character with his brother's name who
metaphorically kills a character with his father's name) to ease this "already
sufficiently obsessive environment" and to transform his sexuality.[37]

Auden's desire for celibacy grows out of and is understood by him to exist in simultaneously ethical and homophobic sites: "Real artists are not nice people,—all their best feelings go into their work, and life has the residue." Here, Auden offers a strange rewriting of sublimation where the symptom is not sublimated into art, but rather the artist's best feelings go into art, leaving the artist evacuated of feeling and thus "not nice." The artist-celibate is not fit for participation in life because he can only inflict his mean "residue" on those around him. Similarly, Flaubert warns: "If you participate actively in life, you don't see it clearly: you suffer from it too much or enjoy it too much." In place of active participation or playing by the rules, Auden posits celibacy as a way of "cheating," referring to it as "the most satisfactory cheating of life bar[ring] perhaps the religious life." His theorization of celibacy as a kind of "cheating" is reinforced by the sexual cheating in the addition of the word "cuckold" in his letters to his brother. In order to cheat one must be extremely familiar with the rules, carefully following them almost all the time. Auden's celibacy enables him to occupy a space both inside and outside the rules—the space of the cheater—who "see[s] it [life] clearly." Rather than slavishly adhering to the rules of citizenship that would exclude him, Auden realizes that the practice of celibacy and the institution of marriage offer raw materials for bridging the gaps in the state's homophobic and uneven distribution of citizenship.[38] He is able to cheat the state, stealing modes of belonging—queer citizenship—for himself and others where and when the state is most blind. Auden's modality of queer citizenship takes both literal and figurative forms; he acquires queer citizenship directly for himself and Mann, but his status as a kind of queer laureate suggests that his ability to transmit or confer citizenship also takes less direct routes.

Is There a Queer Citizen before Stonewall?

In the remainder of this chapter, I will argue that the coexistence of "homosexuality" and "citizenship" is only possible, according to the letter of 1940s American law, in a geography of enforced celibacy. Auden's *The Sea and the Mirror: A Commentary on Shakespeare's "The Tempest"* (1944) is Auden's response to the explosive controversy around his move from his native England to New York in 1939, as well as a text that theorizes his queer citizenship in relation to the legal requirements of celibacy.[39] Most important, however, it is a didactic text that instructs others in how to deploy celibacy as an instrumental disguise to forge a livable queer citizenship. Auden's text teaches queers how to use celibacy to access American citizenship at a historical moment when homosexuals (theoretically) could not become citizens.

The now overlooked *Sea and the Mirror* (which Auden's early readers considered his magnum opus) takes the incompatibility of sexuality and nationality as its primary subject. It is an extremely dense and variegated text, containing a range of verse forms as broad as any poem in English.[40] Auden composed *The Sea and the Mirror* between August 1942 and February 1944, transplanting William Shakespeare's play into an American milieu and foregrounding the problems of his own cultural transformation from an Englishman to an American.[41] Drawing on the resources of Shakespeare's New World play, Auden rewrites *The Tempest* (1611) to stage the shedding of his European identity. Moreover, *The Tempest* stages a reascendance to power, as Auden saw America revivifying his poetry and enabling his eventual return to Europe. Throughout the poem, Auden identifies with Prospero and with Caliban, experimenting with each identification in order to forge a good (queer) life. This identification with Caliban is particularly important, since Caliban's exclusion figures the prohibition of queers from American citizenship. Thus, Auden's interpretation of *The Tempest* (which is subtitled "a commentary") captures and comments on the overlapping juridical, social, and cultural implications of his departure from England and subsequent American naturalization.[42] Even though Auden moved to New York on January 26, 1939, it was not until May 20, 1946, that he became a full U.S. citizen.[43] Therefore, while the text was written on American soil, Auden was technically still a British national at the time of its creation. This liminality is crucial to understanding both Auden's and the text's politics of queer citizenship.

How is it possible that Auden, whose candor about homosexuality barred him from military service in 1942, came to receive a U.S. military pass in 1945 (along with the uniform and the rank of major) and became naturalized as a U.S. citizen in 1946?[44] Certainly Auden's confessions of homosexuality could have been used as evidence of "moral turpitude." Auden's acquisition of these technologies of naturalization, as well as naturalization itself, is even more surprising in light of his engagement with Marxist thought.[45] Auden's self-description in the title of his poem "A Communist to Others" (1932) should have further disqualified him from citizenship as a number of cases in the 1930s ruled that since communism was incompatible with the principles of the Constitution, communist aliens were ineligible for citizenship.[46] However, because the state was not particularly thorough or effective at policing homosexuality and was almost certainly not familiar with Auden's communist poetry, and because by the late 1930s, when Auden immigrated to America, the "public charge" clause had been stripped of its ability to bar homosexual immigrants, the state had virtually no tools for enforcing its citizenship prohibitions.[47] In light of this homophobic legal framework, Auden writes his American citizenship, a citizenship that his homosexuality should not have made possible, dialectically in relation to celibacy. *The Sea and the Mirror* rejects Prospero's politics of renunciation (and the younger Auden's views on celibacy, which Prospero embodies) in favor of forging queer belonging through what I will call Caliban's active instrumentalized celibacy.[48]

Prospero's speech to Ariel occupies the majority of the first section of *The Sea and the Mirror* and provides a mode of acquiring citizenship through ascetic renunciation. Prospero depicts himself as a man who has ceded his desires in exchange for political belonging: "I am glad that I did not recover my dukedom till / I do not want it" (5). Allegorically, Prospero fulfills the requirements of the celibate American citizen—desireless, surrendering in order to gain acceptance. Reading this speech next to Auden's letters to his brother from 1927 and 1928, Prospero is immediately recognizable as the Flaubertian celibate artist withdrawn from life that Auden hopes to be: "I am glad I freed you, [Ariel] / So at last I can really believe I shall die. / For under your influence death is inconceivable" (5). Here, Prospero sees Ariel as the embodiment of pure artistry and spirituality, a vehicle that transports him away from the realities of existence like death. While in the previous chapters celibacy is a mode of engagement, here Prospero figures celibacy as total reclusion. This position of passivity is coupled with a promotion of silence and detachment: "But we have only to learn to sit still and give no orders" (6) and "I never suspected the way of truth / Was a way of silence" (11). Prospero literally embodies "the pursed mouth" of asceticism, which Auden describes in his earlier letters to his brother as devoid of "enjoy[ment]" and life's vital forces. Prospero's aesthetic and ascetic theory is crucial to understanding *The Sea and the Mirror* as a whole, for Auden described the work as "my Ars Poetica, in the same way I believe *The Tempest* to be Shakespeare's ie I am attempting something which in a way is absurd, to show in a work of art, the limitations of art" (xi). The Prospero section embodies these limitations; Prospero offers an older model of art, one grounded in the nineteenth-century affect of Flaubertian disengagement, the nineteenth-century tradition of reading Shakespeare as Prospero, and the aesthetic theories of the younger Auden.[49]

Auden criticizes celibacy for imagining "the future within moderate, very moderate, limits" (41). He further elucidates this position in "Henry James and the Dedicated" (1944), which was published in the same year as *The Sea and the Mirror*:

> James certainly did not imagine that intellectual vocations were the only ones. It is possible, I think, that he would share my belief that the vocation to which the majority of mankind is called is also the highest and hardest, and that to be a good husband and father is a larger achievement than becoming the greatest artist or scientist on earth.
>
> At the same time James thought, and I agree with him, that if you *are* called to the intellectual life, then you had better remain single and if possible, celibate. Outside the totalitarian countries, the temptations of Philistia are still her age-old ones of money and fame, which the really gifted man can resist fairly easily so long as he is alone. But give him a wife and it becomes his duty to be a parent; give him a family and in many cases he will soon be faced with the choice between being unfaithful to the demands of his work, and unfaithful to his responsibilities for those he has promised to love, and will only too often end up being faithful to neither.
>
> Maybe that is why many a writer, James among them, have suffered from physical or psychological troubles which made marriage impossible; their disability was in fact, not as some psychologists assert, the cause for their gift, but its guardian angel.[50]

While Auden retains his pathologized view of celibacy (in both senses) from the late 1920s (celibacy as a symptom of "disability"), he supplements and complicates that vision by positing a special relationship between celibacy and the literary: celibacy is the necessary condition of artistic production. This connection is reinforced most obviously in *The Sea and the Mirror* when Caliban directly councels "gay apprentice[s]" who seek to become artists to keep a "single bed" (36). Less obviously, the artist is described as possessing prodigious powers of observation—"No perception however *petite*, no notion however subtle, escapes your attention or baffles your understanding" (37, his emphasis)—inscribing him in the tradition of celibate observer that I have described earlier. In addition to a celibate detachment that enables observation, Auden's essay here tropes on writing as a birth or production that requires labor (in both senses) to suggest that celibacy enables certain kinds of (re)production. But such production is not the "highest" aim—the final section of "Caliban to the Audience" and Ariel's "Postscript" offer a new vision of the artist as an ambitious, politically engaged queer citizen. Caliban is the poem's most important figure and allegorizes the difficulty queer artists experience when they attempt to subscribe and belong to normative modes of nationalism.

While Prospero's asceticism grants him admission to the house of the *"native Muse"* (a figure for America), which Caliban describes at the beginning of his address to the audience, this admission comes at a *"price"* (34, his emphasis). Refusing to pay, Caliban is the sole exclusion, *"the solitary exception,"* left out of the *"tout le monde"* invited *"to drop in at any time"* (29, 27, 27, his emphasis). In my reading, the native Muse's house straightforwardly allegorizes America in its open-armed welcomeness. Caliban describes the native Muse (represented as a society woman) as more democratic and permissive than either her *"Grecian aunt or Gallic sister"* (28, his emphasis), both of whom represent pinnacles of the democratic spirit. The native Muse's house is full of every accent, rank, age, and taste—*"the mixed perfected brew"*—a veritable melting pot (28, his emphasis). It is a place with completely open borders where everyone is invited, everyone except Caliban.

Caliban is excluded for a variety of reasons. According to Jonathan Goldberg, his two major liabilities for appropriation and rewriting as a hero are the rape of Miranda and his limited (if inventive) language skills:[51]

PROSPERO: [T]hou didst seek to violate
The honour of my child.
CALIBAN: O ho, O ho! Would't had been done!
Thou didst prevent me—I had peopled else
This isle with Calibans.

CALIBAN: You taught me language, and my profit on't
Is I know how to curse.[52]

Auden potentially exonerates Caliban of both of these charges by transforming Caliban into Henry James—the famous celibate whose eloquent linguistic circumlocutions astound. I say "potentially" because Auden seems to want to keep, or perhaps cannot help but keep, Caliban's dangerous sexuality from peeking out from under the cloak of celibate Jamesian prose.[53] That is, even a Jamesian circumlocutory disguise cannot smuggle Caliban past the border guards of belonging into the native Muse's house.[54]

Caliban's desire to belong—the central aim of his address—is compromised from his first depiction. In his opening words, he stands in a posture of shame:

> If now, having dismissed your hired impersonators with verdicts
> ranging from the laudatory orchid to the disgusted and disgusting
> egg, you ask and, of course, notwithstanding the conscious fact of
> his irrevocable absence, you instinctively *do* ask for our so good, so
> great, so dead author to stand before the finally lowered curtain
> and take his shyly responsible bow for this, his latest, ripest produc-
> tion, it is I—my reluctance is, I can assure you, co-equal with your
> dismay—who will always loom this wretchedly into your picture, for,
> in default of the all-wise, all-explaining master you would speak *to*,
> who else at least can, who else indeed must respond to your bewil-
> dered cry, but its very echo, the begged question you speak to him
> *about*. (27, his emphasis)

Auden nicknamed Caliban "The Prick" (xviii) in several letters to friends. With this in mind, Caliban speaks reluctantly ("who else at least can, who else indeed must respond to your bewildered cry") because he feels vulnerable and ashamed—an exposed set of genitals. This dangerous exposure, familiar to any reader of James's autobiographical writing, fuels Caliban's compensating, flaunting sexuality: the audacity and insult that his nickname implies. Here, Caliban is unequal to the task of standing in for an author-celebrity who refuses to speak on his own behalf. He posits a mediating gap between the actuality of expression and its skewed representation before the social. Caliban's "echo" is constituted by the "author," as well as the judgments ("the laudatory orchid" and "the disgusted and disgusting egg") of the "audience." That is, this ambassadorial figure is simultaneously an authorial self-representation and a symptom of the author's celebrity manifested by the audience.[55] The text conflates the celebrity of Auden and Shakespeare (this is a production where Caliban refers to the "author") and summons the shade of the failed dramatist James (in the references to the "all-explaining master" and his "shyly responsible bow").[56] An embarrassing ambassador, Caliban is shameful not just for Shakespeare (a trope that threads through Caliban's address) but also to the native Muse who associates him with Sycorax's witchcraft and "*unrectored chaos*" (29, his emphasis). But the pinnacle of Caliban's offense for the native Muse—its "*gross climax*"—is the "*horror unspeakable*" of making "*a pass at her virgin self*" (29, his emphasis). That is, he will bring the gritty underbelly of sexuality into the "innocent" home of the native Muse. Here, the trope of preterition ("*horror unspeakable*") as well as Caliban's queer associations with unnaturalness, monstrosity, and witchcraft suggest that his exclusion from the Muse's virginal home is a homophobic one: homosexuality and American citizenship, as I have argued earlier, are inimical.[57]

This homosexual exclusion of Caliban is personalized by Auden to stage the limits of his own citizenship. Along these lines, the text establishes a strong identification between Auden and Caliban. Caliban not only is an authorial representation within the textual imaginary but also shares many biographical details with Auden. For example, Caliban describes "*incest in a dream*" (34, his emphasis), which refers to a dream Auden recounts in a letter: "I suddenly had a violent longing to be fucked by him [Auden's father.]"[58] Additionally, the young Auden made a special effort to be selected for the role of Caliban in a school play.[59] Moreover, Caliban's relationship to James further identifies him with Auden as James's move and naturalization are the mirror image of James's transatlantic passage.[60]

This identificatory network implicitly whitens Caliban, obscuring the way that the polarization between homosexuality and American citizenship was significantly diminished by the privilege of whiteness. Black queer writers like Claude McKay, James Baldwin, and Langston Hughes had significantly less ability to move in and out of America's borders than white authors like Auden. This is one reason that Baldwin does not fit into my revised description of queer commuters. For example, as William Maxwell's phenomenal work has argued, "The FBI was tailing globetrotter Claude McKay . . . and directing customs officials to retain the poet and his effects at every U.S. port of entry."[61] Surveillance by the FBI was similarly the catalyst for Baldwin's flight from the United States in 1964.[62] Langston Hughes appeared on the Hoover Security Index—a list of those considered dangerous enough to be interned in case of war.[63] Rather than attributing this increased surveillance merely to the perceived communism and radical ties of these black writers, Maxwell notes the FBI's "distinct" interest in sexuality as a motivation.[64] For example, McKay's bureau reputation as "bohemian reprobate" was crucial to his identity as a "notorious negro revolutionary."[65] Similarly, Baldwin is flagged as "a well-known pervert."[66] Thus, while Auden, Caliban, and Auden's queer commuters are certainly wise to employ caution (and celibacy), they enjoy relative mobility in relation to their black contemporaries.

The homophobic context of *The Sea and the Mirror* has escaped notice, as virtually the entire critical history of the text aestheticizes it as Auden's Christian *ars poetica* and reads it in a social, historical, and political vacuum.[67] Caliban's vision of the poetic "damag[ing]" the real will precisely map the assault *The Sea and the Mirror* makes upon constructions of citizenship: *"Is it possible that, not content with inveigling Caliban into Ariel's kingdom, you have also let loose Ariel in Caliban's. . . . For if the intrusion of the real has disconcerted and incommoded the poetic, that is a mere bagatelle compared to the damage which the poetic would inflict if it ever succeeded in intruding upon the real. We want no Ariel here, breaking down our picket fences in the name of fraternity, seducing our wives in the name of romance, and robbing us of our sacred pecuniary deposits in the name of justice"* (35, his emphasis). Caliban articulates his own condemnation on behalf of the audience. Like Caliban, Auden seems to be preempting his own bad British reviews (the reviews of the volume were divided along national lines between scathing British reviews and glowing American ones) represented in the lack of applause at the end of Caliban's address and engaging the accusations of shame and failure put forward by his critics. Auden rebukes them for letting his perceived politics befog his poetry to the point of opaqueness ("the intrusion of the real has disconcerted and incommoded the poetic"). The closing portion of the quotation is not just a satire of bourgeois desires for home, marriage, and wealth but Auden's defensive assault on those snarling critics who see him as a threat to their way of life. The geographic description of the imbrication between art and life (the unleashing of Caliban and Ariel into each other's respective realms) implies a heteronormative order—each man has a wife who is not to be seduced by another man. The geography of the nation-state, both in the text and as imagined in the immigration legislation prior to the McCarran-Walter Act, is either a heteronormative or a celibate one.

A Queer National Space

In representing America through an elaborate geographic metaphor depicting not only the native Muse's house but also its *"interesting alcove,"* *"stair[s],"* *"front door,"* and back (28, 28, 29, his emphasis), the text draws attention to the exclusionary nature of all geographies:[68]

Must we—it seems oddly that we must—remind you that our existence
does not, like hers [our native Muse], enjoy an infinitely indicative
mood, an eternally present tense, a limitlessly active voice, for in our
shambling, slovenly makeshift world any two persons, whether domestic
first or neighbourly second, require and necessarily presuppose in both
their numbers and in all their cases, the whole inflected gamut of an
alien third, since, without a despised or dreaded Them to turn the back
on, there could be no intimate or affectionate Us to turn the eye to; that,
chez nous, Space is never the whole uninhibited circle but always some
segment, its eminent domain upheld by two co-ordinates. There always
has been and always will be not only the vertical boundary, the river
on this side of which initiative and honesty stroll arm in arm wearing
sensible clothes, and beyond which is a savage elsewhere swarming with
contagious diseases, but also its horizontal counterpart, the railroad
above which houses stand in their own grounds, each equipped with a
garage and a beautiful woman, sometimes with several, and below which
huddled shacks provide a squeezing shelter to collarless herds who eat
blancmange and have never said anything witty. . . . For without these
prohibitive frontiers we should never know who we were or what we
wanted. It is thanks to them that we do know with whom to associate,
make love, exchange recipes and jokes, go mountain climbing or sit side
by side fishing from piers. It is thanks to them, too, that we know against
whom to rebel. We can shock our parents by visiting the dives below the
railroad tracks, we can amuse ourselves on what would otherwise have
been a very dull evening indeed, in plotting to seize the post-office across
the river. (31–32)

Here, Caliban suggests that the very segregation between Us and Them is
constituted in and through geography. That is, geographies and "prohibitive
frontiers" are constitutive of the first-person identity and the second-person
horizontality of national identification. But the passage playfully calls for
a transgression of these frontiers (that we "*shock our parents by visiting the
dives below the railroad tracks*"), so as to seize control of and transform how
the national circulates within these geographies ("*seize the post-office across
the river*"). In other words, Caliban here suggests that geographic transgression enables the rewriting of the operations and flows of the national
(humorously embodied in the postal system).

The text imbues geography with enormous power. Many critics have tried to locate the island of *The Tempest*, but the work refuses any easy association with a particular geography or fixed location. Gonzalo's address in *The Sea and the Mirror* provides much of what geographic information about the island exists at all (as he does in the Shakespearean original):

I look back
For the last time as the sun
Sets behind that island where
All our loves were altered (16)

While Gonzalo literally speaks of the island on which *The Tempest* takes place, Auden's readers (judging from the preoccupations of his reviewers) would probably have also heard "Auden" reflecting on his departure from England.[69] Auden's belief that *The Tempest* was Shakespeare's farewell highlights this reading.[70] But Auden does not merely laminate the island of *The Tempest* onto England; rather, he deploys *The Tempest*'s inherent deterritorialized and deterritorializing capacity, what Derrida has called, in a different context, its *hypertopicality*.[71] Auden draws on the *hypertopical—both placeless and overplaced*—character of *The Tempest* to forge his queer citizenship.[72] *Hypertopicality* posits particular geographies as multi-sited, giving the impression of being overplaced (in many places at once) and in no place at all, placeless (because the location cannot be fixed or located). To put this another way, *The Sea and the Mirror* fluidly maps three islands (Manhattan, England, and Circe's island) onto the island of *The Tempest* (for a total of four) to dislocate and universalize cultural and national identities.[73]

Circe's mythical island highlights the imbricated islands' transformative powers: "As all the pigs have turned back into men / And the sky is auspicious and the sea / Calm as a clock, we can all go home again" (13). Here, Antonio angrily sees the men return home changed and, changed, change home. Caliban and Auden are able to effect a conversion, performing their entitlement to belonging. This flamboyant compensation is already evident in the work's "Preface":

The aged catch their breath,
For the nonchalant couple go
Waltzing across the tightrope
As if there were no death
Or hope of falling down;
The wounded cry as the clown

Doubles his meaning, and O
How the dear little children laugh
When the drums roll and the lovely
Lady is sawn in half. (3)

Here, the circus offers a place where high and low freely intermingle and change places, where tightrope walkers appear fearless even as the "wounded cry" of the clown suggests the very real possibility of danger. These lines narrate Auden's cultural transformation, dramatizing the dangers of moving across space (mirroring Auden's migration as a "nonchalant couple" with Isherwood to America away from the politics and death in Europe). But even without reading so strongly, these lines clearly foreground transformation as the clown's puns move words from one register into another and the "Lady" is changed into a grotesque spectacle of her formerly "lovely" self. *The Sea and the Mirror* moves from appearing to feel shameless in order to effect change as the tightrope couple does, to actually being shameless in what Caliban calls "the full bloom of the unbothered state" (53). *Hypertopicality*'s avoidance of surveillance substitutes for the achievement of the real goal—"the unbothered state"—of being a queer subject unbothered by the judgments of both the social and the self.

Before arriving at the utopian "unbothered state," Caliban articulates a "transcend[ent]" vision free "of *any* condition" or "obligation to inherit or transmit" (47, his emphasis):

Again, other selves undoubtedly exist, but though everyone's pocket is bulging with birth certificates, insurance policies, passports and letters of credit, there is no way of proving whether they are genuine or planted or forged, so that no one knows whether another is his friend disguised as an enemy or his enemy disguised as a friend (There is probably no one whose real name is Brown), or whether the police who here as elsewhere are grimly busy, are crushing a criminal revolt or upholding a vicious tyranny, any more than he knows whether he himself is a victim of the theft, or the thief, or a rival thief, a professionally interested detective, or a professionally impartial journalist. (48)

Here, identity papers do not enable the state to police its borders. This lack of useful surveillance (attempts seem futile) decriminalizes identity shifts and explains away the state's nondifferentiation of enemy and friend. In other words, Caliban suggests that the identity markers of homosexuality or communism, or an attempted parliamentary condemnation that locates one as an enemy, might not be misrecognitions but instead victimizing injustices. Their status as injustices suggests that these exclusions should be remedied and that citizenship should be granted. But this "transcend[ent]" vision is nightmarish as it is produced "where all is need and change" (47). This passage creates a space where identity is not legible to anyone, even the individual himself. It is the practical solution that celibacy as closetedness and *hypertopicality* as illegibility create to produce the queer citizen in secret at the cost of "seeing ourselves as we are" (52).

This queer national space is unlivable for Auden and for Caliban—they need the "unbothered state" of acceptance. This shame-free space receives its clearest articulation in the poem's closing "Postscript" spoken by Ariel to Caliban with the Echo by the Prompter:

> Spare me a humiliation,
> > To your faults be true:
> I can sing as you reply
> > *. . . I*
> Wish for nothing lest you mar
> The perfection in these eyes . . .
> > —only
> > As I am can I
> > Love you as you are. (55–56)

Here, Ariel accepts, loves, and further in the "Postscript" even incorporates Caliban into herself, referring to him as "we" (56). Rather than the solitary and individualized legal space carved out by celibacy to hide faults, Ariel creates a place of unconditional love, a livable queer national space. The Prompter's "I" has a wide range of attachment. It can be read as a separate utterance of identity, a response to Ariel, and/or as creating declaratives of the imperatives that begin each line of each new stanza ("I wish for nothing lest you mar"). This range of attachment enables the queer citizen to associate with whomever he wants as well as keeping to himself if he so chooses. It is my hope that this examination of how *The Sea and the Mirror* manages the politics of shame—the public assaults on Auden's citizenship, residence, and national and cultural belonging on the one hand, and the attacks on his sexual politics on the other—has begun to suggest that any map of pre-Stonewall queer citizenship is incomplete without reference to celibacy.[74] Questions about queer citizenship do not erupt spontaneously with Stonewall but were negotiated by Auden and many others at least a quarter century earlier. Within the confines of pre-Stonewall America, celibacy is not just the result of shame but a tactic of survival in an environment of real fear. This pre-Stonewall queer citizen looks different than his post-Stonewall counterpart. Rather than a strategy of recognition, the celibate queer citizen deploys multiple kinds of national belonging, strategies for transforming national spaces, and solitary disguises all in the service of manipulating U.S. immigration law to forge a queer national identity. Thus, the pre-Stonewall queer is less concerned with aspirations and concepts than with pure and perhaps even crude practicality.

Chapter Five | Philosophical Bachelorhood,
Philosophical Spinsterhood, and
Celibate Modernity

Celibate Heaven, or How to Get from "A" to "V"

The January 1981 cover of *Penthouse Forum* features a surprising image: Andy Warhol stands beside a sultry blonde wearing a T-shirt that reads, "ANDY WARHOL IS A VIRGIN" (fig. 5.1).[1] The seductive woman's garter and stockings peek out of the translucent surface of the white shirt on which Warhol's virginity is proclaimed. Reading the woman's sartorial presentation, we could see the striking juxtaposition of T-shirt and garter implying that just below the surface, covered only by the thin veneer of Warhol's virginity (embodied in a T-shirt) resides an effeminate sexuality (in the form of a sexy woman). However, this queer reading is at odds with those that my project has striven to articulate and at odds with Warhol's own pose on the cover. Rather than Warhol's famed "swish" gender presentation (which is the alleged cause for Jasper Johns's and Robert Rauschenberg's frosty relations with him), we see something much closer to the neutrality described by John Wilcock: "I've thought of him as being a mirror, a seismograph, all those things which are almost totally neutral themselves but reflect what is poured into them."[2] Without for a moment so much as glancing over at the woman who appears to be offering herself to him, Warhol stands unfazed in what the art critic and curator Mario Amaya refers to as his "completely empirical kind of attitude."[3] The T-shirt suggests that Warhol, rather than lacking a sexual interest in women, is not sexually interested, or at least has not been intimate with anyone. While we might imagine the cover as offering two versions of Warhol's celibacy, one stony and untouchable (represented by him) and the other teasing and sexy (represented by the model), this chapter takes the cover as beginning to theorize a sociable celibacy—one characterized by alloeroticism and born of the interaction between Warhol and the blonde model beside him. While much of this chapter will be concerned with elaborating Warhol's alloerotic celibacy, I want to define it provisionally as a celibacy in relation; this sexuality's coordinates of desire, pleasure, and fantasy are oriented outward in geometries involving at least two people.

Returning to the cover image, the plain text reading of the T-shirt's assertion that "Andy Warhol is a virgin" is echoed about a month later in Warhol's own published diaries, where he writes in February 1981:

> Yesterday I was watching a game show, *Blockbusters* with Bill Cullen, and it was two black guys, a warden and his cousin, against a white girl and the category was "Letters" and the question was: "Andy Warhol is a 'V.'" And (*laughs*) she got the answer right, she said, "Virgin." And then Bill Cullen said, "That's right, at fifty-one." She won $500 and she got it up to $12,000.
>
> Oh, and I got a letter from Germany written in German about *Bad*—it was official-looking and the only sentence I can read is so funny: "In this film they kill a man under a *Volkswagen*!"[4]

Reading the cover with this entry in mind, we see Warhol affirming the T-shirt's message, circulating a discourse of his celibacy. The passage is somewhat surprising in that Warhol is most forcefully associated with the signifier "A" in relation to his *a: a novel* (1968) and *The Philosophy of Andy Warhol (From A to B and Back Again)* (1975) and its concomitant chain of associations: Andy, artist, adultery, amphetamine, albino, and so forth.[5] This passage seems to offer an alternative signifier for Warhol and one that I hope will recast our understanding of him.[6] Even as Warhol's declarative statement that "she got the answer right" suggests that we read the "V" as standing transparently for "Virgin," the passage also opens a second "right" answer: that "V" stands for "Volkswagen." The position of "Volkswagen" as the final word in the entry and the fact that it is the only other word in the entry beginning with "V" highlight this reading. Warhol's oft-quoted contention—"I want to be a machine"—is here fulfilled by his becoming Volkswagen. Like fellow filmmakers Buster Keaton, Charlie Chaplin, and Dziga Vertov, Warhol casts himself as a machine.[7] He is literally a man

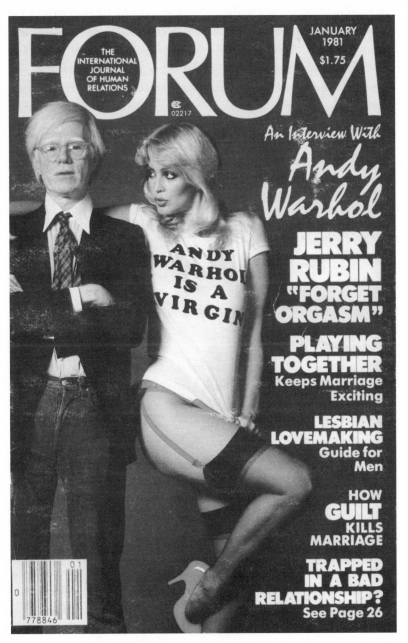

FIGURE 5.1. Andy Warhol on the cover of *Penthouse Forum*, January 1981.
Photograph by Mark Wiener.

killer, the object of consumer and sexual desire, but also curiously sexless. The voraciousness of desire for him—he is the "people's car" giving everyone an automotive and sexual ride—is only matched by his mechanic untouchability.

What is so striking is how dissimilar this understanding of Warhol is from standard accounts. In the opening paragraph of *Pop Out*—the most important edited collection about Andy Warhol's sexuality—the editors put forward a very different genealogy of Warhol's sexuality: "Andy Warhol was queer in more ways than one. To begin with, he was a fabulous queen, a fan of prurience and pornography, and a great admirer of the male body. This queerness was 'known,' in one way or another, by the gay audiences who enjoyed his films, the police who censored them, the gallery owners who excluded his sketches of male nudes from exhibits, the artists who were made uncomfortable by his swishiness, not to mention the drag queens, hustlers, speed freaks, fag hags, and others who populated the Factory."[8] The editors here offer a queer Warhol in response to the majority of scholars and members of the art establishment who "have 'de-gayed' him."[9] When references to Warhol's sexuality have occurred, the editors tell us it has either been to "moralize about the 'degraded' quality of Warhol's art" or to nominate him as "'asexual' or 'voyeuristic'" rather than "[mention] that he was *gay*."[10] While recognizing, as the editors do, that these nominations frequently function as closeting gestures that censor, straighten, and normalize Warhol's gay sexuality, this chapter is only ancillarily interested in deploying celibacy to unsettle gayness in order to suggest that "gayness" is not a category that we can know in advance. Instead, this chapter is centrally interested in how Warhol positions himself within a tradition of celibate philosophers. I argue that this tradition underwrites the Factory's new modes of government and theorizes a concept of group celibacy. The chapter closes by reading Valerie Solanas's SCUM *Manifesto* (1968) as offering an opposing modality of sociable celibacy; she posits SCUM as an insurrectionary critique and alternative to Warhol's style of governance. Reading the celibate reign of Warhol over the Factory and of Solanas over SCUM, I hope to elucidate the relationship between these philosophical celibates and their styles of government as well as to theorize the relationship between celibacy and philosophy more generally.

In addition to his self-presentation on the cover of *Penthouse Forum*, Warhol propounded his celibacy frequently in interviews. For example, in the interview with Scott Cohen from this same issue of *Penthouse Forum*,

Warhol remarks, "Well, I never have sex" and "Yeah. I'm still a virgin."[11] Similarly, George Gruskin says to Warhol in a 1973 interview: "There is another area I would like to discuss with you; namely your family life, love life, romantic involvement. Your sex life, to put it bluntly." Warhol responds: "I don't have any."[12] The editorial frame of *Pop Out* is prepared for Warhol's assertion of his own virginity/sexlessness/celibacy, positioning those around Warhol as authenticators of his queer provenance: "This queerness was 'known,' in one way or another," by "gay audiences," "the police," "gallery owners," and "artists," "not to mention the drag queens, hustlers, speed freaks, fag hags, and others who populated the Factory." But those in Warhol's circle often understood him in terms of celibacy as well. For example, Viva, one of the Factory Superstars, asserts: "I don't think he [Warhol] has any sex life." Similarly, Billy Name, another Superstar, calls Warhol "a true monk."[13] More important, however, these claims for Warhol's celibacy by members of the Warhol circle suggest that the Factory might exist as a celibate milieu alongside more familiar claims of it being, in Kelly Cresap's phrase, "Queer Central," or as Wayne Koestenbaum puts it (mapping the complex interrelation between effeminate men, beautiful women, and cats): "Pussy Heaven."[14]

This celibate version of Warhol and of the Factory is tantalizingly evoked by an anonymous observer in Victor Bockris's biography of Warhol: "Philip [Fagan] was definitely not selling sex, recalled another observer, which would have worked out just fine there in 'celibate heaven,' as I thought of the Factory. But Andy and Philip seemed to be very close, like two little girls in a way, and they baked cakes together, so Fagan had found a niche in which he didn't have to put out but could get supported and hang out."[15] This gossipy moment in Bockris's not fully scholarly biography of Warhol suggests something amazing—the Factory as a celibate sociality. Rather than dismiss this alternative genealogy of the Factory as hearsay, I follow such queer thinkers as Eve Sedgwick, Gavin Butt, and Henry Abelove in understanding gossip as one of the best sources of sexual knowledge.[16] It is not clear from the anonymous observer's comments whether Fagan's selling of sex "would have worked out just fine" because everyone in the Factory was celibate, did not want to be, and thus would have purchased sex, or whether it "would have worked out just fine" because he was not selling sex and thus would fit in perfectly with all the other celibates at the Factory. In either reading, the Factory circa 1964 is characterized by a version of celibacy, or even, as the baking of cakes suggests, a celibate domesticity. This celibate

Factory is elaborated by Ultra Violet, one of Warhol's Superstars, who refers to Viva as "still celibate," and Janet Palmer, who describes Factory regular Michael Post as "determined to stay a virgin until he was twenty-one."[17] POPism: The Warhol Sixties (1980) describes "the running question about" Paul Morrissey as "did he have a sex life or not?"[18]

More than the celibacy of the individual members of the Warhol circle, Gerard Malanga suggests how celibacy organized life at the Factory: "It was almost as if he [Warhol] was sexless. He cringed from physical contact. It was that celibacy which gave him enormous manipulative power over the magnificently beautiful people he brought together. But it was congenial."[19] The éclat of life at the Factory and its "magnificently beautiful people" is orchestrated by Warhol's celibacy.[20] Warhol similarly places celibacy at the center of the Factory when he remarks in the context of his friend Henry Geldzahler moving in with a boyfriend, "I could only be really good friends with unattached people." While Warhol and Geldzahler used to spend hours talking on the phone, now when Warhol calls, Henry is no longer "available" (in the double sense of being able to talk as well as sexually), suggesting nonattachment as a source of "immediacy" for Warhol and life at the Factory.[21]

Though Warhol is not primarily thought of as a philosopher, the alloeroticism of Warhol's celibacy described by Malanga and Warhol himself only emerges when we consider him as such. While certainly a nontraditional philosophical text, The Philosophy of Andy Warhol investigates questions of aesthetics, ethics, politics, eschatology, temporality, and many other avowedly philosophical concerns. Philosopher and art critic Arthur Danto has argued that Warhol "had the greatest philosophical acuity of any modern artist."[22] My investment in understanding Warhol as a philosopher takes its cue less from Danto than from John Guillory's wonderful essay "The Bachelor State: Philosophy and Sovereignty in Bacon's New Atlantis," which notes: "Between 1600 and 1800 nearly every one of the greater philosophers was unmarried: Descartes, Hobbes, Spinoza, Locke, Leibniz, Hume, Adam Smith, Kant (the major exception is Berkeley). To this number we must also add the most important scientists, Robert Boyle, Robert Hooke, and Isaac Newton, who would have been known in their own time as philosophers rather than scientists."[23] Guillory posits that this remarkably uniform type might have emerged out of "a socially sanctioned association between the unmarried state and intellectuality."[24] Freedom from the institution of marriage is not only a freedom from "its responsibilities and distractions," but also a "freedom from constraint in a deeper sense": "Marriage can be said to stand in for social institutions generally, inasmuch as these might constrain both freedom of action and freedom of thought."[25] These new social freedoms open the possibility for Guillory that the philosophical bachelor is able to create new styles of government (the philosopher-king provides Guillory's most recognizable example). Philosophical bachelorhood for Guillory largely ends in the early nineteenth century with Kant, Kierkegaard, and Schopenhauer.

While Guillory sees this tradition as continuing in the twentieth century only with Wittgenstein and through the philosophical memory of such common logical examples as "All unmarried men are bachelors" or "No bachelors are married," I will argue that this tradition is a bit more expansive.[26] From the nineteenth century, we might include Lewis Carroll, particularly given the importance of celibacy in *Alice's Adventures in Wonderland* (1865) and *Through the Looking Glass and What Alice Found There* (1871).[27] The twentieth-century tradition certainly must include George Santayana, whose theorization of nonsexual and unconsummated erotic friendship resides at the heart of his philosophy.[28] We could also add Nietzsche and Sartre and even Foucault.[29] Most important, I understand Warhol to continue this celibate tradition and theorize a style of governance, one that performs what Michael Warner calls philosophy as "a counternormative way of living."[30]

Warhol's marriage to his tape recorder is the most important event of his philosophical bachelorhood and begins to explain his promotion of himself as celibate in the twin etymological senses of virginity and of bachelorhood.[31] Nietzsche's reading of Socrates as ironically married and still a part of the tradition of celibate philosophers will provide the basis with which to read Warhol within this genealogy of celibate modernity.[32] Warhol attributes his nonnormative marital choice to "missing some responsibility chemicals and some reproductive chemicals." The "chemicals" in this account summon an explanation that is part biological and part mechanical, making him simultaneously vulnerably human and coldly mechanistic. This opposition suggests a particularly queer development of his life: "If I had them [the missing chemicals] I would probably think more about aging the right way and being married four times and having a family—wives and children and dogs."[33] Warhol's inability to age "the right way" is embodied in his silver wig, which prematurely ages him and links him to the celibate temporality that I described in chapter 2. In particular, the wig's silver color would have associated Warhol with the futurity of the past that characterizes celibate temporality: "Silver was the future, it was spacy—the astronauts wore silver suits. . . . And silver was also the past—the Silver Screen—Hollywood actresses photographed in silver sets."[34] "Aging the right way" not only suggests celibate temporality but also installs queerness into the heart of heteronormativity by magnifying and multiplying heterosexuality to make it unrecognizable by encompassing "being married four times."

Warhol's reference to the number four lays the groundwork for his alternative marital narrative:

> When I got my first TV set, I stopped caring so much about having close relationships with other people. . . . So in the late 50s I started an affair with my television which has continued to the present, when I play around with as many as *four* at a time. But I didn't get married until 1964 when I got my first tape recorder. My wife. My tape recorder and I have been married for ten years now. . . . The acquisition of my tape recorder really finished whatever emotional life I might have had, but I was glad to see it go. (my emphasis)

Here, Warhol has four adulterous affairs with his four TVs that he "play[s] around" with—one for each marriage. The tape recorder and TVs are particularly easy to anthropomorphize and ascribe agency to because they seem to possess a trait that is (wrongly) thought to be definitional of humanity: the capacity for speech. Embodying the neutrality and detachment described by Wilcock and Amaya, Warhol eschews traditional marriage and emotional life. Later in *The Philosophy*, he describes his reasons for marrying: "I have no memory. Every day is a new day because I don't remember the day before. . . . That's why I got married—to my tape recorder."[35] The act of marriage is a turn toward memory and contemplation. Here, Warhol's marriage and affairs suggest him as participating in the tradition of "freedom of action and freedom of thought" described by Guillory; the tape recorder remembers everything for him so that he does not have to spend his time recollecting.

In fact, Warhol expressly articulates this freedom of mind in relation to his unwillingness to marry (despite enormous family pressure to do so):

> A person can cry or laugh. Always when you're crying you could be laughing, you have the choice. Crazy people know how to do this best because their minds are loose. So you can take the flexibility

your mind is capable of and make it work for you. You decide what you want to do and how you want to spend your time. Remember, though, that I think I'm missing some chemicals, so it's easier for me than for a person who has a lot of responsibility chemicals, but the same principle could still be applied in a lot of instances.[36]

Here, Warhol sees responsibility (which he has characterized as involving marriage, children, and pets) as antithetical or at least a roadblock to "flexibility" of mind. His choice to marry his tape recorder is a marriage to himself (as it literally repeats and records him) that is also a same-sex marriage between Warhol and his tape recorder double. At the same time, it is a promiscuous marriage to any number of others (as the recorder chronicles Ondine and other members of his entourage in *a: a novel*).[37] The simultaneity of this marriage as marriage to self and marriage as polygamy underpins Warhol's alloerotic celibacy: "That's why I seek out people with minds like tape recorders to be with. My mind is like a tape recorder with one button—Erase."[38] Here, those he "seek[s] out"—his friends and his entourage—are conflated with and are competition for his wife, serving the same function of remembrance and generating a remarkable proximity between conjugal and other modes of intimacy. The marriage to his tape recorder and potential marriageability between Warhol and his friends create new modes of alliance and affiliation, tapping into what Elizabeth Freeman calls "a queer desire to imagine and represent something different from the social choices at hand."[39] Anyone can stand in for and be endowed with the social and economic intimacy and power that reside at the heart of the couple.

Warhol makes social relations with objects and allows them to organize his social field as much as people do and in some cases more so (as he relates to people as objects, seeking those "with minds like tape recorders").[40] Warhol's mobilization of marriage is particularly important, since marriage is the only affiliation that supersedes consanguine bonds. This willingness to endow nonhuman actors with the ability to reorganize kinship structures is a key component of Warhol's sociable celibacy. The eroticization of objects and people as objects clarifies some of the mysteriousness of Charles Henri Ford's comment that "everything is sexual to Andy without the sex act actually taking place."[41] Ford suggests Warhol's profound intimacy and ability to make relations with objects that do not exist in the realm of normative sexuality. His celibacy operates at a zero degree of desire—he likes everything.[42] That is, he does not just desire his tape recorder but desires as a tape recorder would—taking in everything with an all-encompassing Eros. To understand how this alloerotic celibacy moves increasingly outward, I will consider *My Hustler* (1965) as one of the most expansive representations of alloeroticism in the Warhol oeuvre.

Sociable Celibacy

My Hustler thematizes the processes described by Malanga, exploring the operations by which Warhol's celibacy "congenially" enables him to manipulate others. I will call the erotics of celibacy that the film elaborates "cockblocking" to capture the sexual pleasure involved in interrupting others' sexual acts and the resulting celibacy of the film. By reading Warhol as a more powerful version of a Queen Ed–like figure—surrounded by "beauties" as Ed is in *My Hustler*—we can further understand the dynamics of the Factory's governance and the Eros native to it.

The title of Andy Warhol's *My Hustler* raises the question that animates the film: Which character authors the possessive "my" of the film's title? Or, to put this question of reference more simply: Whose hustler is Paul America? This question would seem to have a simple answer—Paul America is the middle-aged Queen Ed's hustler. Ed "dialed-a-hustler," and Paul America headed to the famously homosexual Fire Island to lie out in the sun. Ed then bets his visiting neighbor Genevieve Charbon and the older hustler (John Macdermott, known around the Factory as the Sugar Plum Fairy) that they cannot take Paul away from him. Even before the bet, the film's opening moment complicates the idea of straightforward ownership when Ed calls to his servant, "Cully! What are you doing out of uniform?" While this moment establishes Ed as upper-class and powerful, it also throws his power into question—he is unable to get his servant to adhere to the proper disciplinary protocols. Ed's simultaneous surety of his power and his anxious fear of losing it lead him to remind not just his servant but Genevieve of her "position." Additionally, Ed also attempts to subordinate John, camping: "At least I'm queen of that [Paul] and I don't want any tired old princesses [John] muscling in on it." Here, Ed resignifies his gender identity as a "queen" into a royal status complete with a hierarchy by which he is granted possession of Paul America to become the Queen of America (to borrow a phrase from Lauren Berlant).[43]

Queen Ed's claim to possess the titular hustler is threatened by a second difficulty: namely, determining whether Paul America is in fact a hustler.

That is, the film is haunted by the question of whether it is about a hustler who is not one. At first glance, Paul is certainly a hustler; his employment by Dial-a-Hustler led to his having been summoned to Fire Island. More subtly, the camera's lingering gaze and reveling in the kinesthetics of Paul's body might imply that he is a hustler. This cinematography suggests that from the outset the film is shot from Ed's point of view. This assumption is highlighted by Ed's command to Genevieve "to get [her] lascivious eyes off that beautiful body," suggesting that he is anxious to continue to control this viewpoint. One story of the shooting of *My Hustler* has Warhol wrestling with Paul Morrissey to prevent him from moving the camera, suggesting that Warhol wanted the cinematography of the film to be even more closely aligned with gazing at Paul America.[44] In being the object of an anxiously controlled homosexual gaze, Paul seems at least partially interpellated into homosexual availability. Paul's availability is further heightened by his assertion that he did not serve in the military because of his "4F" classification that he describes as being due to his "bad knee." While the "4F" was given to men unfit for military service, it was also frequently given to homosexuals (Auden received the same classification).[45] The older hustler's incredulous smirk and assent to Paul's story about his knee with a sarcastic "Yeah, sure" heighten the homosexual connotations of Paul's classification.

But the film's second half complicates reading Paul straightforwardly as a homosexual or as a hustler. This part of the film takes place in a bathroom where John and Paul discuss Paul's becoming a hustler. At several points, Paul indicates that he is not a hustler, saying, "Actually, I'm unemployed right now. I don't have a job." He also seems ignorant about hustling and its basic vocabularies, asking the older hustler, "What do you mean 'john'? What's a 'john'?" Moreover, Paul America is described as "that virgin boy" and "fresh," which might refer either to Paul's newness to hustling or to his celibacy. Pressing on Michael Moon's reading of the film, we might interpret this uncertainty about Paul's status as a hustler as part of the fantasy. Reading Warhol's film as theorizing the encounter between "a 'straight-acting' hustler and a trade-seeking john" as "a particularly complex kind of epistemology of the closet," Moon argues that "the john wants a virile youth and consequently (to his mind) a straight-identified one, but what he really requires is a youth who will at least pretend to be straight."[46] Paul's seeming ignorance of homosexuality and the world of trade make him seem all the more "straight." Rather than seeing the old queen's bet as "self-defeating," as Moon does, we might understand the bet that neither Genevieve nor the older hustler can wrest Paul America away from Ed as a fantasy-heightening effect.[47] In other words, by possessing a potentially erotic interest in Genevieve, Paul America's heterosexuality is further credentialed and his claims to virility are strengthened, thereby increasing Ed's desire for Paul. Rather than operating on Moon's assumption that Ed desires queer sex, I will argue that the film is characterized as much by sexlessness as by sex (as Warhol himself is).[48]

Genevieve has "stolen" many of Ed's erotic interests: "You certainly have stolen enough. What were their names? Poor boy Gordon back in Cambridge. You remember Achilles?" Here, the countless men signified by Gordon and Achilles would seem to prevent an intelligent man like Ed from foolhardily betting that Genevieve will not or cannot do it again. However, if we understand Genevieve's theft as an erotic arrangement ("cockblocking") that gives her pleasure and also gives Ed pleasure, the bet makes a great deal of narrative sense. Sedgwick's conception of cuckoldry helps us to further elaborate the definition of cockblocking: "'To cuckold' is by definition a sexual act performed on a man, by another man."[49] While Genevieve is obviously not a man, cockblocking shares the hierarchical and indirect sexual performance that Sedgwick sees as characterizing cuckoldry. In fact, while Sedgwick's understanding of cuckoldry as an act between men might put under erasure the sexual experience transpiring between the extramarital man and woman, cockblocking is a sexual act characterized solely by celibacy.

The text explicitly describes Genevieve's pleasure in cockblocking when Ed asks her, "Do you like to have sex with them [Ed's erotic interests]?" "You know very well I don't. The only thing that amuses me is just going down there and distracting them long enough to, ah, make you suffer about it a little bit and sweat a little bit and run out there and screech and send your silly bodyguard and all that nonsense you go through." The dislocation of the bodyguard (moving away from Ed and interposing himself between Genevieve and Paul) suggests the complex route of desire in this film. Ed's body is in fact in need of guarding as Genevieve's luxuriation in the details of his discomfort and discomposure constitute a sexual axis not between Paul America and her but between Ed and her. Ed is blind to (or at least feigns blindness to) Genevieve's pleasure when he says: "You don't get any sexual pleasure. You get some kind of perverse psychological enjoyment out of stealing them away from faggots, don't you?" But her response—"Well, stealing them away from you in particular"—establishes Ed as her sexual object rather than suggesting that she possesses a kind of sexual orientation toward cockblocking. This specificity toward Ed and away from Paul or Gordon or Achilles is made even clearer in the following exchange:

G: You always bring it [the conversation] back on your sex subject. In point of fact all it is is your thwarting me and me thwarting you. And that is simply what the entire game is all about. . . .

E: And what would you do? You would get him all hot and bothered and frustrated and then you'd drop him.

G: I have absolutely no interest in getting him hot and bothered and frustrated.

Genevieve's insistence that she has "absolutely no interest" in anything involving Paul America and that the entirety of the "game" is in the "thwarting" relation between her and Ed begins to suggest cockblocking as a celibate act that is both auto- and alloerotic. In contrast to the celibate plotting that I elaborated in chapter 1 that operates in tandem with the courtship and marriage plots, here cockblocking offers a celibate plot that stands independently of these other plots, offering its own autoerotic pleasures as well as the more counterintuitive pleasures of alloeroticism.[50]

This alloeroticism fits comfortably into neither the object-based understandings of the hetero/homo binary nor the gender-based understandings of insertive/receptive and active/passive that define normative constructions of modern sexuality. Rather, the mediated and eminently substitutable object of Paul or Gordon or Achilles in the cockblocking between Genevieve and Ed enables us to develop the Eros of celibate plotting. Building on that discussion, I want to suggest that the alloeroticism of cockblocking is celibate in that it is not the object itself that gives the desiring subject pleasure, but the autoerotic satisfaction of keeping another desiring subject from pleasure. In this way, the negation of alloerotic pleasure (even as the negation binds both desiring subjects together) produces a relational autoeroticism. This relational autoeroticism is autoerotic in a broad sense (rather than the more narrow version of the masturbatory) in that it has a nongenital organization of self-pleasuring. While a wide range of activities might be described as autoerotic, the turn away from phallic sexuality inherent in the word "cockblocking" foregrounds the nongenital nature of this sexual practice. The indecipherability of this practice within normative sexual frameworks begins to explain why Genevieve is continually understood as "sexless" and is asked whether or not she is a virgin. Virginity is a category that repeatedly fails to encompass queer sexualities.[51] While War-hol and the Factory are often placed at the center of new modes of desiring and sexual configurations, I want to build on my reading of *My Hustler* and the philosophical Warhol to place him in a new register: as a theorist of political economy. That is, rather than imagine Warhol as apolitical as he often is in the context of his paintings of Mao and comments like "I love every 'lib' movement there is," I will read Warhol's governance in relation to Valerie Solanas, charting Warhol's intense interest in and preoccupation with theories of government.[52]

Andy Warhol Is a Vampire Not a Valerie

Solanas not only personally felt Warhol's "enormous manipulative power" to lack the purported "congenial[ity]" described by Malanga, but also ob-jected on theoretical grounds, establishing scum as an organization with its own celibate structure to counter Warhol's Factory. That is, Solanas of-fers a limit case for thinking about Warhol's governmentality. Solanas is most famous for shooting Warhol and writing the scum *Manifesto*. The story goes that Solanas attempted to assassinate Warhol because he lost the only copy of her play *Up Your Ass* (1966) and because, as she explained, "he had too much control of my life."[53] While readings of the shooting po-sition the two figures as polar opposites engaged in a clash between gay liberation and feminism or fighting "a war of technologies," with Solanas's "low tech writing apparatus . . . up against the reproductive panache of the Warhol machine," I understand Solanas's statement that "he had too much control of my life" as a complaint about Warhol's style of governance, emerg-ing from her competing tradition of philosophical bachelorhood.[54] While Guillory excavates a long male tradition of bachelor philosophers, we might find a similar early modern warrant for women in Mary Astell and see the tradition continuing with Emma Goldman, Simone de Beauvoir, Shulamith Firestone, Solanas, and (following my discussion of celibate ethics in chap-ter 2) Marianne Moore in the nineteenth and twentieth centuries.[55]

Like Warhol, Solanas self-consciously understands herself as a philoso-pher interrogating both the meaning of "a Philosophical Good" (75) and the social role of philosophy (52, 53). Moreover, she positions herself in rela-tion to two of our philosophical celibates—Sartre and Beauvoir (who she calls "overrated windbags") (6), rejecting them to carve her place within this tradition. Avital Ronell has argued that we should see Solanas as an important philosopher in the traditions of Nietzsche, Heidegger, Hegel, Derrida, Genet, Beauvoir, Sartre, Butler, Bataille, Deleuze, and countless others: "She belongs with them [philosophers and theorists], even if only as a limping straggler and wounded anomaly."[56] Understanding Solanas and Warhol as philosophical interlocutors, we can see them sharing an intellectual investment in celibacy but disagreeing over styles of governance.

The influence of Solanas on Warhol is plainly evident, for example, in *Women in Revolt* (1971), where Jackie Curtis plays a thinly veiled Solanas character who runs a SCUM-like organization called P.I.G (Politically Involved Girls) that preaches female superiority. Like Solanas, Curtis begs for money, engages in lesbian sex, and makes revolutionary pronouncements. Warhol's *Philosophy*, *Autobiography*, and *POPism* are all also haunted by Solanas as he fears she will try to shoot him again. Similarly, Warhol's impact is evident in Solanas's SCUM *Manifesto* when she praises automation and when she rails against "'Great Art'" and "'Great Artists'"—an attack at least partially directed at Warhol.[57]

While not about celibacy per se, the dedication of *Up Your Ass* (the play that began much of the trouble between Solanas and Warhol) offers a fascinating vantage from which to begin to inquire into Solanas's governance: "I dedicate this play to ME a continuous source of strength and guidance, and without whose unflinching loyalty, devotion and faith this play would never have been written, additional acknowledgements: Myself—for proof reading, editorial comment, helpful hints, criticism and suggestions and an exquisite job of typing. I—for independent research into men, married women and other degenerates."[58] Here, Solanas makes a strong claim for the ownership of her labor (and valuation of female labor more generally), positing what Breanne Fahs calls "her strict reliance upon herself as the sole textual authority."[59] I would add that the baroqueness of this gesture suggests not only a kind of stinginess (akin to Warhol's own) insofar as the dedicatory page is generically a place of generosity to others, but also a paranoid relation to influence. This rejection of outside influences is also a distinctly anti-Pop gesture; in *POPism* Warhol writes: "I was never embarrassed about asking someone, literally, 'What should I paint?' because Pop comes from the outside."[60] For Solanas absolute autonomy is imperative as a mode of authorship. It receives an even more expansive treatment in the SCUM *Manifesto*.

The SCUM *Manifesto* offers Solanas's rationale for celibacy and is the text with which she is most closely identified. SCUM is an acronym (which

Solanas occasionally repudiated) that stands for the Society for Cutting Up Men.[61] Solanas's SCUM differs from its radical feminist contemporaries—the groups of Ti-Grace Atkinson, Andrea Dworkin, Cell 16, and Women Against Sex (WAS)—as well as the antecedent feminist organizations that advocate celibacy (that I considered in chapters 1 and 2) in agitating for change through criminal practices rather than civil disobedience.[62] The manifesto calls women to action, attempting to incite them "to overthrow the government, eliminate the money system, institute complete automation, and destroy the male sex."[63] While the text is genocidal in its hopes for the destruction of men as a species, it is not, as it is often imagined, a call for the obliteration of the human race.

The manifesto is often understood in these apocalyptic terms because after explaining that society should no longer reproduce men, Solanas asks, "Why produce even females? Why should there be future generations?"[64] Rather than causing the end of humanity, these questions must be read in the context of her claim that "it is possible, therefore, never to age and to live forever."[65] For this reason she follows her harrowing question "Why should there be future generations?" with two more questions that help to contextualize the new social order that she imagines: "What is their purpose? When aging and death are eliminated, why continue to reproduce?"[66] Instead, Solanas imagines an all-female celibate society that does not age and cannot die. This society is similar to the one described in Charlotte Perkins Gilman's *Herland* (1915) except that eternal youth and immortality replace Gilman's mode of parthenogenetic reproduction. In a famous passage, Solanas describes this new celibate state and its importance: "Sex is not part of a relationship: on the contrary, it is a solitary experience, noncreative, a gross waste of time. The female can easily—far more easily than she may think—condition away her sex drive, leaving her completely cool and cerebral and free to pursue truly worthy relationships and activities . . . when the female transcends her body, rises above animalism, the male, whose ego consists of his cock, will disappear."[67] Here, cockblocking is not a sexual form but a modality of genocide. Warhol's repeated claim that he would rather devote time to artistic production than sex suggests that he shares Solanas's understanding of sex as "a gross waste of time."[68] Moreover, Solanas's valorization of "cool[ness]" suggests that she shares his most identifiable affect.

Despite this convergence, their respective styles of governance could not be more different. Solanas is often depicted as "an outcast among outcasts" or as "a loner," but her relationship to organized politics is more complicated than straightforward rejection.[69] Toward the end of the manifesto, Solanas begins to chart a plan for destroying the economy and overthrowing the government: "If a large majority of women were SCUM, they could acquire complete control of this country within a few weeks simply by withdrawing from the labor force, thereby paralyzing the entire nation."[70] However, after briefly elaborating this plan, Solanas rejects it: "But SCUM is too impatient to wait for the de-brainwashing of millions of assholes [women who have not yet taken on SCUM's ways of seeing and thinking]."[71] Instead, she summons a "small handful of SCUM"—this elite cadre "consists of individuals; SCUM is not a mob, a blob."[72] Rather than a large group, SCUM posits a parodic Warholian coterie that deftly attacks its patriarchal structure. Where Warhol's coterie positions him at the center—the "cultish kind of set up" described by Nat Finkelstein—SCUM's individualism is paradoxically deindividuated.[73] By the time of Warhol's shooting there is a remarkable impersonality in Solanas's autonomy as she declares, "Read my manifesto and it will tell you what I am."[74] In place of telling people *who* she is, Solanas allows her organization to speak abstractly on her behalf.

Where for Solanas the self is tightly protected in a citadel, Warhol flauntingly disseminates himself, using his own name to cover over those of his Factory coterie in a deindividuating stroke. The Factory members are treated "like tape recorders" whose tapes Warhol can fill himself up with, pouring himself into his vassals and extending himself as he erases his Superstars.[75] The condition of their appearance as Superstars is disappearance as Warhol's brand effaces them. Thus, Warhol hystericizes his coterie into pleasing him, working for him, and even working as him.[76] Solanas's insistence on absolute control requires that she operate on the older models of celibate authorship in which celibacy excludes collaboration (as I discussed in chapter 1). In contrast, Warhol's style of governance and "flexibility" of mind enable him to pioneer a celibate mode of collaboration characterized by intimacy that supplants or exists outside of sexual intimacy.[77] These new types of intimacy (like the new modes of desire in *My Hustler*) are dependent on Warhol being either unmarried or publicly celibate, as when he is imagined by a friend to be either "the first nonmarried President" or at least someone who does not have sex with his wife:

You'd be just right for the Presidency. You would videotape everything. You would have a nightly talk show—your own talk show as

President. You'd have somebody else come on, the other President that's the President for you, and he would talk your diary out to the people, every night for half an hour. And that would come before the news, What the President Did Today. So there would be no flack about the President does nothing or the President just sits around. Every day he'd have to tell us what he did, if he had sex with his wife. . . . You'd have to say you played with your dog Archie. . . . You'd have to say how many long-distance phone calls you made that day. You'd have to tell what you ate in the private dining room, and you'd show on the television screen the receipts you paid for private food yourself.[78]

Here, the taboo around the public discussion of the President's sex life makes possible new connections, new relations with his dog. Similarly, when a little later in the same passage Warhol is imagined as "nonmarried," a new social order emerges, one where "there'd be no more First Lady. Only a First Man."[79] While it is not the case that Warhol would have been "the first nonmarried President," as I discussed in the introduction, the fantasy that he could be highlights the revolutionary newness of the social relations that the passage instantiates. In addition to creating new social configurations, Warhol's philosophical bachelorhood generates a new kind of governance.

Here, the President both does something, keeping him from the charge of "doing nothing," and radically shifts the political structure of America by having another person—"the other President that's the President for you" (much as Warhol would allow other Factory members to pose as him in interviews and appearances)—carry on the act of governance. Warhol appears to cede all control (letting someone else run the country), while retaining all the power (the "President that's the President" for Warhol reads what Warhol writes down in his diary on a show that Warhol runs). The reduction of all worldly affairs to the mundane contents of a diary (consisting of personal matters like what phone calls he made, what he ate, and how he paid for his food), suggests Warhol's limitless ability to transform the world into a proxy for himself or incorporate it into himself. He is a true "receiving station," taking it all in, usurping autonomy, and consolidating paternal power to become Solanas's nightmare.[80] The mistake of both Solanas's and Queen Ed's governance for Warhol is that they take too active a role.[81] Warhol governs by "shut[ting] up" and letting people "doubt themselves" rather than getting "aggressive" and "tell[ing] someone what to do" because he has learned that "you actually have more power when you shut up."[82] His governmentality operates at the border between activity and passivity that Stephen Koch describes as Warhol's "master[y] of passive power."[83] That is, while members of the Factory experienced Warhol's rule as possessing the absoluteness of monarchy, Warhol positions himself as an absent executive with a puppet or figurehead appearing to govern while Warhol makes all the decisions. Describing his ideal work environment in another passage from *The Philosophy*, Warhol writes: "When I think about what sort of person I would most like to have on a retainer, I think it would be a boss. A boss who could tell me what to do, because that makes everything easy when you're working."[84] Here, the "boss" is in Warhol's employ "on a retainer," subordinate to him and advising him. While the boss creates an enabling scene of constraint, keeping him from having "to dream up . . . tasteless things to do," Warhol is undoubtedly in power if not in charge, since he is paying the retainer.[85] This eschewal of freedom constitutes a fascinating abdication of the American dream of being one's own boss and is instead replaced with maintaining authority by increasing passivity.

Warhol's complex governance is embodied in his Factory nickname, Drella (a name that combines the virginal Cinderella with the sexual Dracula). In Bram Stoker's *Dracula* (1897), Dracula's leeching power is as much about control of writing and technology as it is about blood and hypnosis.[86] Mina's phonographic ability to record Dracula's thought as her own kind of receiving station is crucial to securing Dracula's demise and protecting England, suggesting that modalities of recording are endowed with tremendous energies for organizing the social in Stoker's text and Warhol's Factory.[87] Similarly, the Cinderella half of Warhol's nickname also occasions a new beginning at the level of nation (the Prince ultimately seeks Cinderella to produce a royal heir), creating new hopes and as yet unrealized opportunities—"the opportunity of the White House" to "start the country over from scratch."[88] The country is imagined as being restored of its resources—a newly virgin land: "We can start the country over from scratch. We can get the Indians back on the reservations making rugs and hunting for turquoise. And we can send Rotten Rita and Ondine out to pan for gold."[89] While any reading of this passage must certainly attend to the vampiric environmental damage of mining gold and turquoise, the tremendous pain of relocation and the reservation system, as well as the gendering and imperialist overtones of nominating the land virginal, I think the spirit of the passage is one of the productivity of rug manufacture, of rich resources, and of resetting social relations. This reconfiguration of social relations is the opportunity of the White House and of the Factory.

Perhaps the greatest opportunity afforded by both Solanas's and Warhol's governance is a new relation to modernity. Rather than positing an alternative modernity, Solanas theorizes an alternative to modernity: one in which women "create a magic world."[90] This enchanted world is a stateless one ruled not by "government, laws, or leaders" but by "rational beings capable of empathizing with each other."[91] The new freedoms of this utopian world grow out of rationality and the abolition of competition for sex and money (since these latter systems of oppression have been eradicated). This stateless condition enables the flowering of individuality in an environment that lacks surveillance, laws, and authority. That Solanas must destroy the state while Warhol works within it (maintaining presidents, bosses, and other structures of authority) speaks to the uneven access to celibacy's power that is granted to men and women. Solanas must destroy modernity to enact her individuality, whereas Warhol is able to work within its strictures.

Famously commenting on these constraints and helping us to chart Warhol's relation to modernity, Max Weber differentiates in his *Protestant Ethic and the Spirit of Capitalism* (1905) between the otherworldly asceticism of monks and hermits and the worldly asceticism that he understands as underwriting capitalism. While worldly asceticism initially possesses a religious underpinning, Weber sees worldly asceticism eschewing its Protestant origins and transforming religious virtues into the economic values of work, time, thrift, punctuality, and self-control. While Warhol grew up in a religious Greek Catholic home and continued to be religious throughout his life, one can scarcely imagine a more concrete embodiment of worldly asceticism—Warhol is a veritable incarnation of hard work, thrift, and self-control. Along these lines, Steven Shaviro posits two common readings of Warhol's work: one that exposes "the institutional structures of commodity capitalism and the art world" and one that sees Warhol "being in complicity with these same institutional structures."[92] To the extent that Warhol's oeuvre escapes the logics of commodity fetishism and Weber's crushing "iron cage," sexual celibacy provides the blueprint for this transcendence. Margreta de Grazia, Maureen Quilligan, and Peter Stallybrass explain that "commodification is . . . not only the vanishing point of the subject into the commodified object, but also of the object into pure exchangeability."[93] Warhol's sexual celibacy as a mode of consumption might begin to reorient this understanding of commodity fetishism. His sexualizing of objects cannot recover the disguised labor of the commodity, but it can reinject the object into a world of social relations by encountering it as an agent of his desire. Escaping the reduction to "pure exchangeability," the object is endowed with a use-value—that of being an object of sexual desire and pleasure and, in the case of Warhol's tape recorder, of love. Pop truly is as Warhol says, a way of "liking things."[94] Desiring at the zero degree, Warhol teaches us to enjoy the "deadening and meaningless routin[ization]" and "standardization" of the iron cage.[95] Reproduced Marilyns, the routines of sleeping, eating, drinking, and working—Warhol makes them numinous again. While for Weber celibacy hides in the monastery, Warhol's alloerotic celibacy enables him to enjoy everything, reenchanting the object world; to quote Charles Henri Ford again, "Everything is sexual to Andy without the sex act actually taking place."[96] This way of relating to the world around him through the prism of sexualized celibacy enables celibate modernity for Warhol (if not for others) to be another name for modernity without the iron cage.

Warhol & Moore celibacy attempt to embody and make their bodies as the public sphere - why does this still fall black bodies?

Conclusion

Asexuality / Neutrality / Relationality

Hymenoplasties, True Love Waits, Promise Keepers, and abstinence-based education: we live in a moment when celibacy has become a public, political topic again. In her recent essay "Starved," Lauren Berlant imagines the possibility of "an 'epidemic of celibacy' in the UK or the United States."[1] While Berlant acknowledges the difficulties of describing such an outbreak, she argues that it describes an important structure of feeling in our time. I would add that it is also a topic that has been ceded to the American political Right.[2] By depicting celibacy only as repressive, an explosion of recent literary production (ordinarily a stronghold of leftist thought)—including Ian McEwan's *On Chesil Beach* (2007), Tom Perrotta's *The Abstinence Teacher* (2007), Stephen MacCauley's *Alternatives to Sex* (2006), Janice Eidus's *The Celibacy Club* (1997), Walter Keady's *Celibates and Other Lovers* (1997), and Michael Arditti's *The Celibate* (1993)—has bolstered celibacy as the property of the Right.[3]

While it is always a mistake to cede any discourse to your political opponents, it seems an egregious mistake to surrender a discourse like celibacy that has been so instrumental in definitions of gender roles, sex and sexuality, and the conditions for marriage throughout the nineteenth and twentieth centuries. In January 2006, President George W. Bush's Administration for Children, Youth, and Families mobilized this classificatory power, defining abstinence and sexual activity: "Abstinence means voluntarily choosing not to engage in sexual activity until marriage. Sexual activity refers to any type of genital contact or sexual stimulation between two persons including, but not limited to, sexual intercourse."[4] I cite this definition not to talk about the Bush administration's well-known assault on premarital sex, reprehensible dissemination of falsehoods regarding condoms and other contraceptives, or homophobic insistence on celibacy as a Christian alternative to homosexuality, but rather to highlight the ways in which the Right deploys its control over the meaning of celibacy to control the meaning of sexuality. That is, the Right presents the battle between "sex" and "not sex" as a zero-sum game, rather than (as I have repeatedly argued throughout this book) a shifting, overlapping, and highly contested terrain. The Left must not forfeit control over this territory. My attempt to think about the sociality of celibacy, resexualizing the nongenital in order to imagine a celibacy animated by sexual currents, desires, identifications, and pleasures, has constituted one strategy for wresting celibacy back from the political Right.

The Asexuality Movement, or the A-Pride Movement, constitutes the most visible modality for multiplying the meanings of the nonsexual today and is the most important heir to the leftist progressive impulses pioneered by celibacy.[5] The Asexuality Visibility and Education Network (AVEN) is at the center of this movement and has "two distinct goals: creating public acceptance and discussion of asexuality and facilitating the growth of an asexual community."[6] However, the history of asexuality predates AVEN and largely remains to be written. Of course, how we historicize asexuality depends on our definition of it. If we mean a gender identity rather than a sexual one, the history of asexuality might take its cue from Nancy Cott's field-altering essay "Passionlessness" (1978). Cott traces the "revers[al] and transformat[ion]" between the seventeenth and the nineteenth centuries" of "a traditionally dominant Anglo-American definition of women as *especially* sexual" into a conception that women "were *less* carnal and lustful than men."[7] Her essay lays the groundwork for historicizing asexuality as a gender ideal.

If, however, asexuality is defined as a discrete group of people, one early precursor for asexual identity might be Ralph Werther's description of "cold anaphrodites" who are said to compose "one-half of one per cent of all adult males."[8] According to Werther, Isaac Newton, Immanuel Kant, and St. Paul number among famous anaphrodites. He explains that cold anaphrodites "shudder violently at the very thought of *any kind* of association grounded on sex differences."[9] Here, any thought of sex is met with revulsion. He further contends: "Since anaphrodites are not suffused with adoration for any type of human, the vast majority are the more inclined to lift their thoughts to their Creator."[10] Such a history might continue with Alfred Kinsey's "rating X," which describes the experience of having "no socio-sexual response."[11] Kinsey segments the population according to sexual practice, here providing a distinct category for asexuals that might be a kind of forebear to modern asexual identity. He creates and describes the kind of medically disqualified category that has typically undergirded the formation of sexual minority cultures.[12] Finally, if by asexual identity we mean an organized political and emotional community, we might look to the historically later emergence of online communities like LiveJournal and AVEN. At the heart of these historical and historiographical questions are theoretical ones.

The editors of the forthcoming volume *Asexualities: Feminist and Queer Perspectives* call for us to move beyond "acceptance and legitimization of asexuality . . . to a critical examination of the ways in which we categorize and index sexualities, desires, and practices."[13] This critical examination of asexuality might borrow from the strategies I have used to chart celibacy, historicizing asexuality and theorizing its proximity to and distance from adjacent sexual formations (celibacy, friendship, love, asceticism) and re-lationalities (familial, nonrelational, nonsexual). It is my hope that such an endeavor will enrich the theorization of asexuality. In the first half of this conclusion, I will survey the geography of asexuality, attempting to describe its topography and the way that it arrests (at least momentarily) the hegemonic operation of the hetero/homo binary.[14] In the second half, I will chart the relationship between celibacy and asexuality in order to sharpen the distinctions between the two.

Roland Barthes's concept of the "Neutral" (which can also be translated as the "Neuter") provides a helpful point of orientation for exploring asexuality in relation to the hetero/homo binary. Barthes defines the Neutral as "every inflection that, dodging or baffling the paradigmatic, oppositional structure of meaning, aims at the suspension of the conflictual basis of discourse."[15] He understands the Neutral to "unthread," "outplay," "outsmart," "baffle," "fake out," and "parry" the binary construction of meaning,[16] which is especially important given the sexual character with which Barthes's autobiography describes his erotic relation to binaries: "For a certain time, he [Barthes] went into raptures over binarism; binarism for him became a kind of erotic object."[17] Barthes associates the Neutral (or the grammatical "Neuter") with such an asexual exemption from the sexual (in the senses of "sexuality" and "primary sexual characteristics" perhaps closest to contemporary Neutrois identity, which exists outside the gender binary). Clarifying this escape, he associates the Neutral with androgyny and drones (male honeybees), "which have no sexual organs, which can't mate."[18] The connotation of being outside both biological sex (Neuter and androgyny) and reproductive sexuality (drones) suggests that asexuality as a figuration of the Neutral has the potential to reconfigure both gender and sexual systems of signification. To the degree that there is a core of this emerging possibility, the core is a multiplication of the meanings of sexual and nonsexual practices. Where the Right offers orthodoxy, regimentation, and fixed meanings for sexuality, asexuality intensifies the level of play in the system.

Before proceeding to unpack the implications of these reconfigurations, we should divide the Neutral between celibacy and asexuality. Celibacy outplays, outsmarts, parries, and fakes out the hetero/homo binary by occupying neither term and both terms simultaneously. When celibacy stays within the binary, the promise of marriage and marriageability shield the celibate with respectable heterosexuality at the same time that the extended period of remaining unmarried associates the celibate with nonnormative sexuality, especially homosexuality (what I have called the potentiality model). Simultaneously, celibacy as a sexuality exceeds the boundaries of the hetero/homo binary, requiring a rethinking of sexual categories and the concept of sex as such.

In contrast, asexuality, I will argue, baffles, dodges, and unthreads the hegemony of hetero- and homosexuality. Of course, not all asexualities puzzle the binary in the same way. One distinction within the asexual community is between romantic and aromantic asexuals. The important difference is that romantic asexuals seek coupled or paired relations which are (or at least appear) more normative in relation to gender and sexual expectations and closely resemble romantic friendship, whereas aromantic asexuals do not.[19] Additional distinctions among kinds of romantic asexuals can be made along the lines of sexual orientation (homoromantic, biromantic, etc.). Aromantics are usually easier for sexual people to understand and are usually what is imagined when the term "asexual" is used in an unmarked way by those unfamiliar with asexuality. Rather than violence, aromantic asexuals usually summon confusion, baffling the hetero/homo binary far more than their romantic counterparts. While aromantic asexuality offers the possibility of theorizing sexuality absent attraction, love, and sex, romantic asexuality—perhaps more than any other sexual formation—seems to proffer the possibility of theorizing attraction and love without the interference or noise of sex. For the purpose of understanding asexuality as baffling the hetero/homo binary, I will be speaking exclusively of aromantic asexuality. I will chart three potentialities opened by asexuality's baffling of the hetero/homo binary.

First, asexuality unthreads the relationship between drives and modern systems of sexuality. In fact, asexuality interrogates whether or not sex is a drive more than any other sexual formation because it is a sexuality that is not underpinned by a sexual drive. In the introduction, I theorized what I call "the expressive hypothesis," which posits that the well-intentioned effort to make certain that nonnormative identities, desires, and pleasures are not suppressed has the unintentional result of canalizing sexuality into forms of sex that aspire to normative sexual acts. While both asexuality and celibacy are engaged in attempts to resist compulsory sexuality, theorizing asexuality as Neutrality expands my "expressive hypothesis." This additional postulate of the expressive hypothesis surmises that our description of sexuality as functioning according to drives comes with the demand that everyone must express sexuality; everyone must possess a drive. By "express," I mean here that sexuality not only must take shape in or seek what we recognize as normative sexual acts but also must exist as a desire or fantasy before using sexual acts as its vehicle. Whether or not we engage in sex acts, we have the drives. The existence of this organizing desire or fantasy both creates an account of itself and produces a requirement to be accountable, even if this narrativization is one of closetedness, sublimation, or a residual and now vestigial phase. Contemporary sexual mores stigmatize both those who do not engage in sexual acts (labeling them "repressed") and those who do not experience desire at all. There can be no sexuality or orientation without a preceding operation of desire, incitement, or urge.

A second potentiality activated by asexuality's momentary cessation of the hetero/homo binary, of its Neutralization of this binary, is the augmentation or elaboration of alternate relationalities. While this project has explored a rich array of possibilities for the formation of modes of alliance (as I argued earlier about Boston marriage and cockblocking), the theorization of "contact" in Samuel Delany's *Times Square Red, Times Square Blue* (2001) gestures toward the kind of relationality that I see asexuality making possible:

Contact is the conversation that starts in the line at the grocery counter with the person behind you while the clerk is changing the paper roll in the cash register. It is the pleasantries exchanged with a neighbor who has brought her chair out to take some air on the stoop. It is the discussion that begins with the person next to you at a bar. It can be the conversation that starts with any number of semi-officials or service persons—mailman, policeman, librarian, store clerk or counter person. As well, it can be two men watching each other masturbating together in adjacent urinals of a public john—an encounter that, later, may or may not become a conversation.[20]

While for Delany "contact" certainly encompasses "casual sex" and "public sexual relations," he seems as interested in the "nonsexual friendships and/or acquaintances" that emerge from such contact whether contact began as a sexual encounter or as neighborly chitchat. Delany does not in fact distinguish between the two, seeing desire "as inseparable from the public contact situation."[21] Moreover, he sees "nonsexual" contact as organized by pleasure: "pleasure in its most generalized form (though pleasure no less important or social for that): the pleasant."[22] While for Delany one kind of pleasure (nonsexual) always seems on the verge of shading into another (sexual), I think that the kind of generalized pleasure that he describes might usefully provide a framework for theorizing the enjoyments of asexuality. That is, this pleasure in "the pleasant" in nonsexual modes of contact that do not acquire a specific object but remain "generalized," begins to provide an underpinning for asexual pleasure.

Delany's model here remains within an economy of drives. Within a drive-based model, we might understand asexuality as taking other-than-sexual objects. For romantic asexuals this could be a romantic object. Many asexuals also describe an aesthetic attraction that is an experience of appreciation rather than sexual attraction.[23] However, I think much of asexuality's potential and interest for sexuality studies is its ability to exceed this drive- and object-based economy, its baffling of the hetero/homo binary through its nonengagement with these economies of desire and pleasure. This is a possibility opened by Leo Bersani's essay on Claire Denis's depiction of the French Foreign Legion in *Beau travail* (1998). Bersani describes an "extraordinary scene in which each Legionnaire flings himself into the arms of another Legionnaire with whom he has been paired for the exercise; each pair repeats several times the rushing together and a rapid movement away from the other's body."[24] Bersani's description of this scene's mode of relationality provides one of the most promising descriptions for the theorization of the physical life of asexuality that I know:

> In describing the embracing exercise I wrote "paired" instead of "coupled" in order to avoid any suggestion of a sexual bonding between one Legionnaire and another as the grounding of their collective sociality. Indeed, it is as if the very possibility of such an intimacy were exhausted by the exhausting repetition of a strenuous and *fundamentally indifferent* coming together. An energetic choreography stifles the movements of desire before they can become psychic designs. Sensuality, de-psychologized, is prevented from mutating into the sexual. The pleasures into which the Legionnaires exercise themselves are nonpurposive pleasures of touch, of each body having its place in a formal, mobile unity of communal repetition. The men, Rob White has written in a perceptive essay on *Beau travail*, are not masking violence; rather, they engage in "a shadow theater of violence in order to achieve mere gesture," thereby evacuating meaning. I would add that the Legionnaires' progressively more choreographed bodies initiate what Foucault calls a "new relational mode," an as yet contentless sociality that seductively sets the stage for the invention of other manifestations of nonsadistic movement, both within the individual psyche and between the human subject and the world.[25]

Bersani's use of the phrase "nonpurposive pleasures" opens the possibility of a model rooted not in drives or purpose or motive (whether conscious or unconscious) but in movement. At first glance, it seems that the phenomenon Bersani is describing might just be sublimation (dance is an archetypical example of sublimation's binding of sexual energies). His description of "sensuality . . . prevented from mutating into the sexual," however, reverses sublimation's temporality. He begins not with a sexuality that is put in the service of something but with its opposite: forces that never coagulate into sexuality. This respite from drive-based sexuality is also accompanied by a suspension of object-based systems of sexuality. Bersani's deliberate stress on his choice of the word "paired" over "coupled" emphasizes that the exhaustion of desire moves us outside the framework of sexuality organized by sexual objects. Strikingly, this passage's reversal of sublimation opens the possibility of forces other than exhaustion that dissipate the sexual from ever coming into being, thereby preventing the actualization of sexual subjects or objects. This is one of the possibilities of asexuality. While I theorize celibacy as a sociable sexuality, one that is alloerotic and interpersonal, asexuality's sociability is characterized by the "contentless sociality" that is alloerotic but not meaningfully so because asexuality eschews sexual possession. About possession, Barthes asserts "that there is a passion of the Neutral but that this passion is not that of a will-to-possess."[26] In a wonderful essay about the nature of sexual possession, Sarah Dowling writes: "Typically, the discourse of sexual possession suggests that it is appropriate to think of a lover as 'mine.' . . . To do so creates confusion between thinking of one's own body and thinking of another body as one's own. To call 'your body' 'mine' creates a slippage between 'your body,' which is 'mine' because I possess it (or you) sexually, and 'my body,' which is also 'mine,' although not in the same way."[27] Asexuality's Neutralization of "the discourse of sexual possession" constitutes a utopian escape from object-based sexuality, unthreading the tie between sexual possession and its objects. This is what makes the sociality contentless—it does not contain sexual objects.

Finally, asexuality reconfigures both the realm of available sexual identities and the gendered order. This transformation is evident in Samuel Delany's early representation of asexuality in his famous science fiction short story "Aye, and Gomorrah . . ." (1966). Delany's text richly imagines a range of new sexual and gender identities emerging as a consequence of asexuality. It explores the relationship between "spacers" (astronauts who have been surgically neutered before puberty, which prevents the identification of their birth sex and the experience of sexual arousal) and those who fetishize this particular body morphology. The latter are derogatorily called "frelks" and are said, in more clinical terminology, to suffer from "free-fall-sexual-displacement complex."[28] The plot of the story turns on the refused transaction between the spacer narrator and a frelk who is a former art history student. The former student attempts to initiate sex with the spacer, who declines. While the text's version of asexuality is dependent on body modification in a way that does not capture the experience of most asexual people, I read this as an important historiographical point, namely, asexual people (and, as I pointed out in the introduction and chapter 1, celibates) have often been associated with particularly body morphologies:

ly with eunuchs (and contemporary eunuch communities), cas-
disabled individuals. Moreover, the text's interest in sterilization
to the histories of forced sterilization that accrue around the
categories of not just disability but also age, race, class, and gender.

In addition to elaborating a sex/gender system that converts body morphology (sex) into a particular gender and sexual identity (spacer), the text
also raises several intriguing sexual possibilities. The title, for example, implicitly asks, "How queer is asexuality?" On the one hand, "Aye, and Gomorrah . . ." substitutes the more familiar "Sodom" with "Aye" (connoting both
asexuality and affirmation), suggesting in its "and" a conjunction of asexuality and queerness (represented by "Gomorrah"). This reading is highlighted by the synecdochical relationship between "Aye" and the final syl-
lable of "sodomy," suggesting sodomy contains within it asexuality. On the
other hand, the ellipsis leaves this conjunction in doubt, asking if one can
be homosexual and asexual simultaneously. Does asexuality preclude com-
bination or concurrence with other sexualities? More strikingly, the frelks
write asexuality back into a sexual economy along the lines suggested by my
expanded expressive hypothesis. The former art history student imagines
that frelks should by all rights be spacers ("the sexually retarded ones they
miss").[29] Here, the desire of frelks for spacers endows the spacers with a
sexual drive which they are lacking, but which the expressive hypothesis
demands. When the former student asks if the narrator regrets having "no
sex," he replies, "'We've got you.'"[30] Here, the frelks desire vicariously on
behalf of the spacers.[31] This co-optation back into the sexual and back into
the will-to-possession diagnosed by Dowling is due to the temporality and
temporariness of the Neutral. Barthes distinguishes between the law of the
Neutral and "a desire for the Neutral," creating a differentiation between
the permanence of a utopian escape from binary meaning (law) and the
temporary reprieve from such meaning activated by desire.[32] While this
desire for the Neutral is "produced against signs" or "outside of signs," it
is "very quickly recuperated as a sign."[33] While Delany describes a culture
thick with monetary and sexual transaction between frelks and spacers,
tarrying a little with the desire for the Neutral brings out new sexual formations and surprising alliances. For example, the former student describes
her desire to the narrator in the following way: "I want you because you
can't want me. That's the pleasure. If someone really had a sexual reaction
to . . . us, we'd be scared away. I wonder how many people there were before there were you, waiting for your creation. We're necrophiles. I'm sure

grave-robbing has fallen off since you started going up [doing the work of spacers]."[34] Here, asexuality seems to make necrophilia or at least its fantasy (relatively) socially acceptable. Moreover, the figuration of spacers as completely passive in relation to the activity of frelks is undercut by the text's short-circuiting this "erotic"—for lack of a better word—encounter. That is, while the text makes clear that frelks regularly give money to spacers, its central pairing between a frelk and a spacer fails to find a currency to exchange. While the narrator insists, "'Look, I don't *need* money! I said *any*thing would do!,'" the frelk demands the impossible—that the desireless spacer desire her: "'You really don't understand I just don't want to buy you?'"[35] This dynamic casts the frelk as engaging in a version of celibacy if not of asexuality. Nonparticipation might here provide a useful category between active and passive sexual acts. Delany's text posits the spacer as a child loved unrequitedly and one-sidedly by the frelk, making the ideal, unconditional familial bond an available mode of stranger sociability. The spacer narrator wants part of the frelk's "ego," something useless to the narrator but valuable to the frelk. In short, the narrator wants a token of love.[36] While I agree with asexuality theorist Eunjung Kim that asexual people can be celibate too—sexual people do not have a monopoly on celibacy—I would add that the practice of celibacy has very different meanings for sexual and asexual people.[37] Along these lines, to the extent that the frelk's desire is erotic, it takes the shape of the kind of sexualized celibacy that has been the focus of this book. However, I think it is also possible to see the frelk as merely frustrated or repressed, "scared" to have a reciprocated sexual response. These two meanings of the frelk's desires are very different from a third reading, which understands the frelks as being as asexual as the spacers. This final reading would interpret the encounter between narrator and frelk as a kind of romantic asexuality or perhaps a way of alleviating loneliness.

Until recently, the difference between asexuality and celibacy has seemed particularly clear around the question of sexual choice, as AVEN's home page makes evident: "Unlike celibacy, which is a choice, asexuality is a sexual orientation."[38] While AVEN's definition of celibacy describes it as a behavior and practice in contrast to asexuality's figuration as a (lack of) desire and as an identarian orientation, *Celibacies* muddies the waters between these distinctions, creating significant overlap between celibacy and asexuality as well as helping to clarify some of the fault lines between the two sexualities. This book's continual efforts to chart the historical processes by which celibacy has been sexualized differentiate it from current scholarly understandings of asexuality. However, by rooting this sexualization in reiterative desire (as theorized in chapter 2) rather than in a singular sexual act, my project draws celibacy closer to the desire- and identity-based understandings of asexuality. While I have mapped an overlap between celibacy and asexuality on the axis of desire, recent scholarship in asexuality has marked its proximity to celibacy by moving toward choice: "Asexuals have 'chosen to actively disidentify with sexuality.'"[39] Here, choice for asexuals occurs in the realm of identity if not of desire.

Sexuality studies and popular wisdom both concur that whatever your understanding of sexual etiology (whether it derives from nature, nurture, or somewhere in between), the end result is that sexuality is profoundly determined without much recourse to personal agency. This relative lack of agency underwrites Leo Bersani's assault on the idea that "radical sex means or leads to radical politics."[40] In other words, because one does not choose one's sexual orientation, it cannot be connected to a political position or worldview. While Bersani's argument is persuasive in the figure of his slumlord who has wild gay sex (we might also think of the Pink Pistols or Log Cabin Republicans), I want to leave open the possibility that radical sex often coalesces, supplements, or enhances radical politics. This is a middle position between the incommensurability that Bersani sees between radical sex and radical politics and positions like the lesbian feminist mantra—"feminism is the theory; lesbianism is the practice"—that posit radical sex itself as a sign of radical politics.

Lesbian feminism seems (contra Bersani) to imagine sexuality or a set of sexual practices or identifications as having a particular political content. This is also a possibility that I see celibacy activating and activating differently than lesbian feminism. While lesbianism's enactment of feminist theory excludes on the grounds of sex and perhaps sexual orientation (though this latter seems mitigated by "the primary intensity" of Adrienne Rich's lesbian continuum), celibacy offers a sexual political choice which is (in theory) open to everyone.[41] As the previous chapters make clear, however, whites and middle- and upper-class people have historically had greater access to celibacy. The question of celibate choice seems to align at least to some extent with the relationship between acts and identities. An act-based model might see celibacy as a choice whereas an identity-based model would leave only wiggle room for, as Butler might put it, improvisation within a scene of very powerful restraint. My discussion of Auden's three possibilities for himself in his letter to his brother might complicate this relationship between choice and determinism. Auden tells his brother that there are three ways he can manage his desire: middle-aged sentimentalism, London buggery, and asceticism. Here, his desire is already determined, and he has the choice to control or manage it in three different ways. The state in the figure of the policeman whom the London bugger "sucks off," as Auden puts it, strongly stigmatizes and controls the conditions of at least one of the sexual choices and may also condition his decision to be celibate. While celibacy's relation to choice is not what makes it so radical, I think retaining the possibility of choice and improvisation, of "three courses," as Auden says, is crucial to a history of celibacy and to sexuality as a whole. Because the dangers and benefits of identity are well known from feminist and queer theory, I will not rehearse them here. Rather, I want to focus on the pitfalls and advantages of sexual choice. Perhaps the greatest danger, which has been lately activated by the Right in the figure of the ex-gay, is the requirement that if sexual choice or sexual lifestyle is self-determined, then one might be coerced to choose a "better" lifestyle. And yet, the idea of sexual political choice is important not just for the multiplication of life narratives that it might effect (for education, career advancement, travel, or personal fulfillment), but also because it opens the possibility that one's sexual practices might themselves be engaged in sexual revolution in the face of state or cultural constraints.

I do not want to suggest that this possibility for choice means that anyone practicing celibacy will be part of the political Left. On the contrary, as I have emphasized many times in the course of this project, and as a celibate in Bersani's own essay—Cardinal Law—makes clear, celibacy is certainly not always connected to progressive politics, and in the case of the cardinal can be connected to abominable political practices. What I am suggesting is that historically celibacy was a choice, and this choice was a site of radical politics, of feminist organizing, of black activism, queer citizenship, and other leftist interventions. Before we decide to cede celibacy to the Right, we might want to consider reclaiming the radical political potential that nineteenth- and twentieth-century artists and activists found in the practices of celibacy.

Notes

Introduction

1. James H. Jones, *Alfred C. Kinsey* (New York: Norton, 1997), 307.

2. On the question of "the content of sex," see Valerie Traub, "Making Sexual Knowledge," *Early Modern Women* 5 (2010): 251–259, especially 254.

3. Michael Warner, *Publics and Counterpublics* (New York: Zone Books, 2002), 52.

4. Michel Foucault, *The History of Sexuality*, vol. 1, *An Introduction*, trans. Robert Hurley (New York: Vintage, 1990), 27.

5. Eve Kosofsky Sedgwick, *Epistemology of the Closet* (Berkeley: University of California Press, 1990), 164–168.

6. Sedgwick, *Epistemology of the Closet*, 188–195.

7. Bridget Hill, *Women Alone: Spinsters in England, 1660–1850* (New Haven, CT: Yale University Press, 2001), 1.

8. Foucault, *History of Sexuality*, 7.

9. Foucault, *History of Sexuality*, 12.

10. Lisa Duggan, "Censorship in the Name of Feminism," in *Sex Wars: Sexual Dissent and Political Culture*, ed. Lisa Duggan and Nan D. Hunter (New York: Routledge, 2006), 32.

11. My project is informed by Stephen Heath's *The Sexual Fix*, which attempts a critique of the conformity of sexual liberation that is "not anti-sex and pro-repression" at a moment when "there is no longer any need to defend 'sexual liberation.'" Stephen Heath, *The Sexual Fix* (New York: Schocken Books, 1984), 4–5.

12. Leo Bersani, *Homos* (Cambridge, MA: Harvard University Press, 1995), 20. For another example of this sentiment, see Douglas Crimp, "How to Have Promiscuity in an Epidemic," in *AIDS: Cultural Activism, Cultural Analysis*, ed. Douglas Crimp (Cambridge, MA: MIT Press, 1988), 237–271.

13. Rei Terada uses the same phrase "expressive hypothesis" in a different context. Rei Terada, *Feeling in Theory: Emotion after the "Death of the Subject"* (Cambridge, MA: Harvard University Press, 2001), 11.

14. Wendy Brown, *Edgework: Critical Essays on Knowledge and Politics* (Princeton, NJ: Princeton University Press, 2005), 86.

15. Eve Kosofsky Sedgwick, *Touching Feeling: Affect, Pedagogy, Performativity* (Durham, NC: Duke University Press, 2003), 126, her emphasis.

16. John Shoptaw, *On the Outside Looking Out: John Ashbery's Poetry* (Cambridge, MA: Harvard University Press, 1994), 66.

17. For examples of this depthless reading practice, see Stephen Best and Sharon Marcus, "Surface Reading: An Introduction," *Representations* 109, no. 1 (2010): 1–21; and Sharon Marcus, *Between Women: Friendship, Desire, and Marriage in Victorian England* (Princeton, NJ: Princeton University Press, 2007), 73–76.

18. Terry Castle, *The Apparitional Lesbian: Female Homosexuality and Modern Culture* (New York: Columbia University Press, 1993); Carla Freccero, *Queer/Early/Modern* (Durham, NC: Duke University Press, 2006); Annamarie Jagose, *Inconsequence: Lesbian Representation and the Logic of Sexual Sequence* (Ithaca, NY: Cornell University Press, 2002); Heather Love, *Feeling Backward: Loss and the Politics of Queer History* (Cambridge, MA: Harvard University Press, 2007); Valerie Traub, *The Renaissance of Lesbianism in Early Modern England* (Cambridge: Cambridge University Press, 2002); Valerie Traub, "The Present Future of Lesbian Historiography," in *A Companion to Lesbian, Gay, Bisexual, Transgender, and Queer Studies*, ed. George Haggerty and Molly McGarry (Oxford: Blackwell, 2007), 124–145.

19. As Katherine Holden points out, the bachelor is more indeterminate than the spinster, and thus his history is more difficult to recover in part because he does not change titles when he changes marital status. Katherine Holden, *The Shadow of Marriage: Singleness in England, 1914–60* (Manchester: Manchester University Press, 2007), 5.

20. For a historically earlier example of this potentiality model, see Vincent J. Bertolini, "Fireside Chastity: The Erotics of Sentimental Bachelorhood in the 1850s," in *Sentimental Men: Masculinity and the Politics of Affect in American Culture*, ed. Mary Chapman and Glenn Hendler (Berkeley: University of California Press, 1999), 20–21.

21. Love, *Feeling Backward*, 12.

22. Joseph A. Boone, "Modernist Re-orientations: Imagining Homoerotic Desire in the 'Nearly' Middle East," *Modernism/Modernity* 17, no. 3 (2010): 566.

23. Stephen Spender, *The Temple* (New York: Grove, 1988), 185.

24. George Bernard Shaw, "Preface to Androcles and the Lion: On the Prospects of Christianity," in *Androcles and the Lion; Overruled; Pygmalion* (New York: Dodd, Mead, 1916), lxxxvii; Friedrich Nietzsche, *Beyond Good and Evil*, trans. Judith Norman (Cambridge: Cambridge University Press, 2002), 45; Remy de Gourmont, *The Natural Philosophy of Love*, trans. Ezra Pound (New York: Liveright, 1932), 247; Mina Loy, *The Lost Lunar Baedeker* (New York: Farrar, Straus and Giroux, 1996), 155.

25. Loy, *Lost Lunar Baedeker*, 216.

26. Loy, *Lost Lunar Baedeker*, 154.

27. Loy, *Lost Lunar Baedeker*, 22.

28. Loy, *Lost Lunar Baedeker*, 42.

29. For an alternative reading of virginity in Loy's work, see Jessica Burstein, *Cold Modernism: Literature, Fashion, Art* (University Park: Pennsylvania State University Press, 2012), 151–197, esp. 166–172.

30. Loy, *Lost Lunar Baedeker*, 153–156. This association between celibacy as a sexual identity and economic security is clear in a faux anthropology of the infamous early twentieth-century radical feminist Heterodoxy Club in which the "true resistant" (the parody of the celibate) confesses that her "economic status depended upon virginity." Florence Guy Woolston, "Marriage Customs and Taboo among the Early Heterodites," reprinted in Judith Schwarz, *Radical Feminists of Heterodoxy: Greenwich Village, 1912–1940* (Lebanon, NH: New Victoria, 1982), 95–96. On marriage bars in England that forge the connection between celibacy and economics, see Mary Abbott, *Family Affairs: A History of the Family in 20th Century Britain* (New York: Routledge, 2003), 28.

31. David Eng's work on Asian American bachelors suggests that the imposition of celibacy can be as harmful as forced sexualization. David Eng, *Racial Castration: Managing Masculinity in Asian America* (Durham, NC: Duke University Press, 2001), 167–203.

32. T. S. Eliot, "The Idea of a Christian Society," in *Selected Prose of T. S. Eliot*, ed. Frank Kermode (New York: Harvest, 1975), 290.

33. There are also a surprising number of twentieth-century mathematicians and scientists who were lifelong celibates: Nikola Tesla, G. H. Hardy, Srinivasa Ramanujan, and Paul Erdös. On Tesla's possible heterosexuality, see Marc Seifer, *Wizard: The Life and Times of Nikola Tesla: Biography of a Genius* (Secaucus, NJ: Birch Lane Press, 1996), 412–413, 465–467, and esp. 17.

34. Carolyn Burke, "The New Poetry and the New Woman: Mina Loy," in *Coming to Light: American Women Poets in the Twentieth Century*, ed. Diane Wood Middlebrook and Marilyn Yalom (Ann Arbor: University of Michigan Press, 1985), 43–47; Charles O. Hartmann, *Free Verse: An Essay on Prosody* (Princeton, NJ: Princeton University Press, 1980), 7.

35. Charles Baudelaire, *Intimate Journals*, trans. Christopher Isherwood (Hollywood: Marcel Rodd, 1947), 97. I have slightly altered Isherwood's translation.

36. George Chauncey, *Gay New York: Gender, Urban Culture, and the Making of the Gay Male World, 1890–1940* (New York: Basic Books, 1994); Sedgwick, *Epistemology of the Closet*.

37. Adrienne Rich, "Compulsory Heterosexuality and the Lesbian Existence," *Signs* 5, no. 4 (1980): 648, 648, 635. Even scholarship that attempts to move away from the lesbian continuum like Sharon Marcus's *Between Women* continues to conflate lesbianism and celibacy. Marcus describes her use of the term "female marriage" as encompassing sex, shared households, and durability and adds that "the diaries and correspondence of . . . [the American actress] Charlotte Cushman provide solid evidence that nineteenth-century women had genital contact and orgasms with other women." When we arrive at a letter between Elizabeth Barrett Browning and her sister, however, describing Cushman's "vows of celibacy & eternal attachment" to Matilda Hays, Marcus has no trouble reading this celibacy as "predicat-

ing" female marriage. Marcus, *Between Women*, 44, 201–202. I return to this moment in chapter 1.

38. Amy M. Froide, *Never Married: Singlewomen in Early Modern England* (Oxford: Oxford University Press, 2005), 12. Froide credits Judith M. Bennett with helping her to come up with the term "ever-married." Froide's distinction also (largely) enables me to bracket the very different relations to parenting/childlessness that "never-married" and "ever-married" people experience.

39. While celibacy was not commonly available to lower classes and racial groups, Irish women were able to access it. Maureen Fitzgerald, *Habits of Compassion: Irish Catholic Nuns and the Origins of New York's Welfare System, 1830–1920* (Urbana: University of Illinois Press, 2006), 25.

40. Henry Abelove, *Deep Gossip* (Minneapolis: University of Minnesota Press, 2003), 21–28.

41. Simone de Beauvoir, *The Second Sex* (New York: Vintage, 1989), 425.

42. Katherine V. Snyder, *Bachelors, Manhood, and the Novel, 1850–1925* (Cambridge: Cambridge University Press, 1999), 3–4.

43. Davida Pines's *The Marriage Paradox* provides an interesting hybrid of the impossibility of celibacy on the one hand and the failure of it on the other by arguing that bachelors and spinsters are part of a "modernist literary and cultural critique of marriage" that "seems to challenge the strength and importance of the institution" but which "perpetuates the status quo" (4). Between the marriage plot and the queer plot, there is no terrain available for the celibate; in Pines's narrative, the celibate even fails at critique. Davida Pines, *The Marriage Paradox: Modernist Narratives and the Cultural Imperative to Marry* (Gainesville: University Press of Florida, 2006).

44. Kathryn R. Kent, *Making Girls into Women: American Women's Writing and the Rise of Lesbian Identity* (Durham, NC: Duke University Press, 2003), 21.

45. Arnold I. Davidson, *The Emergence of Sexuality: Historical Epistemology and the Formation of Concepts* (Cambridge, MA: Harvard University Press, 2001), 53. On purity, see also Michel Foucault, "The Battle for Chastity," in *Ethics: Subjectivity and Truth. The Essential Works of Michel Foucault, 1954–1984*, vol. 1, ed. Paul Rabinow (New York: New Press, 1994), 185–197.

46. Kathleen Coyne Kelly and Marina Leslie, "Introduction: The Epistemology of Virginity," in *Menacing Virgins: Representing Virginity in the Middle Ages and Renaissance*, ed. Kathleen Coyne Kelly and Marina Leslie (Newark: University of Delaware Press, 1999), 16.

47. Traub, *Renaissance of Lesbianism*, 15.

48. This work is in dialogue with an increasingly large body of historical and religious scholarship that chronicles nuns, women religious, eunuchs, and castrati's entwinement with power; see, for example, Sharon T. Strocchia, *Nuns and Nunneries in Renaissance Florence* (Baltimore: Johns Hopkins University Press, 2009); Amy Leonard, *Nails in the Wall: Catholic Nuns in Reformation Germany* (Chicago: University of Chicago Press, 2005); Matthew Kuefler, *The Manly Eunuch: Masculinity, Gender Ambiguity, and Christian Ideology in Late Antiquity* (Chicago: University of Chicago Press, 2001); Mary M. Anderson, *Hidden Power: The Palace Eunuchs of Imperial China* (Buffalo, NY:

Prometheus, 1990); David Ayalon, *Eunuchs, Caliphs and Sultans: A Study of Power Relation* (Jerusalem: Magnes Press, Hebrew University, 1999); Penelope Delafield Johnson, *Equal in Monastic Profession: Religious Women in Medieval France* (Chicago: University of Chicago Press, 1994). This work is also in dialogue with scholarship about the liberatory potential of celibacy within religious institutions; see, for example, Margaret M. McGuinness, *Called to Serve: A History of Nuns in America* (New York: New York University Press, 2013); Sally L. Kitch, *Chaste Liberation: Celibacy and Female Cultural Status* (Urbana: University of Illinois Press, 1989); Barbara Mann Wall, *Unlikely Entrepreneurs: Catholic Sisters and the Hospital Marketplace, 1865–1925* (Columbus: Ohio State University Press, 2005); John J. Fialka, *Sisters: Catholic Nuns and the Making of America* (New York: St. Martin's, 2004); Carol K. Coburn and Martha Smith, *Spirited Lives: How Nuns Shaped Catholic Culture and American Life, 1836–1920* (Chapel Hill: University of North Carolina Press, 1999); and John S. Haller and Robin M. Haller, *The Physician and Sexuality in Victorian America* (Carbondale: Southern Illinois University Press, 1995), xii. For an example of the ill use to which celibacy continues to be put, see Lisa Isherwood's work on the Christian organization True Love Waits in *The Power of Erotic Celibacy: Queering Heteropatriarchy* (New York: T. and T. Clark, 2006).

49. While unmarried woman are usually understood to feel the pressures of matrimony more strongly than their male counterparts, Pierre Bourdieu offers a reverse case. Pierre Bourdieu, *The Bachelors' Ball: The Crisis in Peasant Society in Béarn*, trans. Richard Nice (Chicago: University of Chicago Press, 2008).

50. One important exception to the ubiquitous practice of separating bachelors and spinsters is Holden, *Shadow of Marriage*.

51. Israel Zangwill, *The Celibates' Club: Being the United Stories of the Bachelors' Club and the Old Maids' Club* (New York: Macmillan, 1905). On the marketing of the choice between marriage and celibacy, see Emma Liggins, "'The Life of a Bachelor Girl in the Big City': Selling the Single Lifestyle to Readers of *Woman* and the *Young Woman* in the 1890s," *Victorian Periodicals Review* 40, no. 3 (2007): 216–238.

52. Lynn Wardley, "Bachelors in Paradise: The State of a Theme," in *The Return of Thematic Criticism*, ed. Werner Sollors (Cambridge, MA: Harvard University Press, 1993), 217–241. See also Rebecca Jennings, *Tomboys and Bachelor Girls: A Lesbian History of Postwar Britain, 1945–1971* (New York: Manchester University Press, 2007).

53. William Faulkner, *The Sound and the Fury* (New York: Vintage, 1984), 78.

54. Eric J. Sundquist, *Faulkner: A House Divided* (Baltimore: Johns Hopkins University Press, 1985), 16, 20, 52.

55. Faulkner, *The Sound and the Fury*, 116.

56. Faulkner, *The Sound and the Fury*, 78.

57. Faulkner, *The Sound and the Fury*, 116.

58. Giovanna Zapperi, "Marcel Duchamp's *Tonsure*: Towards an Alternate Masculinity," *Oxford Art Journal* 30, no. 2 (2007): 289–303.

59. I borrow this phrase, if not its exact meaning, from Leo Bersani's essay of the same title. Leo Bersani, "Genital Chastity," in *Homosexuality and Psychoanalysis*, ed. Tim Dean and Christopher Lane (Chicago: University of Chicago Press, 2001), 351–366.

60. Bruce Burgett, "Sex, Panic, Nation," *American Literary History* 21, no. 1 (2009): 73–74.

61. Sherwood Anderson's Wing Biddlebaum exemplifies such a celibate nongenital sexuality. Sherwood Anderson, *Winesburgh, Ohio: A Group of Tales of Ohio Small-Town Life* (Wickford, RI: North Books, 1998).

62. Kathryn Bond Stockton, "Growing Sideways, or Versions of the Queer Child: The Ghost, the Homosexual, the Freudian, the Innocent, and the Interval of Animal," in *Curiouser: On the Queerness of Children*, ed. Steven Bruhm and Natasha Hurley (Minneapolis: University of Minnesota Press, 2004), 283. The fact that Cornell, Warhol, and Moore all lived with their respective parents for much of their lives no doubt contributes to this "childlike" quality.

63. The 1840s also witnessed women banding together with threats of sexual abstinence to convince their husbands to abandon alcohol. Daniel Okrent, *Last Call: The Rise and Fall of Prohibition* (New York: Scribner, 2010), 15.

64. Elle Carol DuBois, *Feminism and Suffrage: The Emergence of an Independent Women's Movement in America, 1848–1869* (Ithaca, NY: Cornell University Press, 1980), 27–28.

65. Marie Anne Pagliarini, "The Pure American Woman and the Wicked Catholic Priest: An Analysis of Anti-Catholic Literature in Antebellum America," *Religion and American Culture* 9, no. 1 (winter 1999): 116.

66. Pagliarini, "Pure American Woman," 116, 98.

67. Fitzgerald, *Habits of Compassion*, 25.

68. Fitzgerald, *Habits of Compassion*, 26.

69. For a legal history of coverture laws, see Laura Hanft Korobkin, *Criminal Conversations: Sentimentality and Nineteenth-Century Legal Stories of Adultery* (New York: Columbia University Press, 1998).

70. Korobkin, *Criminal Conversations*, 40, her emphasis.

71. Norma Basch, *In the Eyes of the Law: Women, Marriage, and Property in Nineteenth-Century New York* (Ithaca, NY: Cornell University Press, 1982), 27.

72. Basch, *In the Eyes of the Law*, 123.

73. Basch, *In the Eyes of the Law*, 28.

74. Korobkin, *Criminal Conversations*, 137–138.

75. Joel Perlmann and Robert A, Margo, *Women's Work? American Schoolteachers, 1650–1920* (Chicago: University of Chicago Press, 2001), 112–115.

76. Sharon Hartman Strom, *Beyond the Typewriter: Gender, Class, and the Origins of Modern American Office Work, 1900–1930* (Urbana: University of Illinois Press, 1992), 332–333.

77. Perlmann and Margo, *Women's Work?*, 112–115.

78. Susan M. Reverby, *Ordered to Care: The Dilemma of American Nursing, 1850–1945* (Cambridge: Cambridge University Press, 1987), 49–51.

79. Reverby, *Ordered to Care*, 85.

80. Florence Nightingale, *Notes on Nursing* (New York: Dover, 1969), 134.

81. Theodore Roosevelt, "On American Motherhood," in Theodore Roosevelt, *Addresses and Papers*, ed. Willis Fletcher Johnson (New York: Sun Dial Classics, 1909), 242.

82. Dagmar Herzog, *Sex in Crisis: The New Sexual Revolution and the Future of American Politics* (New York: Basic Books, 2008), 165.

83. Herzog, *Sex in Crisis*, 123, 121.

84. Kent, *Making Girls into Women*, 21.

85. Kent, *Making Girls into Women*, 21.

86. Kent, *Making Girls into Women*, 42, 24.

87. I borrow the term "conjugal imperative" from D. A. Miller's *Jane Austen, or The Secret of Style* (Princeton, NJ: Princeton University Press, 2003), 50. Lee Virginia Chambers-Schiller, *Liberty, a Better Husband: Single Women in America: The Generations of 1780–1840* (New Haven, CT: Yale University Press, 1984), 11. On the paucity of colonial spinsters, see also Carl. N. Degler, *At Odds: Women and the Family in America from the Revolution to the Present* (New York: Oxford University Press, 1980), 151–152. This claim is also supported by more recent scholarship on bachelors. See Mark E. Kann, *A Republic of Men: The American Founders, Gendered Language, and Patriarchal Politics* (New York: New York University Press, 1998), 52–78; and Peter Laipson, "'I Have No Genius for Marriage': Bachelorhood in Urban America, 1870–1930" (PhD diss., University of Michigan, 2000), 18–28.

88. Zsuzsa Berend, "Cultural and Social Sources of Spinsterhood in Nineteenth-Century New England" (PhD diss., Columbia University, 1994). Published portions of this dissertation appear as Zsuzsa Berend, "'The Best or None!': Spinsterhood in Nineteenth-Century New England," *Journal of Social History* 33, no. 4 (2000): 935–957; and Zsuzsa Berend, "'Written All Over with Money': Earning, Spending, and Emotion in the Alcott Family," *Journal of Historical Sociology* 16, no. 2 (2003): 209–236.

89. Chambers-Schiller, *Liberty, a Better Husband*, 17.

90. Margaret Fuller, "The Great Lawsuit: Man *Versus* Men. Woman *Versus* Women," in *Transcendentalism: A Reader*, ed. Joel Myerson (Oxford: Oxford University Press, 2000), 419.

91. On Fuller's vast knowledge of Catholicism, see Kimberly VanEsveld Adams, *Our Lady of Victorian Feminism: The Madonna in the Works of Anna Jameson, Margaret Fuller, and George Eliot* (Athens: Ohio University Press, 2001), 31.

92. Catherine Beecher to Sister Sarah Buckingham Beecher, August 20, 1843, in *The Limits of Sisterhood: The Beecher Sisters on Women's Rights and Woman's Sphere*, ed. Jeanne Boydston, Mary Kelley, Anne Margolis (Chapel Hill: University of North Carolina Press, 1988), 239.

93. Boydston, Kelley, and Margolis, *Limits of Sisterhood*, 240.

94. Okrent, *Last Call*, 18.

95. Fitzgerald, *Habits of Compassion*, 42.

96. Kimberly VanEsveld Adams, *Our Lady of Victorian Feminism*, 118–147.

97. Hasia R. Diner, *Erin's Daughters in America: Irish Immigrant Women in the Nineteenth Century* (Baltimore: Johns Hopkins University Press, 1983), 48–54.

98. Chambers-Schiller, *Liberty, a Better Husband*, 40, 228n41. See also Sharon R. Ullman, *Sex Seen: The Emergence of Modern Sexuality in America* (Berkeley: University of California Press, 1997), 22. For a detailing of unmarried women's involvement in moral reform, not social reform, in the South, see Christine Jacobson Carter, *Southern Single Blessedness: Unmarried Women in the Urban South, 1800–1865* (Urbana: University of Illinois Press, 2006), 118–149.

99. Chambers-Schiller, *Liberty, a Better Husband*, 40, 228n41; Laura L. Behling, *The Masculine Woman in America 1890–1935* (Urbana: University of Illinois Press, 2001), 1–59. Celibacy thus extends the body of scholarship that does not draw a sharp distinction between the spheres, exemplified by Cathy N. Davidson and Jessamyn Hatcher, eds., *No More Separate Spheres!* (Durham, NC: Duke University Press, 2002); Monika M. Elbert, ed., *Separate Spheres No More: Gender Convergence in American Literature, 1830–1930* (Tuscaloosa: University of Alabama Press, 2000); and Rosalind Rosenberg, *Beyond Separate Spheres: Intellectual Roots of Modern Feminism* (New Haven, CT: Yale University Press, 1982).

100. DuBois, *Feminism and Suffrage*, 15. See also Trisha Franzen, *Spinsters and Lesbians* (New York: New York University Press, 1996).

101. Arthur Riss, *Race, Slavery, and Liberalism in Nineteenth-Century American Literature* (Cambridge: Cambridge University Press, 2006), 12.

102. See, for example, Jasbir Puar, *Terrorist Assemblages: Homonationalism in Queer Times* (Durham, NC: Duke University Press, 2007); David Eng, *The Feeling of Kinship: Queer Liberalism and the Racialization of Intimacy* (Durham, NC: Duke University Press, 2010); Lisa Duggan, *The Twilight of Equality: Neoliberalism, Cultural Politics, and the Attack on Democracy* (Boston: Beacon Press, 2003); and especially Warner, *Publics and Counterpublics*, 31–44.

103. Warner, *Publics and Counterpublics*, 56.

104. Warner, *Publics and Counterpublics*, 119.

105. Warner, *Publics and Counterpublics*, 124.

106. While accounting for just a minuscule fraction of this enormous drop in the marriage rate, the free love movement, which John C. Spurlock terms a "*middle-class radicalism*," had an outsized impact on the assault on marriage. The ranks of celibacy swelled in part because of the agitation of this roughly historically contemporaneous radicalism. John C. Spurlock, *Free Love: Marriage and Middle-Class Radicalism in America, 1825–1860* (New York: New York University Press, 1988), 2, his emphasis. See also Louis J. Kern, *An Ordered Love: Sex Roles and Sexuality in Victorian Utopias—The Shakers, the Mormons, and the Oneida Community* (Chapel Hill: University of North Carolina Press, 1981).

107. Laipson, "'I Have No Genius for Marriage,'" 52.

108. Degler, *At Odds*, 152.

109. Chauncey, *Gay New York*, 76, 136.

110. Clelia Duel Mosher, *The Mosher Survey: Sexual Attitudes of 45 Victorian Women*, ed. James MaHood and Kristine Wenburg (New York: Arno, 1980).

111. John D'Emilio and Estelle B. Freedman, *Intimate Matters: A History of Sexuality in America* (New York: Harper and Row, 1988), 175, 176.

112. D'Emilio and Freedman, *Intimate Matters*, 190. On the relationship between bachelorhood and class, see Laipson, "'I Have No Genius for Marriage,'" 110–124.

113. The western United States also has an important relationship to celibacy inasmuch as the frontier was conceptualized, as Henry Nash Smith's classic American studies text argues, as a "virgin land." See Henry Nash Smith, *Virgin Land: The American West as Symbol and Myth* (Cambridge, MA: Harvard University Press, 2005). While

this trope elides the colonization and slaughter of American Indians and feminizes the land for heterosexual conquest by men, it suggests the crucial role of women in "settling" the West. Lobbying for suffrage was often couched in the West in the language of marriageability: "I would call upon all of the bachelors in this Convention to vote for it. . . . It is the best provision to get us wives that we can introduce." Here, future Union general Henry Wager Halleck's comment suggests the extent to which celibacy as marital prospect helped both to further the colonial project of Manifest Destiny and win the vote. Rebecca Mead, *How the Vote Was Won: Woman Suffrage in the Western United States, 1868–1914* (New York: New York University Press, 2004), 39. On the relationship between marriageable women and empire in the British context, see Rita S. Kranidis, *The Victorian Spinster and Colonial Emigration: Contested Subjects* (New York: St. Martin's, 1999).

114. Chambers-Schiller, *Liberty, a Better Husband*, 3, 27–33.

115. John D'Emilio, "Capitalism and Gay Identity," in *The Lesbian and Gay Studies Reader*, ed. Henry Abelove, Michèle Aina Barale, and David M. Halperin (New York: Routledge, 1993), 469.

116. Ben Barr Lindsey and Wainright Evans, *The Companionate Marriage* (New York: Boni and Liveright, 1927), 187.

117. Floyd Dell, *Love in the Machine Age: A Psychological Study of the Transition from Patriarchal Society* (New York: Octagon Books, 1973), 11, 118.

118. Margot Canaday, *The Straight State: Sexuality and Citizenship in Twentieth-Century America* (Princeton, NJ: Princeton University Press, 2009), 91–93.

119. Christina Zwarg, *Feminist Conversation: Fuller, Emerson, and the Play of Reading* (Ithaca, NY: Cornell University Press, 1995), 180. For Adams, Fuller's celibacy is primarily spiritual rather than physical. While I do not disagree that Fuller's celibacy has a spiritual component, all the passages that Adams discusses in relation to Fuller's spiritual celibacy are drawn from the later, and I would argue more conservative, *Woman in the Nineteenth Century* rather than the more radical "Great Lawsuit" that I am discussing. See Adams, *Our Lady of Victorian Feminism* 118–147, esp. 122–129.

120. Fuller, "Great Lawsuit," 412, my emphasis. On the Pauline tradition of celibacy, see Henry C. Lea, *History of Sacerdotal Celibacy in the Christian Church* (London: Watts, 1932), esp. 9 and 19. For a period discussion of the relationship between Paul and celibacy, see *Single Blessedness; Or, Single Ladies and Gentlemen against the Slanders of the Pulpit, the Press, and the Lecture Room* (New York: C. S. Francis, 1852), 167–189.

121. Fuller, "Great Lawsuit," 413.

122. Chauncey, *Gay New York*, 76–86; Laipson, "'I Have No Genius for Marriage,'" 125–165; Howard P. Chudacoff, *The Age of the Bachelor: Creating an American Subculture* (Princeton, NJ: Princeton University Press, 1999).

123. Haller and Haller, *Physician and Sexuality in Victorian America*, 211–225.

124. Henry David Thoreau, *Walden and Civil Disobedience*, ed. Sherman Paul (Boston: Houghton Mifflin, 1960), 151.

125. See Michael Warner, "Thoreau's Bottom," *Raritan* 11, no. 3 (1992): 53–79; Michael Warner, "Thoreau's Erotic Economy," in *Comparative American Identities: Race,*

Sex, and Nationality in the Modern Text, ed. Hortense Spillers (New York: Routledge, 1991), 157–174; and Abelove, *Deep Gossip*, 29–41.

126. Still other celibacies might find the rubric of masturbation to be too genitally organized.

127. Leo Bersani, "Ardent Masturbation," *Critical Inquiry* 38, no. 1 (2011): 6.

128. Kevin P. Murphy, *Political Manhood: Red Bloods, Mollycoddles, and the Politics of Progressive Era Reform* (New York: Columbia University Press, 2008), 31.

129. Henry Adams, "The Education of Henry Adams," in *Henry Adams*, ed. Ernest Samuels and Jayne N. Samuels (New York: Library of America, 1983), 1075.

130. Thomas Gold Appleton, *A Sheaf of Papers* (Boston: Roberts Brothers, 1875), 234.

131. Appleton, *Sheaf of Papers*, 234. The pact to eschew marriage that famed labor organizer, social progressive, and diplomat Raymond Robins makes with his equally famous reformer sister Elizabeth Robins in 1900 suggests that the connection between celibacy and reform persists after the demise of the Mugwumps. Neil V. Salzman, *Reform and Revolution: The Life and Times of Raymond Robins* (Kent, OH: Kent State University Press, 1991), 56–61. While Elizabeth Robins would keep her Alaskan promise to her brother throughout her successful acting and writing careers, as well as throughout her suffrage campaigning alongside Elizabeth Pankhurst, Raymond Robins would marry a short time afterward. On radical English attitudes toward celibacy, see Elaine Showalter, *Sexual Anarchy: Gender and Culture at the Fin de Siècle* (New York: Viking, 1990), 22.

132. The other president was James Buchanan. On Buchanan, see John Gilbert McCurdy, *Citizen Bachelors: Manhood and the Creation of the United States* (Ithaca, NY: Cornell University Press, 2009), 198–200.

133. David J. Pivar, *Purity Crusade: Sexual Morality and Social Control, 1868–1900* (Westport, CT: Greenwood Press, 1973), 113–114; Dr. B. F. DeCosta, *The White Cross Society Christian Union*, March 3, 1887.

134. Okrent, *Last Call*, 42.

135. Okrent, *Last Call*, 26.

136. Dr. B. F. DeCosta, *The White Cross Society Christian Union*, January 29, 1885.

137. Dr. B. F. DeCosta, *The White Cross: Its Origin and Progress* (Chicago: Sanitary Publishing, 1887), 5.

138. DeCosta, *The White Cross: Its Origin and Progress*, 6.

139. Frederic M. Thrasher, *The Gang: A Study of 1,313 Gangs in Chicago* (Chicago: University of Chicago Press, 1927), 242.

140. Thrasher, *The Gang*, 461.

141. Lillian Faderman and Stuart Timmons, *Gay L.A.: A History of Sexual Outlaws, Power Politics, and Lipstick Lesbians* (New York: Basic Books, 2006), 112.

142. Valerie Solanas, SCUM *Manifesto* (New York: Verso, 2004), 30; A Southern Women's Writing Collective, "Sex Resistance in Heterosexual Arrangements," in *The Sexual Liberals and the Attack on Feminism*, ed. Dorchen Leidholdt and Janice G. Raymond (New York: Pergamon Press, 1990), 140–147.

143. Moran argues that "mature single women had been the backbone of first-wave feminism." Rachel F. Moran, "How Second-Wave Feminism Forgot the Single Woman," *Hofstra Law Review* 33, no. 1 (2004): 226.

144. Along these lines, see also Richard Rambuss, "After Male Sex," *South Atlantic Quarterly* 106, no. 3 (2007): 578.

145. Henry James, *The Bostonians*, ed. Pierre A. Walker (New York: Modern Library, 2003), 17, 77.

146. Henry James, *Henry James Letters*, vol. 4, *1895–1916*, ed. Leon Edel (Boston: Belknap, 1984), 307, and quoted in Leon Edel, *Henry James: A Life* (New York: Harper and Row, 1985), 233.

147. Sedgwick, *Epistemology of the Closet*, 1.

148. John Guillory, "The Bachelor State: Philosophy and Sovereignty in Bacon's New Atlantis," in *Politics and the Passions, 1500–1800*, ed. Victoria Kahn, Neil Saccamano, and Daniela Coli (Princeton, NJ: Princeton University Press, 2006), 49–74.

149. Heather Love, "Gyn/Apology: Sarah Orne Jewett's Spinster Aesthetics," *ESQ: A Journal of the American Renaissance* 55, nos. 3–4 (2009): 309.

150. This photograph—Portrait of a Man (1938)—has been graciously supplied by the Museum of Decorative Art in Prague and Joseph Sudek's executor Anna Farova.

151. Little is known about Sudek's relationship to Jan Sampalik (1903–1984). Sampalik was an officer of Czechoslovak State Railways and survived internment in a concentration camp during World War II. Frantisek Tichy is also known to have painted several portraits of him.

Chapter One. The Longue Durée of Celibacy

1. David M. Halperin, *How to Do the History of Homosexuality* (Chicago: University of Chicago Press, 2002), 108.

2. Halperin, *How to Do the History of Homosexuality*, 108.

3. Halperin, *How to Do the History of Homosexuality*, 108. Elizabeth Abbott and Dale Launderville have both attempted to write cross-cultural transhistoric histories of celibacy. See Elizabeth Abbott, *A History of Celibacy: From Athena to Elizabeth I, Leonardo da Vinci, Florence Nightingale, Gandhi, and Cher* (New York: Scribner, 2000); and Dale Launderville, *Celibacy in the Ancient World: Its Ideal and Practice in Pre-Hellenistic Israel, Mesopotamia, and Greece* (Collegeville, MN: Liturgical Press, 2010).

4. While this chapter will not be able to fully explore this connection between vocation and homosexuality, the sense of "calling" in both, as well as the suffusion of the language of work in contemporary terminology for sex acts (blow job, hand job, rim job), for sex professionals (working girl), and for sexualized gender presentations (workin' it), further underwrite this hypothesis. I am grateful to Stephanie Alexander for helping me to understand this. On the erotics of career during this period, see Kathryn R. Kent, *Making Girls into Women: American Women's Writing and the Rise of Lesbian Identity* (Durham, NC: Duke University Press, 2003), 66, 72, 132.

5. Kathryn M. Ringrose, *The Perfect Servant: Eunuchs and the Social Construction of Gender in Byzantium* (Chicago: University of Chicago Press, 2003), 83.

6. Ringrose, *Perfect Servant*, 22.

7. John Boswell, *Christianity, Social Tolerance, and Homosexuality: Gay People in West-*

ern Europe from the Beginning of the Christian Era to the Fourteenth Century (Chicago: University of Chicago Press, 2005), 250, 378–380.

8. Thomas L. Mack, *Thomas Gray: A Life* (New Haven, CT: Yale University Press, 2000), 35. On queerness and Gray, see George E. Haggerty, *Men in Love: Masculinity and Sexuality in the Eighteenth Century* (New York: Columbia University Press, 1999); and Robert F. Gleckner, *Gray Agonistes: Thomas Gray and Masculine Friendship* (Baltimore: Johns Hopkins University Press, 1997).

9. Thomas Gray to Charles Victor de Bonstetten, April 12, 1770, in *The Works of Thomas Gray in Prose and Verse*, ed. Edmund Gosse (New York: AMS Press, 1968), 3:361–362.

10. Mack, *Thomas Gray*, 35. The relationship between celibacy and philosophy will be explored more fully in chapter 5.

11. A. J. A. Symons, *The Quest for Corvo: An Experimental Biography* (New York: NYRB Classics, 2001), 248.

12. Ralph Werther, *Autobiography of an Androgyne*, ed. Scott Herring (New Brunswick, NJ: Rutgers University Press, 2008), 26, 76.

13. Quoted in Justin Spring, *Secret Historian: The Life and Times of Samuel Steward, Professor, Tattoo Artist, and Sexual Renegade* (New York: Farrar, Straus and Giroux, 2010), 29.

14. Elizabeth Drexel Lehr, *"King Lehr" and the Gilded Age* (Philadelphia: Lippincott, 1935), 58. For a wonderful article on queerness in Lehr's book, see Stephanie Foote, "The Little Brothers of the Rich: Queer Families in the Late Nineteenth Century," *American Literature* 79, no. 4 (2007): 701–724.

15. Quentin Crisp, *The Naked Civil Servant* (New York: Holt, Rinehart, and Winston, 1977), 53, 34.

16. By prelesbian, I mean a model or pattern that contributes to the formation of the modern lesbian, rather than preceding the emergence of the term "lesbian." For a long history of the lesbian, see Halperin, *How to Do the History of Homosexuality*, 48–80.

17. Desiderius Erasmus, *Erasmus on Women*, ed. Erika Rummel (Toronto: University of Toronto Press, 1996), 31.

18. Valerie Traub, *The Renaissance of Lesbianism in Early Modern England* (Cambridge: Cambridge University Press, 2002); Theodora Jankowski, *Pure Resistance: Queer Virginity in Early Modern English Drama* (Philadelphia: University of Pennsylvania Press, 2000); Kathleen Coyne Kelly and Marina Leslie, eds., *Menacing Virgins: Representing Virginity in the Middle Ages and Renaissance* (Newark: University of Delaware Press, 1999).

19. Traub, *Renaissance of Lesbianism*, 150–151, 231.

20. Traub, *Renaissance of Lesbianism*, 252.

21. Heather Love, *Feeling Backward: Loss and the Politics of Queer History* (Cambridge, MA: Harvard University Press, 2007), 77.

22. Lillian Faderman, *Surpassing the Love of Men: Romantic Friendship and Love between Women from the Renaissance to the Present* (1981; repr., New York: Perennial, 2001), 297.

23. Martha Vicinus, *Intimate Friends: Women Who Loved Women, 1778–1928* (Chi-

cago: University of Chicago Press, 2004); Alan Bray, *The Friend* (Chicago: University of Chicago Press, 2003).

24. Love, *Feeling Backward*, 77.

25. Lillian Faderman, "Romantic Friendship and Boston Marriage," in *Encyclopedia of Lesbian, Gay, Bisexual, and Transgender History in America*, ed. Marc Stein (New York: Scribner, 2004), 3:47. On the history of Boston marriage, see Helen Lefkowitz Horowitz, *The Power and Passion of M. Carey Thomas* (New York: Knopf, 1994), 166–181; Carl N. Degler, *At Odds: Women and the Family in America from the Revolution to the Present* (New York: Oxford University Press, 1980); Micaela di Leonardo, "Warrior Virgins and Boston Marriages: Spinsterhood in History and Culture," in *Que(e)ry Religion: A Critical Anthology*, ed. Gary David Comstock and Susan E. Henking (New York: Continuum, 1997); Blanche Wiesen Cook, "Female Support Networks and Political Activism: Lillian Wald, Crystal Eastman, Emma Goldman," in *A Heritage of Her Own: Toward a New Social History of American Women*, ed. Nancy F. Cott and Elizabeth H. Pleck (New York: Simon and Schuster, 1977), 412–445; and Kate McCullough, "The Boston Marriage as the Future of the Nation: Queerly Regional Sexuality in Diana Victrix," *American Literature* 69, no. 1 (1997): 67–103.

26. Henry James, *The Complete Notebooks of Henry James*, ed. Leon Edel and Lyall H. Powers (Oxford: Oxford University Press, 1987), 19. On the image of the New England woman, see Martha Banta, *Imaging American Women: Idea and Ideals in Cultural History* (New York: Columbia University Press, 1987), 51–58.

27. "Child Lost through Hypnotism," *Chicago Tribune*, December 22, 1892, 4.

28. Susan S. Lanser, "'Queer to Queer': The Sapphic Body as Transgressive Text," in *Lewd and Notorious: Female Transgression in the Eighteenth Century*, ed. Katharine Kittredge (Ann Arbor: University of Michigan Press, 2003), 36. This connection between singularity and lesbianism provides additional evidence of the relationship between celibacy and lesbianism.

29. Pamela Thurschwell, *Literature, Technology, and Magical Thinking, 1880–1920* (Cambridge: Cambridge University Press, 2001), 34. The discourse of mesmerism (which is similar to hypnotism) is eroticized within *The Bostonians* (1886) as well: "He [Basil Ransom] grew more impatient . . . at [Selah] Tarrant's grotesque manipulations, which he resented as much as if he himself had felt their touch, and which seemed a dishonour to the passive maiden [Verena Tarrant]" (57). This passage offers a homoerotics of the hypnotic (Basil imagining Selah's hands on him), as well as the veiled suggestion of an incestuous violation of Verena's sexual purity. Henry James, *The Bostonians*, ed. Pierre A. Walker (New York: Modern Library, 2003). Other references to this work will be cited parenthetically in the text.

30. Madelon Bedell, *The Alcotts: Biography of a Family* (New York: Clarkson N. Potter, 1980).

31. Faderman, "Romantic Friendship and Boston Marriage," 47.

32. Helen Howe, *The Gentle Americans, 1864–1960: Biography of a Breed* (New York: Harper and Row, 1965), 83. Throughout her work, Faderman repeatedly cites this passage as an originary moment for Boston marriage. For instances of this reference, see Faderman, *Surpassing the Love of Men*, 190; and Lillian Faderman, "Nineteenth-

Century Boston Marriage as a Possible Lesson for Today," in *Boston Marriages*, ed. Esther D. Rothblum and Kathleen A. Brehony (Amherst: University of Massachusetts Press, 1993), 29. For more information about Howe, see Rita K. Gollin, *Annie Adams Fields: Woman of Letters* (Amherst: University of Massachusetts Press, 2002), 274–277.

33. Ednah D. Cheney, "Correspondence," *Open Court, a Quarterly Magazine*, January 5, 1893.

34. Cheney echoes Fuller's understanding of celibacy in her early correspondence with Caroline Wells Healey Dall. The correspondence is published in Margaret McFadden, "Boston Teenagers Debate the Woman Question, 1837–1838," *Signs* 15, no. 4 (1990): 841–847. Additionally, *The Bostonians* draws a genealogical connection to Fuller, representing her in the figure of Mrs. Farrinder. A number of contemporary reviews allude to this identification, and this argument is made more recently in Charles Anderson's introduction to the text. *Boston Beacon*, March 27, 1886, 3, and *Springfield [MA] Republican*, April 18, 1886, 4, in *Henry James: The Contemporary Reviews*, ed. Kevin J. Hayes (Cambridge: Cambridge University Press, 1996), 159, 165. See also Charles Anderson, "Introduction," in Henry James, *The Bostonians* (New York: Penguin, 1974), 19. Part of the similarity can be heard in the linguistic proximity of "l" and "r" sounds and the names' shared "f" beginning and "er" ending.

35. Terry Castle, *The Apparitional Lesbian: Female Homosexuality and Modern Culture* (New York: Columbia University Press, 1993). The early death of Seth Cheney, Ednah Cheney's husband, left her a young widow. Her memoir, *Reminiscences* (1902), describes her friend Augusta R. Curtis moving in with her for at least a year after her husband's death: "She was devoted to the [Cheneys'] child, and did much to make the empty house a home" (60). This quotation begins to suggest that it is Cheney herself who is "accustomed" both personally and through acquaintance "to the existence of ties between women." This ambiguity in the letter (which also accrues in Cheney's phrase "as I have known") receives further clarification in Cheney's memoir, where she describes a nameless woman who "became ever after one of my dearest and closest companions" (76). The tenderness of this passage suggests a profound love between Cheney and her unnamed companion. Ednah D. Cheney, *Reminiscences of Ednah Dow Cheney* (Boston: Lee and Shepard, 1902).

36. For a literary example of a Boston marriage with lesbian content, see Mary Casal (pseudonym of Ruth Fuller Field), *The Stone Wall: An Autobiography* (Chicago: Eyncourt, 1930).

37. Hugh Stevens, *Henry James and Sexuality* (New York: Cambridge University Press, 1998), 97. On "homosexual chastity," see also Lionel Trilling, *The Opposing Self: Nine Essays in Criticism* (New York: Viking, 1955), 114.

38. Stevens, *Henry James and Sexuality*, 97.

39. Thomas Herbert Dickinson's unpublished play *Winter Bound* (1929) also tells the story of two women who live together and practice celibacy.

40. Katie-Louise Thomas, "A Queer Job for a Girl: Women Postal Workers, Civic Duty and Sexuality 1870–80," in *In a Queer Place: Sexuality and Belonging in British and European Contexts*, ed. Kate Chedgzoy, Emma Francis, and Murray Pratt (Burlington, VT: Ashgate, 2002), 58. Elihu Vedder's painting *The Dead Alchemist* (1868) offers a

slightly earlier version of the conjunction of marriage and work. Alchemy has a long tradition dating back to (at least) Isaac Newton of being associated with hermeticism and celibacy. The alchemist's table/working desk is a marriage chest or cassone, suggesting that in order to achieve his transformation of lead into gold, he has had to forfeit marriage in pursuit of his vocation.

41. James's text obsessively depicts the religio-political overtones of celibacy, referring to suffrage supporters as "converts" (59) and "pilgrims" (30), while depicting Olive and Verena as women engaged in a "holy office" (151), "a kind of priesthood" (134), "at the altar of a great cause" (165), and fighting for "the only sacred cause" (35).

42. Annamarie Jagose, *Inconsequence: Lesbian Representation and the Logic of Sexual Sequence* (Ithaca, NY: Cornell University Press, 2002), 69.

43. Jagose, *Inconsequence*, 70.

44. Margaret Fuller, "The Great Lawsuit: Man *Versus* Men. Woman *Versus* Women," in *Transcendentalism: A Reader*, ed. Joel Myerson (Oxford: Oxford University Press, 2000), 419.

45. Caleb Crain, *American Sympathy: Men, Friendship, and Literature in the New Nation* (New Haven, CT: Yale University Press, 2001), 204.

46. Vicinus, *Intimate Friends*, 9; Sharon Marcus, *Between Women: Friendship, Desire, and Marriage in Victorian England* (Princeton, NJ: Princeton University Press, 2007), 201.

47. Amy Dru Stanley, "Conjugal Bonds and Wage Labor: Rights of Contract in the Age of Emancipation," in *Women and the American Legal Order*, ed. Karen J. Maschke (New York: Garland, 1997), 149–178. Stanley argues in her discussion of the postemancipation extension to slaves of the right to contract that freedom and the ability to contract are virtually synonymous during this period.

48. While Terry Castle's *Apparitional Lesbian* implicitly attacks Lillian Faderman for desexualizing the lesbian content of James's novel as a "Boston marriage," their interpretations are actually quite close. Despite some differing interpretive investments— Faderman wants to see Olive and Verena's relationship as more biographically rooted in that of Alice James and Katherine Loring than Castle does; Faderman emphasizes an American context while Castle emphasizes a French one, etc.—both are invested in depathologizing the text's lesbian erotics and demonstrating its lesbian or lesbian-like content.

49. In 1879 Cooley also posited that "the right to one's person may be said to be a right of complete immunity"; quoted in John W. Johnson, *Griswold v. Connecticut: Birth Control and the Constitutional Right of Privacy* (Lawrence: University Press of Kansas, 2005), 57.

50. Brook Thomas, *American Literary Realism and the Failed Promise of Contract* (Berkeley: University of California Press, 1997), 62–64.

51. Stevens, *Henry James and Sexuality*, 90.

52. Edward Said's *Beginnings* might provide an additional model. Edward W. Said, *Beginnings: Intention and Method* (New York: Columbia University Press, 1985), 137–152.

53. Eve Kosofsky Sedgwick, *Between Men: English Literature and Male Homosocial Desire* (New York: Columbia University Press, 1985), 21.

54. René Girard, *Deceit, Desire, and the Novel: Self and Other in Literary Structure*, trans. Yvonne Freccero (Baltimore: Johns Hopkins University Press, 1976), 11.

55. On Verena as *tabula rasa*, see Jennifer L. Fleissner, *Women, Compulsion, Modernity: The Moment of American Naturalism* (Chicago: University of Chicago Press, 2004), 124–127.

56. Girard, *Deceit, Desire, and the Novel*, 10, 47.

57. Sedgwick, *Between Men*, 22.

58. To the extent that there exists a repressed content in Basil's relationship to Olive, the language of "a firm" might open the specter of a plurality of partners (Olive-Verena-Basil). The possibility of polygamy haunts the novel in Verena's frequent association with the complex marriage practices of the Cayuga community (a lightly veiled proxy for the Oneida) and of course runs counter to my explication of the celibacy plot. However, since Basil's reference to the language of "a firm" is clearly intended to imply a dyadic partnership (much like the unsuccessful partnership he will begin later in the novel), I do not read the passage as polygamous. On the relationship between partnership law and polygamy, see Adrienne D. Davis, "Regulating Polygamy: Intimacy, Default Rules, and Bargaining for Equality," *Columbia Law Review* 110 (2010): 1955.

59. David Kurnick, "An Erotics of Detachment: *Middlemarch* and Novel-Reading as Critical Practice," ELH 74, no. 3 (2007): 596. See also Richard Kaye, *The Flirt's Tragedy: Desire without End in Victorian and Edwardian Fiction* (Charlottesville: University of Virginia Press, 2002).

60. Leslie A. Fiedler, *Love and Death in the American Novel* (Champaign, IL: Dalkey Archive Press, 2003), 25.

61. Fiedler, *Love and Death in the American Novel*, 26. Fiedler is building on D. H. Lawrence's claim that "two childless, womanless men, of opposite races" model a relationship that will become "the nucleus of a new society." This relationship is "deeper than the depths of sex. Deeper than property, deeper than fatherhood, deeper than marriage, deeper than love. So deep that it is loveless." D. H. Lawrence, *Studies in Classic American Literature* (New York: T. Seltzer, 1923), 64, 59. W. H. Auden, who was an avid admirer of Lawrence's work, certainly read American literature as a literature of isolation rather than coupling: "The American literary tradition, Poe, Emerson, Hawthorne, Melville, Henry James, T. S. Eliot, is much nearer to Dostoievski than to Tolstoi. It is a literature of lonely people. Most American books might well start like Moby Dick: 'Call me Ishmael.'" W. H. Auden, *Double Man* (New York: Random House, 1941), 152.

62. Fiedler, *Love and Death in the American Novel*, 12.

63. Christopher Looby, "Innocent Homosexuality: The Fiedler Thesis in Retrospect," in *Mark Twain: "The Adventures of Huckleberry Finn"; A Case Study in Critical Controversy*, ed. Gerald Graff and James Phelan (New York: Bedford Books, 1995), 535–550. While it is beyond the bounds of this study to develop a theory of celibate gender identity, I think there is much to be said on the topic. The emphasis on "non-sensual wifely love" over "*mere* sexual attraction" in Ralph Werther's *Autobiography of an Androgyne* (1918) might provide a starting point. Ralph Werther, *Autobiography of an Androgyne*, ed. Scott Herring (New Brunswick, NJ: Rutgers University Press, 2008), 78–79, my emphasis.

This reading might be developed more fully by considering Werther's contemplation of a career as a monk, his castration, and the articulated objective of Werther's book: the delineation of "the phenomena of androgynism, passive sexual inversion, and psychical infantilism as they manifested themselves in the life of its writer" (17–18). Werther's avowed "psychical infantilism"—what Joanne Meyerowitz sees as his self-presentation as a baby and preoccupation with babyishness—might be read as a part of his celibate gender identity. Here, babyishness functions as a mode of association and learned strategy of attraction (rather than innocence as it might ordinarily be understood). Joanne Meyerowitz, "Thinking Sex with an Androgyne," GLQ: A Journal of Lesbian and Gay Studies 17, no. 1 (2011): 97–105.

64. Halperin, How to Do the History of Homosexuality, 120.

65. My reading of the ending of The Bostonians is influenced by Leslie Petty, Romancing the Vote: Feminist Activism in American Fiction, 1870–1920 (Athens: University of Georgia Press, 2006); and Sara Blair, "Realism, Culture, and the Place of the Literary: Henry James and The Bostonians," in The Cambridge Companion to Henry James, ed. Jonathan Freeman (Cambridge: Cambridge University Press, 1998), 151–168.

66. Wendy Graham, Henry James's Thwarted Love (Stanford, CA: Stanford University Press, 1999), 28.

67. Graham, Henry James's Thwarted Love, 2. James's major biographers, Leon Edel and Fred Kaplan, also see James engaging in lifelong celibacy. Leon Edel, Henry James: A Life (New York: Harper and Row, 1985); Fred Kaplan, Henry James: The Imagination of a Genius: A Biography (New York: Morrow, 1992).

68. Graham, Henry James's Thwarted Love, 39. For an alternate theory of James's celibacy, see Mary Esteve, "Anerotic Excursions: Memory, Celibacy, and Desire in The American Scene," in Questioning the Master: Gender and Sexuality in Henry James's Writings, ed. Peggy McCormack (Cranbury, NJ: Associated University Presses, 2000), 196–216.

69. Tim Dean, Beyond Sexuality (Chicago: University of Chicago Press, 2000), 276.

70. Dean, Beyond Sexuality, 276.

71. Jean Laplanche, "Sublimation and/or Inspiration," Formations: A Journal of Culture/Theory/Politics 48 (2002–2003): 31.

72. James, Complete Notebooks, 218.

73. This reading of the passage from James's journal is heavily indebted to Katherine V. Snyder, Bachelors, Manhood, and the Novel, 1850–1925 (Cambridge: Cambridge University Press, 1999), 104.

74. Michael Warner, "Irving's Posterity," ELH 67, no. 3 (2000): 774.

75. Matt Cohen, "Walt Whitman, the Bachelor, and Sexual Poetics," Walt Whitman Quarterly Review 16, nos. 3–4 (1999): 145; Bryce Traister, "The Wandering Bachelor: Irving, Masculinity, and Authorship," American Literature 74, no. 1 (2002): 111–137.

76. Heather Love, "Gyn/Apology: Sarah Orne Jewett's Spinster Aesthetics," ESQ: A Journal of the American Renaissance 55, nos. 3–4 (2009): 314.

77. This relationship between observation and celibacy extends with particular poignancy to detective novels. Siegfried Kracauer's The Detective Novel (completed in 1925) asserts the necessity of the celibate detective. Kracauer's detective represents pure reason and is detached from and not distracted by the creaturely world of sex.

Auden similarly writes in his essay "The Guilty Vicarage: Notes on the Detective Story, by an Addict" that "in his sexual life, the detective must be either celibate or happily married." W. H. Auden, *The Complete Works of W. H. Auden: Prose*, vol. 2, *1939–1948*, ed. Edward Mendelson (Princeton, NJ: Princeton University Press, 1996), 267. On the relationship between celibacy and the female detective, see Kathy Mezei, "Spinster, Surveillance, and Speech: The Case of Miss Marple, Miss Mole, and Miss Jekyll," *Journal of Modern Literature* 30, no. 2 (2007): 103–120.

78. Henry James, "The Art of Fiction," in *Henry James: Literary Criticism: Essays on Literature, American Writers, and English Writers*, ed. Leon Edel (New York: Library of America, 1984), 1:54.

79. For more information on their collaboration see Wayne Koestenbaum, *Double Talk: The Erotics of Male Literary Collaboration* (New York: Routledge, 1989), 161–162.

80. Walter Besant, *Autobiography of Sir Walter Besant* (New York: Dodd, Mead, 1902), 186–187.

81. Henry James, "The Future of the Novel," in *Henry James: Literary Criticism: Essays on Literature, American Writers, and English Writers*, ed. Leon Edel (New York: Library of America, 1984), 1:103.

82. James, "Future of the Novel," 103.

Chapter Two. Celibate Time

1. On Moore's fame, see Elizabeth Gregory, "Stamps, Money, Pop Culture, and Marianne Moore," *Discourse* 17, no. 1 (1994): 132.

2. Rosenbach Museum and Library (hereafter RML) Marianne Moore Collection, XII:17:16, February 27, 1969.

3. On Moore's relationship to advertising, see Marie Boroff, *Language and the Poet: Verbal Artistry in Frost, Stevens, and Moore* (Chicago: University of Chicago Press, 1979).

4. Kathleen M. Barry, *Femininity in Flight: A History of Flight Attendants* (Durham, NC: Duke University Press, 2007), 175–181.

5. George Lois, *$ellebrity* (New York: Phaidon, 2003), n.p. [50].

6. I quote from my copy of the commercial, though most of the text is available in Lois's book *$ellebrity*. See Lois, *$ellebrity*, n.p. [50]. For more information about the commercial, see RML Marianne Moore Collection, V:34:22. While I would not want to put too much emphasis on the lesbian implications of the tagline "They like our girls," some of the other commercials in the campaign (like the Dalí commercial) do not include this phrase.

7. Many of the commercials in the campaign are animated by hierarchies of power. For example, when Whitey Ford claims that a knuckleball is harder to throw than a screwball, the comedic screwball Salvador Dalí dramatically responds as an authority on the subject: "Oh no, no, no, no, no, Whitey."

8. On Moore and rhyme, see Elizabeth Bishop, "Efforts of Affection: A Memoir of Marianne Moore," in *The Collected Prose*, ed. Robert Giroux (New York: Farrar, Straus and Giroux, 1984), 138–140. Other references to this work will be cited parenthetically in the text.

9. Because there is a paucity of information about the commercial, it is unclear whether the drinks appeared in the aired version. They appear in the publicity still (fig. 2.1) and in Lois's book. However, they do not appear in the copy of the commercial that I have seen, though other commercials in the campaign do feature drinks.

10. Jeanne Heuving, *Omissions Are Not Accidents: Gender in the Art of Marianne Moore* (Detroit: Wayne State University Press, 1992), 18.

11. Denise Riley, "The Right to Be Lonely," in *Impersonal Passion: Language as Affect* (Durham, NC: Duke University Press, 2005), 49–58; Michael Cobb, "Lonely," *South Atlantic Quarterly* 106, no. 3 (2007): 445–457.

12. Marianne Moore, *The Complete Prose of Marianne Moore*, ed. Patricia C. Willis (New York: Viking, 1986), 503.

13. Elizabeth Freeman, "Packing History, Count(er)ing Generations," *New Literary History* 31, no. 4 (2000): 733, 727, her emphasis.

14. Freeman, "Packing History, Count(er)ing Generations," 740.

15. Freeman, "Packing History, Count(er)ing Generations," 740.

16. Rachel F. Moran, "How Second-Wave Feminism Forgot the Single Woman," *Hofstra Law Review* 33, no. 1 (2004): 226.

17. Henry James, *The Bostonians*, ed. Pierre A. Walker (New York: Modern Library, 2003), 17.

18. George Santayana, *The Last Puritan: A Memoir in the Form of a Novel*, ed. William G. Holzberger and Herman J. Saatkamp Jr. (Cambridge, MA: MIT Press, 1986), 21.

19. Freeman, "Packing History, Count(er)ing Generations," 742.

20. Freeman, "Packing History, Count(er)ing Generations," 742.

21. Robert Payne, "On Mariamna De Maura," in *Festschrift for Marianne Moore's Seventy-Seventh Birthday*, ed. Tambimuttu (New York: Tambimuttu and Mass, 1964), 21–27.

22. See also Elizabeth Gregory, *Quotation and Modern American Poetry: "Imaginary Gardens with Real Toads"* (Houston: Rice University Press, 1996), 170–172.

23. Freeman, "Packing History, Count(er)ing Generations," 728.

24. Freeman, "Packing History, Count(er)ing Generations," 735. Freeman slightly misreads Judith Butler in her suggestion that "repetitions with any backwards-looking force [in Butler's formulation of queer performativity] . . . are merely 'citational' and can only thereby consolidate the authority of the fantasized original" (727). Butler would not differentiate between citation and use (this is Derrida's complaint about Searle) and therefore would not see citation as consolidating a fantasized original because she would not imagine a "fantasized original."

25. Bishop highlights the word "burden" ("Efforts of Affection," 147) as having particular significance for the Moore family.

26. Quoted in Vivian R. Pollak, "Moore, Plath, Hughes, and 'The Literary Life,'" *American Literary History* 17, no. 1 (2005): 107.

27. Freeman, "Packing History, Count(er)ing Generations," 727.

28. In some of the only criticism on the volume, Charles Molesworth discusses several of these self-images. Charles Molesworth, *Marianne Moore: A Literary Life* (New York: Atheneum, 1990), 411–414.

29. Linda Leavell, "Marianne Moore, the James Family, and the Politics of Celibacy," *Twentieth Century Literature* 49 (2003): 223.

30. John Ashbery's excellent 1966 review of the volume is perhaps its most extensive treatment. See John Ashbery, "Jerboas, Pelicans, and Peewee Reese: Marianne Moore," in John Ashbery, *Selected Prose*, ed. Eugene Richie (Ann Arbor: University of Michigan Press, 2004), 83–88.

31. Molesworth, *Marianne Moore*, xxii.

32. Kathryn R. Kent, *Making Girls into Women: American Women's Writing and the Rise of Lesbian Identity* (Durham, NC: Duke University Press, 2003), 296n51; John Emil Vincent, *Queer Lyrics* (New York: Palgrave Macmillan, 2002), xvii; Ellen Levy, *Criminal Ingenuity: Moore, Cornell, Ashbery, and the Struggle between the Arts* (New York: Oxford University Press, 2011), xxiii, 42. See also Sabine Sielke, *Fashioning the Female Subject: The Intertextual Networking of Dickinson, Moore, and Rich* (Ann Arbor: University of Michigan Press, 1997), 68–72. In addition, Bishop implies both Moore's lesbianism in her association with "two elderly Boston ladies" and her heterosexuality (flirting with gentlemen), though this could just be a way of relating for her (Bishop, "Efforts of Affection," 148, 134).

33. Moore, *Complete Prose*, 606–607.

34. I found this usage of "explicit" in two different obscenity cases: *United States v. Ginzburg*, 224 F. Supp. 129 (E.D. Pa. 1963), *aff'd*, 338 F.2d 12 (3d Cir. 1964), *aff'd*, 383 U.S. 463 (1964); and *United States v. West Coast News Co.*, 228 F. Supp. 171 (W.D. Mich. 1964), *aff'd*, 357 F.2d 855 (6th Cir. 1966).

35. Another reading is of course possible—that Moore sarcastically describes her noncomprehending audient as "impressive." And yet I would be wary of reading this exchange as anything other than witty flirtation, as this alternate reading underestimates the value that Moore places on clothing—the woman is "strikingly well-dressed."

36. Moore, *Complete Prose*, 607.

37. The Bryn Mawr paper suggests another moment of unachieved desire. That is, whatever "Bryn Mawr" signifies—a community of women, female erotics, educational revolution, etc.—Moore does not seem to be able to communicate her participation fully.

38. D. A. Miller's analysis of Robert Ferrars and his toothpick case might offer another example of this second model. Miller compares Ferrars to "a self-fertilizing flower" that is self-complete and without sexual lack. D. A. Miller, *Jane Austen, or the Secret of Style* (Princeton, NJ: Princeton University Press, 2003), 15.

39. On this model of chastity, see Kasey Evans, "How Temperance Becomes 'Blood Guiltie' in *The Fairie Queen*," sel: *Studies in English Literature, 1500–1900* 49, no. 1 (2009): 37–38.

40. Marianne Moore, *Tell Me, Tell Me: Granite, Steel, and Other Topics* (New York: Viking, 1966), 45. Other references to this work will be cited parenthetically in the text.

41. Bonnie Costello, *Marianne Moore: Imaginary Possessions* (Cambridge, MA: Harvard University Press, 1981), 3.

42. Michael Warner, "Irving's Posterity," elh 67, no. 3 (2000): 774n6.

43. Moore also praises knottedness in "Charity Overcoming Envy" (also in *Tell Me, Tell Me*): "The Gordian knot need not be cut" (19).

44. Linda Leavell makes a similar claim, though she sees Moore's celibacy as a symptom of trauma resulting from her frustrated amorous desires for Peggy James (the daughter of William and the niece of Henry). Leavell, "Marianne Moore," 221–227. This traumatic relation to celibacy is further developed in another essay where Leavell argues that "Marriage" is written as an angry rebuke to Scofield Thayer for proposing to her. While it is outside the scope of this essay to offer a different, less pathologized origin of Moore's celibacy, Leavell's trauma model is at odds with the nonstigmatized model of celibacy that I am elaborating. Moreover, Leavell problematizes her own narrative by suggesting that Moore's identification with bachelorhood came long before she met Peggy. Linda Leavell, "'Frightening Disinterestedness': The Personal Circumstances of Marianne Moore's 'Marriage,'" *Journal of Modern Literature* 31, no. 1 (2007): 64–79.

45. This point is made in Vincent, *Queer Lyrics*, 89. See also Heuving, *Omissions Are Not Accidents*, 12.

46. Cristanne Miller, "Rhythms of Embodiment," Gender and the Poetics of the Visual, *Modernist Studies Association*, Vancouver, October 22, 2004. Miller also breaks from Ashbery's reading, suggesting that when syntax and stanza coincide, orgasmic pleasure results.

47. Marianne Moore, letter to Viking Press, May 2, 1966, RML Marianne Moore Collection, V:67:19.

48. For other sites of this backward reading, see the description of word order in "Subject, Predicate, Object." and "An Expedient—Leonardo da Vinci's—and a Query": "memory / making past present." Additionally, the inclusion of part of "Tell me, tell me" in "A Burning Desire to be Explicit" further suggests the need to read backward.

49. Reading the book as the medium for *Tell Me, Tell Me* might also gesture toward Moore's other poetic sequences like "Pouters and Fantails" (1914), "Part of a Novel, Part of a Poem, Part of a Play" (1932), and "Old Dominion" (1936).

50. The collection's title might signify this backwardness in several ways. The title might allude to the line "tell me, tell me, tell me, elm!" (216.3) from the Anna Livia Plurabelle section of James Joyce's *Finnegans Wake* (1939), which Moore attempted to publish in the *Dial*. This stuttering allusion might signify the importance of "hesitancy" and its crucial role in the Parnell scandal or the backwardness that runs throughout Joyce's text, as when a barrel rolls uphill. It might also allude to Langston Hughes's "Tell Me" (1951), which takes up the questions of loneliness and deferral. Additionally, I think the title draws on the unusual biographical temporality of Virginia Woolf's *Orlando: A Biography* (San Diego: Harcourt, 1928), particularly its interest in "rainbow and granite" (77). In Woolf's essay collection also titled *Granite and Rainbow* (London: Hogarth Press, 1956), the opening essay is titled "The Narrow Bridge of Art," which Moore's collection literalizes and solidifies in the transformation from "rainbow" to "steel."

51. The opening of "The Tailor of Gloucester" emphasizes this backward-directed pastness: "In the time of swords and periwigs and full-skirted coats with flowered lappets—when gentleman wore ruffles, and gold-laced waistcoats of paduasoy and taffeta—there lived a tailor in Gloucester." Beatrix Potter, *The Tailor of Gloucester* (New York: Frederick Warne, 1981), 9.

52. Marianne Moore, *Selected Letters*, ed. Bonnie Costello, Celeste Goodridge, and Cristanne Miller (New York: Penguin, 1997), 5.

53. The mice in "Tell me, tell me" are described with a quotation that Henry James uses in his autobiography to describe his family.

54. The desire for "continuity" resonates with Moore's understanding of the collection as biographical. Additionally, the title of the collection hints at its preoccupation with self-narration and self-image.

55. This "rosette" was worn by Lord Nelson on his tricorn, linking him to Moore's Washington.

56. While Heuving suggests that Moore's later poetry employs overstatement (as in "The Arctic Ox") uncharacteristic of the understatement of the early work, moments such as this suggest a greater continuity.

57. Moore, *Complete Prose*, 321.

58. Moore, *Complete Prose*, 504.

59. I borrow the term "conjugal imperative" from D. A. Miller, *Jane Austen, or the Secret of Style*, 50. Leavell argues that William James's "'passion for distinguishing' is almost by definition celibate" because it is opposed to simplicity, and erotic relations are blurry and vague. Leavell, "Marianne Moore," 238. Moore borrows this phrase from a review of Henry James's *Autobiography*. This point is made in Patricia C. Willis, "Notes," *Marianne Moore Newsletter* 7, nos. 1–2 (1983): 13–14.

60. M. Daphne Kutzer, *Beatrix Potter: Writing in Code* (New York: Routledge, 2003), 7.

61. The Auden group bolsters Potter's queer iconicity in W. H. Auden's admiration of her in his queer homage "Letter to Lord Byron" (1936) and in Christopher Isherwood and Edward Upward's queer realm Mortmere (*The Mortmere Stories* [London: Enitharmon, 1995]). W. H. Auden, *The English Auden: Poems, Essays, and Dramatic Writings 1927–1939*, ed. Edward Mendelson (London: Faber, 1977), 167–199. On the figure of the aunt, see Katherine Moore, *Cordial Relations: The Maiden Aunt in Fact and Fiction* (London: Heinemann, 1966).

62. The poem "Tell me, tell me" also functions as a "told-backward biography": beginning with death and ending with birth. The poem begins in crisis with the speaker's imperative to "tell me, tell me." This imperative reads as a death wish as the speaker seeks refuge in the extinction of "egocentricity" in the suicide of the absorption of the family. And it ends in birth with "captivity" as a pejorative image, a spinster's image, of "confinement."

63. For more on the connection with Crane, see Margaret Holley, *The Poetry of Marianne Moore: A Study in Voice and Value* (Cambridge: Cambridge University Press, 1987), 171. See also Kent, *Making Girls into Women*, 233–234.

64. Maurice Agulhon, *Marianne into Battle: Republican Imagery and Symbolism in France, 1789–1880*, trans. Janet Lloyd (Cambridge: Cambridge University Press, 1981), 9–10, 30–37.

65. "Liberty" might offer another self-reference alluding to the Liberty stanza of "Light Is Speech" in *Tell Me, Tell Me*.

66. Gregory, "Stamps, Money, Pop Culture, and Marianne Moore," 124. See also

Sandra Gilbert, "Marianne Moore as Female Female Impersonator," in *Marianne Moore: The Art of a Modernist*, ed. Joseph Parisi (Ann Arbor: University of Michigan Press, 1990), 27–46.

67. Gregory, "Stamps, Money, Pop Culture, and Marianne Moore," 132.

68. Moore's inhabitation of Washington seems of a piece with Larry Rivers's assertion that he painted his *George Washington Crossing the Delaware* (1953) because he wanted to do something that "no one in the New York art world would doubt was disgusting, dead, absurd—that is, it was a deliberate attempt at painting the artistically and politically retrograde." Frank O'Hara, "Why I Paint as I Do" (interview with Larry Rivers), *Horizon* 2, no. 1 (1959): 98.

69. The lines from "Smooth Gnarled Crape Myrtle" might be instructive here: "One may be a blameless / bachelor, and it is but a step / to Congreve." Congreve may here be a general signifier for bawdiness, or more specifically, following his plays, the blameless bachelor might signify a dirty old man or a sodomite. However, I am more inclined, given the preceding line "Art is unfortunate," to read these lines in terms of Jeremy Collier's 1698 complaint against the immorality of the stage. This polemic took hold of the public imagination, and Congreve felt that he could not write anymore. Here, Congreve's name would be a cautionary tale; the danger of being blameless, of not risking the transgression of crossing the boundaries of politeness, of not having an erotic content in one's writing might cause one to give up writing entirely.

70. John Warner Moore to Marianne Moore, February 22, 1941, RML Marianne Moore Collection, VI:36:03 (his emphasis).

71. For more on Warner's muscular Christianity, see Molesworth, *Marianne Moore*, 95. On muscular Christianity, see Clifford Putney, *Muscular Christianity* (Cambridge, MA: Harvard University Press, 2001). We might consider muscular Christianity's antisentimentality in relation to Moore's poetics. Moore's family also associated her with masculinity, designating her with masculine pronouns in their letters. Additionally, Moore was an adamant suffragist. On the connection between suffrage and masculinity, see, for example, Laura L. Behling, *The Masculine Woman in America, 1890–1935* (Urbana: University of Illinois Press, 2001).

72. Though Washington married, his association with celibacy is heightened by his childlessness.

73. Gregory, "Stamps, Money, Pop Culture, and Marianne Moore," 132.

74. Bishop, "Efforts of Affection," 144.

75. Eve Kosofsky Sedgwick, *Touching Feeling: Affect, Pedagogy, Performativity* (Durham, NC: Duke University Press, 2003), 68.

76. Michel Foucault, "The Battle for Chastity," in *Ethics: Subjectivity and Truth. The Essential Works of Michel Foucault, 1954–1984*, ed. Paul Rabinow (New York: New Press, 1994), 1:185–197.

77. Kent, *Making Girls into Women*, 223.

78. Arnold Rampersad, *The Life of Langston Hughes* (Oxford: Oxford University Press, 2002), 2: 419–420.

79. Rampersad, *Life of Langston Hughes*, 420.

80. As an extension of this democratic project, we might understand Moore to be

reversing the backward temporality that Valerie Rohy and others understand to be historically attached to black subjects. Valerie Rohy, *Anachronism and Its Others: Sexuality, Race, Temporality* (Albany: SUNY Press, 2009).

81. While it might be objected that my reading conflates Moorishness with Negroness, the two were much conflated during the period. Poem 14 in Claude McKay's "The Cycle" (1943), for example, contains the lines: "The New York critics say, when Shakespeare wrote / Othello, that he did not mean to make / A hero out of a Negro, that the Poet / Meant Arab, which the white mind could easier take. / Now everywhere in Europe, the word Moor / Means African black as it did in Shakespeare's day." See Claude McKay, *Complete Poems*, edited by William J. Maxwell (Urbana: University of Illinois Press, 2004), 248. For a historically longer view of this interrelation, see Emily C. Bartels, *Speaking of the Moor: From "Alcazar" to "Othello"* (Philadelphia: University of Pennsylvania Press, 2008).

82. See also Bishop, "Efforts of Affection," 128.

83. Moore, *Complete Prose*, 557.

84. Hilton Kramer, "Freezing the Blood and Making One Laugh," *New York Times*, March 15, 1981.

85. I borrow the phrase "erotics of enclosure" from Cary Howie, *Claustrophilia: The Erotics of Enclosure in Medieval Literature* (New York: Palgrave, 2007). For information about the activities and history of Cell 16, see Roxanne Dunbar-Ortiz, *Outlaw Woman: A Memoir of the War Years, 1960–1975* (San Francisco: City Lights, 2001), esp. 152–161.

Chapter Three. The Other Harlem Renaissance

1. James Baldwin, "Stagolee," in *A Lonely Rage: The Autobiography of Bobby Seale* (New York: Times Books, 1978), ix–x.

2. Jeremiah Moses Wilson's *Black Messiah and Uncle Toms: Social and Literary Manipulations of a Religious Myth* (University Park: Pennsylvania State University Press, 1982) similarly yokes Louis and Divine in his chapter "Waiting for the Messiah: From Joe Louis to Martin Luther King, Jr."

3. Langston Hughes, *The Collected Poems of Langston Hughes*, ed. Arnold Rampersad (New York: Vintage, 1995), 311–312.

4. On Louis, see, for example, Lewis A. Erenberg, *Greatest Fight of Our Generation: Louis vs. Schmeling* (New York: Oxford University Press, 2006); David Margolick, *Beyond Glory: Joe Louis vs Max Schmeling, and a World on the Brink* (New York: Knopf, 2005); and Patrick Myler, *Ring of Hate: Joe Louis vs Max Schmeling: The Fight of the Century* (New York: Arcade, 2005).

5. Jill Watts, *God, Harlem U.S.A.: The Father Divine Story* (Berkeley: University of California Press, 1992), 141–142.

6. R. Marie Griffith, "Body Salvation: New Thought, Father Divine, and the Feast of Material Pleasures," *Religion and American Culture* 11, no. 2 (2001): 119–120. For a description of Father Divine's followers, see Claude McKay, *Harlem: Negro Metropolis* (New York: Harcourt Brace Jovanovich, 1968), 39.

7. On celibacy and Divine, see Griffith, "Body Salvation," 142–144. See also Kenneth E.

Burnham, *God Comes to America: Father Divine and the Peace Mission Movement* (Boston: Lambeth, 1979), 116–118. On food, see Jualynne E. Dodson and Cheryl Townsend Gilkes, "'There's Nothing Like Church Food': Food and the U.S. Afro-Christian Tradition: Re-membering Community and Feeding the Embodied S/spirit(s)," *Journal of the American Academy of Religion* 63, no. 3 (1995): 519–538.

8. Hughes, *Collected Poems of Langston Hughes*, 403–404.

9. Chester Himes, *A Rage in Harlem* (New York: Vintage, 1991), 31.

10. Claude McKay, *Amiable with Big Teeth: A Novel of the Love Affair between the Communists and the Poor Black Sheep of Harlem*, 149, Columbia University Library, Samuel Roth Papers, Box 29, Folder 7.

11. In an earlier essay, "East River, Downtown," Baldwin was less complimentary of Divine: "My first hero was Joe Louis. I was ashamed of Father Divine." But even here, he acknowledges Divine in the register of heroism. See James Baldwin, "East River, Downtown," in *Nobody Knows My Name: More Notes of a Native Son* (New York: Dial, 1961), 72–82.

12. Sterling Brown, letter to Gorham Munson, January 9, 1940, National Archives, Record Group 69, Records of the Works Projects Administration, PI-57, Entry 27, Records of the Federal Writers' Project, Records of the Central Office, Reports and Miscellaneous Records Pertaining to Negro Studies, Box 2, Folder: Negro Studies. See also Joanna V. Gabbin, *Sterling A. Brown: Building the Black Aesthetic Tradition* (Westport, CT: Greenwood Press, 1985), 79–80; and Sterling Brown, *Sterling A. Brown's A Negro Looks at the South*, ed. John Edgar Tidwell and Mark A. Sanders (Oxford: Oxford University Press, 2007), 118–123.

13. There are certainly additional texts that might be influenced by Divine without directly representing him, such as "Fire and Cloud," in Richard Wright's *Uncle Tom's Children: Four Novellas* (New York: Harper, 1938), 221–317; and Robert Hayden's "Witch-Doctor," in *Collected Poems*, ed. Frederick Glaysherp (New York: Liveright, 1997), 35–37. While Hayden says in an interview with Dennis Gendron that "Witch-Doctor" is about Prophet Jones—"[I wrote a character-poem] about Prophet Jones ('Witch-Doctor')"—there also seem to be some elements of Father Divine in the portrait. Robert Hayden, "An Interview with Dennis Gendron," in *Robert Hayden: Essays on the Poetry*, ed. Laurence Goldstein and Robert Chrisman (Ann Arbor: University of Michigan Press, 2001), 15. On Father Divine's presence in this poem, see Robert Burns Shaw, *Blank Verse: A Guide to Its History and Use* (Athens: Ohio University Press, 2007), 179.

14. Watts, *God, Harlem U.S.A.*, 82–86.

15. I would read Divine's influence operating differently in *Quicksand* than Lewis does. Where Lewis reads Divine as a figure of lust akin to Reverend Green, I read *Quicksand* as a novel about the power of celibacy. When Helga abstains from sex, she is lavished with gifts and attention from James Vayle, Axel Olson, and other admirers; it is only when she engages in sex acts with Reverend Green and Robert Anderson that shame and suffering ensue. To put this differently, while Helga will not engage in the bald exchange of sex for money when she cannot find employment in Chicago, she will exchange mystified forms of sex (attraction, flirtation, and sensuality) for mysti-

fied currencies (fancy clothes, jewelry, and other gifts). As long as she exchanges sex for money in these mystified forms (that is, as long as she remains celibate), she both maintains her bourgeois respectability and is lavished with the security and material goods that she desires.

16. David Levering Lewis, *When Harlem Was in Vogue* (New York: Knopf, 1981), 255.

17. Lewis, *When Harlem Was in Vogue*, xvi.

18. Langston Hughes, *The Big Sea* (New York: Thunder's Mouth, 1986), 228.

19. William J. Maxwell, *New Negro, Old Left: African-American Writing and Communism between the Wars* (New York: Columbia University Press, 1999); Barbara Foley, *Radical Representations: Politics and Form in U.S. Proletarian Fiction, 1929–1941* (Durham, NC: Duke University Press, 1993); Barbara Foley, *Spectres of 1919: Class and Nation in the Making of the New Negro* (Urbana: University of Illinois Press, 2003); Tony Martin, *Literary Garveyism: Garvey, Black Arts, and the Harlem Renaissance* (Dover, MA: Majority, 1983); Winston James, *Holding Aloft the Banner of Ethiopia: Caribbean Radicalism in Early Twentieth-Century America* (New York: Verso, 1998); Clare Corbould, *Becoming African Americans: Black Public Life in Harlem, 1919–1939* (Cambridge, MA: Harvard University Press, 2009); James Smethurst, *The New Red Negro: The Literary Left and African American Poetry, 1930–1946* (New York: Oxford University Press, 1999).

20. Robert Weisbrot, *Father Divine and the Struggle for Racial Equality* (Urbana: University of Illinois Press, 1983), 148.

21. Weisbrot, *Father Divine and the Struggle for Racial Equality*, 148.

22. In a reversal of shopworn narratives about the relationship between African Americans and the Communist Party, Father Divine deftly took advantage of the communists. Watts, *God, Harlem U.S.A.*, 119–121. On the dynamism of relations between black and white communists, see Maxwell, *New Negro, Old Left*, 63–124.

23. Smethurst mentions Divine in a footnote; Smethurst, *New Red Negro*, 241n20.

24. For a discussion of the Old Negro's haunting of the New Negro, see Emily Bernard, "The Renaissance and the Vogue," in *The Cambridge Companion to the Harlem Renaissance*, ed. George Hutchinson (Cambridge: Cambridge University Press, 2007), 29–30. On the Peace Mission Movement's views on race, see Weisbrot, *Father Divine and the Struggle for Racial Equality*, 100–103; Watts, *God, Harlem U.S.A.*, 89–90.

25. Kevin K. Gaines, *Uplifting the Race: Black Leadership, Politics, and Culture in the Twentieth Century* (Chapel Hill: University of North Carolina Press, 1996), 2.

26. Gaines, *Uplifting the Race*, 4.

27. Shane Vogel, *The Scene of the Harlem Cabaret: Race, Sexuality, Performance* (Chicago: University of Chicago Press, 2009), 4.

28. Maxwell, *New Negro, Old Left*, 126.

29. This work provides a supplement to Beryl Satter's charting of the changing meanings of celibacy in the Peace Mission Movement. Beryl Satter, "Marcus Garvey, Father Divine and the Gender Politics of Race Difference and Race Neutrality," *American Quarterly* 48, no. 1 (1996): 43–76, esp. 63.

30. On lynching, see Lisa Duggan, *Sapphic Slashers: Sex, Violence, and American Modernity* (Durham, NC: Duke University Press, 2000), 18–19. On black women's virtue, see Evelyn Brook Higginbotham, *Righteous Discontent: The Women's Movement*

in the Black Baptist Church, 1880–1920 (Cambridge, MA: Harvard University Press, 1993), 189–190. Gertrude Stein's "Melanctha" (1909) exemplifies and contributes to this discourse of uncleanliness when she describes Rose Johnson as possessing "the simple, promiscuous unmorality of the black people," in Gertrude Stein, Selected Writings, ed. Carl Van Vechten (New York: Vintage, 1972), 340.

31. Siobhan Somerville, Queering the Color Line: Race and the Invention of Homosexuality in American Culture (Durham, NC: Duke University Press, 2000).

32. McKay's interest in Divine spans his conversion to Catholicism and may provide some clue to his mysterious change of heart.

33. McKay, Harlem, 25.

34. McKay, Harlem, 47.

35. George Hutchinson, The Harlem Renaissance in Black and White (Cambridge, MA: Belknap Press, 1995), 22.

36. McKay, Harlem, 26.

37. The book was written at a time when McKay had difficulty getting published. Moreover, my reading of Harlem: Negro Metropolis seems dissonant with the current critical emphases on movement and travel, offering a more entrenched, more at-home, older McKay alongside the more familiar diasporic younger McKay of such potent commentators as Michelle Ann Stephens and Brent Hayes Edwards. Michelle Ann Stephens, Black Empire: The Masculine Global Imaginary of Caribbean Intellectuals in the United States, 1914–1962 (Durham, NC: Duke University Press, 2005); Brent Hayes Edwards, The Practice of Diaspora: Literature, Translation, and the Rise of Black Internationalism (Cambridge, MA: Harvard University Press, 2003).

38. McKay, Harlem, 28.

39. McKay, Harlem, 18.

40. On rent parties, see James F. Wilson, Bulldaggers, Pansies, and Chocolate Babies: Performance, Race, and Sexuality in the Harlem Renaissance (Ann Arbor: University of Michigan Press, 2010), 12–28. On the "hot bed" system, see Lewis, When Harlem Was in Vogue, 108.

41. McKay, Harlem, 260.

42. McKay, Harlem, 90. Father Divine's frequent description here and elsewhere as "prancing" coupled with his flamboyant sartorial style and Cadillac might enrich Monica Miller's mapping of the interrelationship between black dandyism and black leadership. See Monica L. Miller, Slaves to Fashion: Black Dandyism and the Styling of Black Diasporic Identity (Durham, NC: Duke University Press, 2009); and Elisa Glick, Materializing Queer Desire: Oscar Wilde to Andy Warhol (Albany: SUNY Press, 2009), 83–106.

43. McKay, Harlem, 143.

44. McKay, Harlem, 191.

45. McKay, Harlem, 49, 91–92.

46. McKay, Harlem, 91–92.

47. McKay, Harlem, 71.

48. McKay, Harlem, 48.

49. McKay, Harlem, 71.

50. McKay, *Harlem*, 45.

51. Robert Stein, "Girls' Coöperative Boarding Homes," *Arena* 19 (March 1898): 398.

52. Joanne J. Meyerowitz, *Women Adrift: Independent Wage Earners in Chicago, 1880–1930* (Chicago: University of Chicago Press, 1988), esp. 55, 69–70, 80–81.

53. Weisbrot, *Father Divine and the Struggle for Racial Equality*, 123.

54. McKay, *Harlem*, 18. On Divine's business practices, see John Trinkaus, Alvin Puryear, and Joseph A. Giacaone, "Father Divine and the Development of African-American Small Business," *Journal of Developmental Entrepreneurship* 5, no. 3 (2000): 221–234.

55. Kathleen Coyne Kelly and Marina Leslie, "Introduction: The Epistemology of Virginity," in *Menacing Virgins: Representing Virginity in the Middle Ages and Renaissance*, ed. Kathleen Coyne Kelly and Marina Leslie (Newark: University of Delaware Press, 1999), 17.

56. Satter, "Marcus Garvey, Father Divine," 63.

57. Nancy Cott, "Passionlessness: An Interpretation of Victorian Sexual Ideology, 1790–1850," *Signs* 4, no. 2 (1978): 219–236.

58. Weisbrot, *Father Divine and the Struggle for Racial Equality*, 110–112; Watts, *God, Harlem U.S.A.*, 158. This might also be read as exemplary of the refunctioning of architecture characteristic of the Peace Mission Movement that Leonard Norman Primiano has charted in "'Bringing Perfection in These Different Places': Father Divine's Vernacular Architecture of Intention," *Folklore* 115 (2004): 3–26.

59. McKay, *Harlem*, 63.

60. Mary Poole, *The Segregated Origins of Social Security: African-Americans and the Welfare State* (Chapel Hill: University of North Carolina Press, 2006), 74.

61. Poole, *Segregated Origins of Social Security*, 94.

62. Poole, *Segregated Origins of Social Security*, 96, 36, 39.

63. While Pauline Hopkins's *Of One Blood* (1903) imagines the virgin Queen Candace and her celibate attendants, the scene crucially imagines them as African, not African American. Pauline Hopkins, *Of One Blood or, The Hidden Self* (New York: Washington Square, 2004).

64. Pauline Hopkins, "Higher Education of Colored Women in White Schools and Colleges," in *Daughter of the Revolution*, ed. Ira Dworkin (New Brunswick, NJ: Rutgers University Press, 2007), 198.

65. On this phenomenon among college-age women, see John D'Emilio and Estelle B. Freedman, *Intimate Matters: A History of Sexuality in America* (New York: Harper and Row, 1988), 190.

66. I borrow the term "conjugal imperative" from D. A. Miller, *Jane Austen, or the Secret of Style* (Princeton, NJ: Princeton University Press, 2003), 50; Jessie Redmon Fauset, *Plum Bun: A Novel without a Moral* (Boston: Beacon, 1990), 66.

67. Kathryn R. Kent, *Making Girls into Women: American Women's Writing and the Rise of Lesbian Identity* (Durham, NC: Duke University Press, 2003), 21–22. Kent's reading is supported by the statistical analysis in Peter Laipson's work, which sees blacks as having a much higher marriage rate than other national/racial groups. Peter Laipson "'I Have No Genius for Marriage': Bachelorhood in Urban America, 1870–1930" (PhD diss., University of Michigan, 2000), 53.

68. Lesbianism poses another threat to celibacy. For example, in Wallace Thurman's *The Blacker the Berry* (1929), the "spinster type" Miss Carrington, who accents the "*Miss*," attempts to seduce Emma Lou. Wallace Thurman, *The Blacker the Berry* (New York: Arno, 1969), 134–135.

69. Diane Batts Morrow, *Persons of Color and Religious at the Same Time: The Oblate Sisters of Providence, 1828–1860* (Chapel Hill: University of North Carolina Press, 2002), 1.

70. Morrow, *Persons of Color and Religious at the Same Time*, 9. See also Hazel V. Carby, *Reconstructing Womanhood: The Emergence of the Afro-American Woman Novelist* (New York: Oxford University Press, 1987), 20–39.

71. Morrow, *Persons of Color and Religious at the Same Time*, 50–51.

72. Morrow, *Persons of Color and Religious at the Same Time*, 53–54. For a discussion of the history of vow status, see Maureen Fitzgerald, *Habits of Compassion: Irish Catholic Nuns and the Origins of New York's Welfare System, 1830–1920* (Urbana: University of Illinois Press, 2006), 18.

73. Watts, *God, Harlem U.S.A.*, 2–4.

74. Watts, *God, Harlem U.S.A.*, 14, 180n3.

75. Watts, *God, Harlem U.S.A.*, 21.

76. For a history of the Sisters of the Holy Family by one of its early members, see Sister Mary Bernard Deggs, *No Cross, No Crown: Black Nuns in Nineteenth Century New Orleans*, ed. Virginia Meacham Gould and Charles E. Nolan (Bloomington: Indiana University Press, 2001).

77. On the Healy brothers, see Stephen J. Ochs, *Desegregating the Altar: The Josephites and the Struggle for Black Priests, 1871–1960* (Baton Rouge: Louisiana State University Press, 1990), 10, 26–29.

78. Ochs, *Desegregating the Altar*, 81.

79. Ochs, *Desegregating the Altar*, 69–71.

80. Ochs, *Desegregating the Altar*, 456.

81. Ochs, *Desegregating the Altar*, 123.

82. Ochs, *Desegregating the Altar*, 10–11, 52.

83. Ochs, *Desegregating the Altar*, 70, 80–81.

84. Ochs, *Desegregating the Altar*, 93–94.

85. Watts, *God, Harlem U.S.A.*, 30.

86. Watts, *God, Harlem U.S.A.*, 27.

87. As McKay mentions in *Harlem*, the little-remembered evangelist George Wilson Becton also advocated celibacy before his murder in 1933. Though celibacy was not a crucial element of Becton's World's Gospel Feast Party, he may also have contributed to the authorization of Divine's celibacy. McKay, *Harlem*, 85. For information on Becton, see Hughes, *Big Sea*, 275–278; and Cary D. Wintz and Paul Finkelman, *Encyclopedia of the Harlem Renaissance* (New York: Routledge, 2004).

88. Watts, *God, Harlem U.S.A.*, 40–41.

89. Watts, *God, Harlem U.S.A.*, 80, 107; Weisbrot, *Father Divine and the Struggle for Racial Equality*, 110.

90. McKay, *Harlem*, 71.

91. Elam J. Daniels, *"Father Divine": The World's Chief False Christ* (Winter Garden, FL: Biblical Echo, 1937), 48.

92. For a discussion of shock facing the intimacy between whites and blacks in the Peace Mission Movement, see Satter, "Marcus Garvey, Father Divine," 55.

93. Watts, *God, Harlem U.S.A.*, 164.

94. George Chauncey, *Gay New York: Gender, Urban Culture, and the Making of the Gay Male World, 1890–1940* (New York: Basic Books, 1994), 266.

95. Wallace Thurman, *Infants of the Spring* (Boston: Northeastern University Press, 1992); Richard Bruce Nugent, *Gentleman Jigger* (Cambridge, MA: Da Capo, 2008).

Chapter Four. The Celibate American

1. U.S. National Archives and Records Administration, Record Group INS, File 51787/11, Box 228.

2. U.S. National Archives and Records Administration, Record Group INS, File 51787/11, Box 228.

3. U.S. National Archives and Records Administration, Record Group INS, File 51787/11, Box 228.

4. U.S. National Archives and Records Administration, Record Group INS, File 51787/11, Box 228.

5. U.S. National Archives and Records Administration, Record Group INS, File 51787/11, Box 228.

6. Margot Canaday, "Who Is Homosexual? The Consolidation of Sexual Identities in Mid-Twentieth-Century American Immigration Law," *Law and Social Inquiry* 28, no. 2 (2003): 351–386. See also Siobhan B. Somerville, "Sexual Aliens and the Racialized State: A Queer Reading of the 1952 U.S. Immigration and Nationality Act," in *Queer Migrations: Sexuality, U.S. Citizenship, and Border Crossings*, ed. Eithne Luibhéid and Lionel Cantú Jr. (Minneapolis: University of Minnesota Press, 2005), 75–91.

7. Margot Canaday, *The Straight State: Sexuality and Citizenship in Twentieth-Century America* (Princeton, NJ: Princeton University Press, 2009), 220.

8. Laud Humphreys, *Tearoom Trade: Impersonal Sex in Public Places* (Chicago: Aldine, 1975), 131.

9. Humphreys, *Tearoom Trade*, 135.

10. Henry Abelove, *Deep Gossip* (Minneapolis: University of Minnesota Press, 2003), 73–74.

11. Abelove, *Deep Gossip*, 75.

12. Abelove, *Deep Gossip*, 78.

13. Abelove, *Deep Gossip*, 76.

14. Abelove, *Deep Gossip*, 73.

15. Abelove, *Deep Gossip*, 72.

16. While Baldwin and Auden almost certainly knew each other (possibly through Harold Norse) and respected each other's work, Auden does not seem to have been a role model for or provided a blueprint for Baldwin in the way he does for so many

other queer writers. Undoubtedly, the fact that Baldwin is the only black artist in Abelove's group of "commuters" is a factor here.

17. Elizabeth Bishop, "A Brief Remembrance and a Brief Tribute: Marianne Moore, W. H. Auden," in *Elizabeth Bishop: Poems, Prose, and Letters*, ed. Robert Giroux and Lloyd Schwartz (New York: Library of America, 2008), 729.

18. Sherill Tippins, *February House: The Story of W. H. Auden, Carson McCullers, Jane and Paul Bowles, Benjamin Britten, and Gypsy Rose Lee, under One Roof in Wartime America* (New York: Houghton Mifflin, 2005).

19. Ted Morgan, *Literary Outlaw: The Life and Times of William S. Burroughs* (New York: Holt, 1988), 72.

20. Aidan Wasley, "Auden and Poetic Inheritance," *Raritan* 19, no. 2 (1999): 133–134.

21. Geoff Ward, *Statutes of Liberty: The New York School of Poets* (New York: Palgrave Macmillan, 2001), 94.

22. Ward, *Statutes of Liberty*, 4.

23. Ned Rorem, *Settling the Score: Essays on Music* (New York: Anchor, 1989), 239.

24. George Chauncey, *Gay New York: Gender, Urban Culture, and the Making of the Gay Male World, 1890–1940* (New York: Basic Books, 1994), 11.

25. See Humphrey Carpenter, *W. H. Auden: A Biography* (Boston: George Allen and Unwin, 1981), 288–293; Richard Davenport-Hines, *Auden* (New York: Pantheon, 1995), 205–207; and P. N. Furbank, *E. M. Forster: A Life* (New York: Harcourt Brace, 1978), 237.

26. W. H. Auden to E. R. Dodds, March 11, 1940, in W. H. Auden, *The Map of All My Youth: Early Works, Friends, and Influences*, ed. Katherine Bucknell and Nicholas Jenkins (Oxford: Oxford University Press, 1990), 112–116.

27. Susannah Gottlieb underscores the philosophical importance of marriage in shaping Auden's poetry and poetics. Susannah Young-ah Gottlieb, "'With Conscious Artifice': Auden's Defense of Marriage," *diacritics* 35, no. 4 (2005): 23–41.

28. Aihwa Ong, *Flexible Citizenship: The Cultural Logics of Transnationality* (Durham, NC: Duke University Press, 1999).

29. W. H. Auden to John Auden, n.d. [1926 or 1927?], uncataloged letters in the Berg Collection at the New York Public Library.

30. *The Orators* might provide further evidence for the dating of these letters to 1927 as the Airman writes in his journal: "Very little progress this year. Never quite as bad as that dreadful spring of 1927, but still generally at week-ends. So much better when seeing E." W. H. Auden, *English Auden: Poems, Essays, and Dramatic Writings 1927–1939*, ed. Edward Mendelson (London: Faber, 1977), 91. Here we might read the Airman as a version of Auden; the referenced "progress" is to the Airman's kleptomania—the chief symptom of his homosexuality; the 1927 date here alludes to Auden's attempts at celibacy, which began, only to fail, in this same year. Celibacy's curative powers are ineffectual for treating homosexuality because he is "so much better when seeing E."

31. Davenport-Hines, *Auden*, 66.

32. This attribution of homosexuality to his mother is evident, for example, in his claim that "the bugger got too much mother love, so sheers off women altogether, the

whorer too little, so must always have another." Richard R. Bozorth, *Auden's Games of Knowledge: Poetry and the Meanings of Homosexuality* (New York: Columbia University Press, 2001), 74.

33. Gustave Flaubert, *Correspondance* (Paris: Gallimard, 1973), 1: 720.

34. Gustave Flaubert, *Selected Letters*, trans. Geoffrey Wall (New York: Penguin, 1997), 160. I have slightly altered Wall's translation.

35. Sigmund Freud, *Totem and Taboo: Some Points of Agreement between the Mental Lives of Savages and Neurotics*, trans. James Strachey (New York: Norton, 1989), 176.

36. Davenport-Hines, *Auden*, 66.

37. My discussion later in this chapter of Auden's incestuous desire for his father bears out Judith Butler's claim that the incest taboo is imbricated with the taboo on homosexuality. Judith Butler, *Gender Trouble: Feminism and the Subversion of Identity* (1990; repr., New York: Routledge, 1999).

38. From the late 1920s until his immigration to America, Auden oscillates between seeing celibacy as a phase to be passed through (the "ingrown virginity" in the Hopkins-esque "Petition") on the one hand and a technique for attaining homosexuality's revolutionary power on the other hand (the Bwili initiation in *The Orators* [1932] and his "white" marriage to Mann).

39. Auden is usually said to be silent in the face of the controversy; Carpenter, *W. H. Auden*, 292.

40. Because a complete enumeration of the forms Auden employs is not available in the secondary literature, and those catalogues that attempt to be full often contain omissions or misclassifications, I have compiled a complete list of poems and their verse forms. It is important to note that Auden does not utilize the blank verse of the Shakespearean original. Epigraph—Emily Brontë's "Plead for Me" is written in a fairly regular iambic tetrameter. "Preface"—fairly closely follows an iambic trimeter, but with one anapest to each line. "Prospero to Ariel"—is spoken in elegiacs of unrhymed alternating thirteen- and eleven-syllable lines with interludes of rhymed, loose tetrameter; it closes with a loose two-stress accentual song. Auden described Prospero's speech to Malcolm Cowley as in "couplets of thirteen and eleven syllables, with the vowels elided" (Auden, *The Sea and the Mirror: A Commentary on Shakespeare's "The Tempest,"* ed. Arthur Kirsch [Princeton, NJ: Princeton University Press, 2003], 77). Antonio's words are written in *terza rima*, and the italicized commentaries that he affixes to the other cast members' speeches are in (modified) rhymed common meter quatrains. Ferdinand—a sonnet in hexameter. Stephano—a ballade. Gonzalo—rhyming trochaic tetrameter catalectic. Adrian and Francisco—a solitary heroic couplet. Alsonso—an epistle in syllabics: nine-syllable lines with each twelve-line stanza culminating in a seven-syllable line. Master and Boatswain—a song consisting of six-line stanzas composed of a common meter quatrain followed by a tetrameter couplet. Sebastian—a sestina that slightly violates the end-word order. Trinculo—quatrains in iambic trimeter with rhymes in the second and fourth lines, before becoming decasyllabic *terza rima*. Miranda—a villanelle. "Caliban to the Audience"—a piece of Jamesian prose. Postscript—trochaic tetrameter catalectic. For a particularly good discussion of the work's genre, see Edward Mendelson, *Later Auden* (New York: Farrar, Straus and Giroux, 1999), 205–206. The work is sometimes

understood as a closet drama. This description seems apt in light of Nick Salvato's recent work, which sees closet drama's closet as a key site for working through modernist sexual formations. See Nick Salvato, *Uncloseting Drama: American Modernism and Queer Performance* (New Haven, CT: Yale University Press, 2010). Martin Puchner's insight that closet drama is a space for reimagining the public sphere is also important here for thinking about Auden's text. Martin Puchner, *Stage Fright: Modernism, Anti-theatricality, and Drama* (Baltimore: Johns Hopkins University Press, 2002), 9–11.

41. While saying that Auden transplants the play "into an American milieu" is something of a simplification, as the bulk of my chapter will suggest, there is clearly an Americanizing project at work. For example, Auden's choice to shift the focus of *The Tempest* to those characters whom he saw as the most lonely ("rejected")—Antonio and Caliban—implies a symptomatic move to make the Shakespeare play more suitable for the American canon and for an American audience in light of his (stated) conception of American literature: "'The first feature that strikes a European about characters in American fiction . . . is their extreme loneliness'" (Carpenter, *W. H. Auden*, 282). This reading is further supported by Auden's use of colloquial American words like "picket fences," "back yard," and "sugarloaf sea." The slang phrase "sugarloaf sea" does not sound particularly American, but Auden told the Harvard Shakespearean Theodore Spencer that he copied it out of *The American Thesaurus of Slang* (1942), suggesting his desire to write in an American idiom (as opposed to an English one) by including these phrases and others. The quoted phrases above appear in Auden, *The Sea and the Mirror*, 35, 4, 46. All other references to this work will be cited parenthetically in the text. An examination of the Berg manuscript also reveals an additionally Americanizing variant when one remembers the turkey's indigenousness to the New World: "the Bard / was sober when he wrote" is replaced by "the bard we most often quote / Talked turkey when he wrote" (Auden, *The Sea and the Mirror*, 75). For further elaboration on "sugarloaf sea," see Mendelson, *Later Auden*, 233.

42. "Commentary" is meant in the medieval sense of the term in which seriality dislocates the primary text's continuity and narrative trajectory. Auden is fascinated by Langland throughout much of his career. On this connection, see Nicholas Howe, "Praise and Lament: The Afterlife of Old English Poetry in Auden, Hill, and Gunn," in *Words and Works: Studies in Medieval English Language and Literature in Honour of Fred C. Robinson*, ed. Peter S. Baker and Nicholas Howe (Toronto: University of Toronto Press, 1998), 293–310. *In Time of War* also has a section with the generic designation "Commentary." Auden, *English Auden*, 249–270. For an extended discussion of this designation, see Alan Ansen's unpublished essay "Crisis and Festival: A Study of W. H. Auden's *The Sea and the Mirror*," Berg Collection, Call No. (Auden), 6–9. For recent work in medieval studies on commentary, see Lawler Francesco del Punta, "The Genre of Commentaries in the Middle Ages and Its Relation to the Nature and Originality of Medieval Thought," in *Was ist Philosophie im Mittelalter? / Qu'est-ce que la philosophie au Moyen Âge? / What Is Philosophy in the Middle Ages*, Jan Aertsen and Andreas Speer, 138–151 (Berlin: Walter de Gruyter, 1998). For more on the commentary as genre, see Martin Irvine, review of "*Medieval Literary Criticism and Theory, c. 1100–c. 1375: The Commentary-Tradition*," *Speculum* 66, no. 2 (1991): 451–453.

43. See Carpenter, *W. H. Auden*, 253, 339; and Davenport-Hines, *Auden*, 207.

44. For accounts of the rejection—an incident that took place during the early days of the composition of *The Sea and the Mirror*—see Carpenter, *W. H. Auden*, 324; and Mendelson, *Later Auden*, 207. For an account of Auden's participation in the United States Strategic Bombing Survey, see John Xiros Cooper, "'The Crow on the Crematorium Chimney': Germany, Summer 1945," *English Studies in Canada* 30, no. 3 (2004): 129–144.

45. For a good overview of Auden's relation to Marx and Marxist thinking, see John Lucas, "Auden's Politics: Power, Authority, and the Individual," in *The Cambridge Companion to W. H. Auden*, ed. Stan Smith (Cambridge: Cambridge University Press, 2004), 152–164.

46. For an overview of these decisions, see *United States v. Schneiderman*, 33 F. Supp. 510, 1940. The McCarran-Walter Act redoubled the persecution of queer citizens by targeting communists because both homosexuals and communists were lumped together (in a well-documented link) as threats to national security. The homology between communists and queers stemmed from their supposed abilities to blend into the mainstream, detect one another, and subvert political and social relations. See Canaday, *Straight State*; Somerville, "Sexual Aliens and the Racialized State"; and Lee Edelman, "Tearooms and Sympathy; or, the Epistemology of the Water Closet," in *Homographesis: Essays in Gay Literary and Cultural Theory* (New York: Routledge, 1994), 148–170.

47. Judge Learned Hand ruled that the public charge suggested "dependency not delinquency" and that people could no longer be deported for petty crimes. Mae M. Ngai, *Impossible Subjects: Illegal Aliens and the Making of Modern America* (Princeton, NJ: Princeton University Press, 2005), 81. See also Canaday, *Straight State*, 215.

48. Work on the intersections of sexuality and citizenship has dated the rise of queer citizenship as coextensive with the AIDS crisis. Shane Phelan, *Sexual Strangers: Gays, Lesbians, and Dilemmas of Citizenship* (Philadelphia: Temple University Press, 2001), 1–5; David Bell and Jon Binnie, *The Sexual Citizen: Queer Politics and Beyond* (Cambridge: Polity, 2000), 35; Eric O. Clarke, *Virtuous Vice: Homoeroticism and the Public Sphere* (Durham, NC: Duke University Press, 2000), 1, 18, 47–48, 101–105.

49. This tradition is also importantly echoed by James in his "Introduction to *The Tempest*," as well as by the older Auden in his *Lectures on Shakespeare*. Henry James, "Introduction to *The Tempest*," in *Henry James: Literary Criticism: Essays on Literature, American Writers, and English Writers*, ed. Leon Edel (New York: Library of America, 1984), 1:1205–1220. W. H. Auden, *Lectures on Shakespeare*, ed. Arthur C. Kirsch (Princeton, NJ: Princeton University Press, 2000).

50. W. H. Auden, *The Complete Works of W. H. Auden: Prose*, vol. 2, *1939–1948*, ed. Edward Mendelson (Princeton, NJ: Princeton University Press, 1996), 244.

51. Jonathan Goldberg, *Tempest in the Caribbean* (Minneapolis: University of Minnesota Press, 2004), 20–22.

52. William Shakespeare, *The Tempest*, ed. Stephen Orgel (Oxford: Oxford University Press, 1998), 120–121 (1.2.347–350) and (1.2.362–3).

53. Following Auden's conceptualization of celibacy, I consciously use the idiom of the repressive hypothesis here.

54. In a letter to a friend on Caliban's inability to belong, Auden writes: "Caliban does disturb me profoundly because he doesn't fit in; it is exactly as if one of the audience had walked onto the stage and insisted on taking part in the action." Auden, *The Sea and the Mirror*, xxx.

55. For a different reading of representation in this passage, see Lucy S. McDiarmid and John McDiarmid, "Artifice and Self-Consciousness in *The Sea and the Mirror*," in *W. H. Auden: Modern Critical Views*, ed. Harold Bloom (New York: Chelsea House, 1986), 70.

56. For an almost identical description of the scene at the beginning of Caliban's speech, see Leon Edel, *Henry James: A Life* (New York: Harper and Row, 1985), 369. Additionally, Auden's camp nickname was "The Master" (or "Miss Master"), although it is not clear whether Auden acquired the nickname from writing *The Sea and the Mirror* or whether it was his nickname earlier. See also Nicholas Jenkins, "Auden in America," in *The Cambridge Companion to W. H. Auden*, ed. Stan Smith (Cambridge: Cambridge University Press, 2004), 49; and Dorothy J. Farnan, *Auden in Love* (New York: Simon and Schuster, 1984), 177.

57. Jonathan Goldberg, "Under the Covers with Caliban," in *Shakespeare's Hand* (Minneapolis: University of Minnesota Press, 2003), 286–307. Goldberg's reading of Caliban's monstrous birth (not of woman born) further identifies Auden and Caliban, following Mendelson's reading that Auden believed that his mother's miscarriage (a murderous birth) enabled his life. Mendelson, *Later Auden*, 219–220.

58. Davenport-Hines, *Auden*, 73.

59. Carpenter, *W. H. Auden*, 41.

60. For information about Henry James's citizenship and cultural identity, see Alan G. James, "A Memorable Naturalization: How Henry James Became a British Subject and Lost His United States Citizenship," *Henry James Review* 12, no. 1 (1991): 55–68; and Pamela Thurschwell, "'That Imperial Stomach Is No Seat for Ladies: Henry James, the First World War and the Politics of Identification," in *Modernist Sexualities*, ed. Hugh Stevens and Caroline Howlett (New York: Manchester University Press, 2000), 167–183.

61. William J. Maxwell, "Ghostreaders and Diaspora-Writers: Four Theses on the FBI and African American Modernism," in *Modernism on File: Writers, Artists, and the FBI, 1920–1950*, ed. Claire A. Culleton and Karen Leick (New York: Palgrave, 2008), 27.

62. William J. Maxwell, "F.B. Eyes: The Bureau Reads Claude McKay," in *Left of the Color Line: Race, Radicalism, and Twentieth-Century Literature of the United States*, ed. Bill V. Mullen and James Smethurst (Chapel Hill: University of North Carolina Press, 2003), 45.

63. Stephen G. Kellman, "Raising Muscovite Ducks and Government Suspicions: Henry Roth and the FBI," in *Modernism on File: Writers, Artists, and the FBI, 1920–1950*, ed. Claire A. Culleton and Karen Leick (New York: Palgrave, 2008), 40.

64. Maxwell, "F.B. Eyes," 47.

65. Maxwell, "F.B. Eyes," 47.

66. Maxwell, "F.B. Eyes," 40.

67. See, for example, Monroe K. Spears, *The Poetry of W. H. Auden: The Disen-*

chanted Island (New York: Oxford University Press, 1963), which is still the most important work of scholarship on the text. Edward O'Shea's work provides an exception, as he reads the text as being located at "the nadir of Modernist confidence." Edward O'Shea, "Modernist Versions of *The Tempest*: Auden, Woolf, Tippett," in *The Tempest: Critical Essays*, ed. Patrick M. Murphy (New York: Routledge, 2001), 544.

68. There seems to be a particular shame that accrues around geography—"some *louche* hotel" (40, his emphasis); the "upstairs" "at Dirty Dick's and Sloppy Joe's" (22); "promiscuous pastures" (42)—that is, the shame of sexual acts is heightened by their public location. Moreover, the public location of these acts does not discriminate between kinds of acts—all sex acts in public are shameful. That is, sex when exposed is a universally shameful experience, one that does not attach itself solely to homosexual acts. Because sex cannot be compatible with public life, *The Sea and the Mirror*, particularly Caliban's address, critiques the state's exclusive condemnation of homosexuality and posits the mundanity of sexual shame. The everydayness and universality of this shameful sex undermine the relationship between shame and sex, as well as the specific prohibition against homosexuality with regard to citizenship.

69. See, for example, Louise Bogan, "Verse," rev. of *For the Time Being*, W. H. Auden, *New Yorker*, September 23–30, 1944, 77–78; George Fraser, "Auden in Midstream," in *Essays on Twentieth Century Poets* (Totowa, NJ: Rowman and Littlefield, 1977), 140–141; and Stephen Spender, "Stephen Spender on Argument or Experience, Auden," review of *For the Time Being*, W. H. Auden, *Time and Tide*, August 25, 1945, 711–712.

70. Auden, *Lectures on Shakespeare*, 296.

71. Jacques Derrida, "Living on—Border Lines," in *Deconstruction and Criticism*, ed. Harold Bloom, Paul de Man, Jacques Derrida, Geoffrey Hartman, and J. Hillis Miller (New York: Seabury, 1979), 105.

72. David J. Barker, "Where Is Ireland in *The Tempest*?," in *Shakespeare and Ireland: History, Politics, Culture*, ed. Mark Thornton Burnett and Ramona Wray (London: Macmillan, 1997), 68.

73. For a discussion of the text in relation to another island, "Atlantis," see Alan Ansen, "Atlantis," Berg Collection, Call No. (Auden), 2. Stuart Christie has suggested the importance of islands for Auden in destabilizing national geographies. Stuart Christie, "Disorientations: Canon without Context in Auden's 'Sonnets from China,'" PMLA 120, no. 5 (2005): 1580–1581.

74. My essay might be seen as extending Robert Caserio's work in new ways. Caserio writes: "The elevation of the refugee as the model, and not the antitype, of citizenship is influenced in Auden's case by his homosexuality." Robert L. Caserio, "Auden's New Citizenship," *Raritan* 17, no. 2 (1997): 91.

Chapter Five. Celibate Modernity

1. Mark Wiener, unnamed cover photograph of Andy Warhol, *Penthouse Forum: The International Journal of Human Relations* 10, no. 4 (1981).

2. John Wilcock and a cast of thousands, *The Autobiography and Sex Life of Andy Warhol* (New York: Other Scenes, 1971), n.p. [Sam Green, p. 2]. For Warhol's account

of Johns's and Rauschenberg's opposition to his swishiness, see Andy Warhol and Pat Hackett, *POPism: The Warhol Sixties* (New York: Mariner Books, 1990), 14.

3. Wilcock, *Autobiography and Sex Life of Andy Warhol*, n.p. [Amaya, p. 2].

4. Andy Warhol, *The Andy Warhol Diaries*, ed. Pat Hackett (New York: Warner Books, 1989), February 17, 1981.

5. On Warhol's association with adultery, see Andy Warhol, *The Philosophy of Andy Warhol (From A to B and Back Again)* (New York: Harcourt Brace Jovanovich, 1975), 21. On the misattribution of albinism, see Tony Scherman and David Dalton, *Pop: The Genius of Andy Warhol* (New York: HarperCollins, 2009), 7. For a more expansive list of associations with "a," see Wayne Koestenbaum, *Andy Warhol* (New York: Viking, 2001), 17.

6. For more on the letter "V," see chapter 2. We might also hear the echo of Duchamp's alter ego, Rrose Sélavy, in "Andy Warhol is a 'V.'" For an excellent discussion of this Duchampian identity, see Rosalind Krauss, *Bachelors* (Cambridge, MA: MIT Press, 1999), 1–50.

7. Michael North, *Machine-Age Comedy* (Oxford: Oxford University Press, 2009), 38.

8. Jennifer Doyle, Jonathan Flatley, and José Esteban Muñoz, "Introduction," in *Pop Out*, ed. Jennifer Doyle, Jonathan Flatley, and José Esteban Muñoz (Durham, NC: Duke University Press, 1996), 1.

9. Doyle, Flatley, and Muñoz, "Introduction," 1. José Esteban Muñoz has again recently cautioned against this de-gaying in his *Cruising Utopia: The Then and There of Queer Futurity* (New York: New York University Press, 2009), 36.

10. Doyle, Flatley, and Muñoz, "Introduction," 1–2.

11. *Penthouse Forum: The International Journal of Human Relations* 10, no. 4 (1981): 20, 23.

12. Andy Warhol, *I'll Be Your Mirror: The Selected Andy Warhol Interviews*, ed. Kenneth Goldsmith (New York: Carroll and Graf, 2004), 218.

13. Ultra Violet, *Famous for 15 Minutes: My Years with Andy Warhol* (London: Backinprint, 2004), 245. Scherman and Dalton's biography of Warhol suggests that the presence of "'very prominent hemangiomas, or collections of blood vessels'" on Warhol's scrotum may have contributed to what they call his "well-known discomfort with sex." Scherman and Dalton, *Pop*, 8.

14. Kelly Cresap, *Pop, Trickster, Fool: Warhol Performs Naivete* (Urbana: University of Illinois Press, 2004), 74; Koestenbaum, *Andy Warhol*, 33–52.

15. Victor Bockris, *Warhol: The Biography* (Cambridge, MA: Da Capo, 2003), 209. Fagan was the subject of Warhol's *Screen Test # 1* (New York, 1965).

16. This passage's odd investment in anonymity might suggest a taboo around celibacy as well as homosexuality.

17. Violet, *Famous for 15 Minutes*, 244; Jean Stein, *Edie: American Girl* (New York: Grove, 1994), 398.

18. Warhol and Hackett, *POPism*, 119. Nico is described as having a "medieval monastery look," and Ondine is nicknamed "Pope Ondine." Moreover, Warhol describes Pope Paul VI as giving him "a real lesson in show business and Pop style," summoning his nickname as the "Pope of Pop." Warhol and Hackett, *POPism*, 145, 55, 134. Warhol possessed the ability to make those around him feel like virgins even if they were not.

Ultra Violet describes this effect: "At one revoltingly vile scene of torture, I vomit all over Andy. I have to leave the movie house. Exposure to that film makes me back into a virgin for a whole season." Violet, *Famous for 15 Minutes*, 159–160.

19. Quoted in Bockris, *Warhol*, 185.

20. Another possibility would read all these assertions of celibacy as "put-ons." Many times throughout *The Autobiography and Sex Life of Andy Warhol*, Warhol is accused of being a fraud or a con man: "You Andy Warhol are the greatest put-on since P. T. Barnum. You believe like P. T. Barnum that there's a sucker born every minute." Wilcock, *Autobiography and Sex Life of Andy Warhol*, n.p. [Paul Morrisey, pp. 2–3]. On Warhol's relation to "put-ons," see Cresap, *Pop, Trickster, Fool*; and Nicholas De Villiers, *Opacity and the Closet: Queer Tactics in Foucault, Barthes, and Warhol* (Minneapolis: University of Minnesota Press, 2012).

21. Warhol and Hackett, *POPism*, 139.

22. Arthur C. Danto, "Andy Warhol: Brillo Box," *Artforum International* 32, no. 1 (1993): 128–129. See also Arthur C. Danto, *Beyond the Brillo Box: The Visual Arts in Posthistorical Perspective* (New York: Farrar, Straus and Giroux, 1992).

23. John Guillory, "The Bachelor State: Philosophy and Sovereignty in Bacon's New Atlantis," in *Politics and the Passions, 1500–1800*, ed. Victoria Kahn, Neil Saccamano, and Daniela Coli (Princeton, NJ: Princeton University Press, 2006), 55. We might also add Emanuel Swedenborg to Guillory's list.

24. Guillory, "Bachelor State," 58.

25. Guillory, "Bachelor State," 56.

26. As Guillory notes, Ray Monk's biography of Wittgenstein is full of rich detail about the intersection between the philosopher's sexual life and his philosophical work, including his contemplation of becoming a monk and most people's understanding of him as a virgin. On this latter claim, Wittgenstein's friend Rowland Hutt remembers the philosopher saying something on the order of "Most people would think that I have had no relationship with women, but I have." Ray Monk, *Ludwig Wittgenstein: The Duty of Genius* (New York: Free Press, 1990), 369. I follow Eric Hayot in taking seriously what he terms the "example-effect" of these examples, seeing content in that which seems arbitrary. Eric Hayot, *The Hypothetical Mandarin: Sympathy, Modernity, and Chinese Pain* (Oxford: Oxford University Press, 2009), 25–30.

27. Donald Rackin, "Mind over Matter: Sexuality and Where the 'Body Happens to Be' in the *Alice* Books," in *Textual Bodies: Changing Boundaries of Literary Representations* (Albany: SUNY Press, 1997), 161–183.

28. George Santayana's contention that "sex is not the only object of sexual passion" also provides an important precursor to what I see as Warhol's relation to the object world. George Santayana, *The Sense of Beauty: Being the Outline of Aesthetic Theory* (New York: Scribner's, 1896, repr. Dover, 1955), 40.

29. Virginia Woolf's depiction of Mr. Ramsay in *To the Lighthouse* (1927; San Diego: Harcourt, 1981) would also provide a fictional representation of the necessity of celibacy for great philosophy.

30. Michael Warner, "Uncritical Reading," in *Polemic: Critical or Uncritical*, ed. Jane Gallop (New York: Routledge, 2004), 34.

31. In understanding Warhol's marriage to his tape recorder as an act of philosophical bachelorhood, my reading departs from seeing it as an instance of what Jennifer Terry calls "objectum-sexuality." Jennifer Terry, "Loving Objects," *Trans-humanities* 2, no. 1 (2010): 33–75.

32. Guillory, "Bachelor State," 53.

33. Warhol, *Philosophy*, 111.

34. Warhol and Hackett, *POPism*, 64–65.

35. Warhol, *Philosophy*, 199.

36. Warhol, *Philosophy*, 112.

37. One might imagine that the critique of marriage goes further—that Warhol imagines it as an inhuman relation, one that takes place between man and machine.

38. Warhol, *Philosophy*, 199.

39. Elizabeth Freeman, *The Wedding Complex: Forms of Belonging in Modern American Culture* (Durham, NC: Duke University Press, 2002), x.

40. The Factory even has a party for a videotape machine. Warhol and Hackett, *POPism*, 119.

41. Wilcock, *Autobiography and Sex Life of Andy Warhol*, n.p. [Charles Henri Ford, p. 3]. Ford's definition of Warhol's sexualized celibacy provides a rich description of Warhol's cult classic *Blow Job* (New York, 1963) and dovetails with my earlier claim that celibacy is a sexuality without a normative aspiration to sexual acts.

42. Roland Barthes, *Writing Degree Zero*, trans. Annette Lavers and Colin Smith (New York: Hill and Wang, 1968).

43. Lauren Berlant, *The Queen of America Goes to Washington City: Essays on Sex and Citizenship* (Durham, NC: Duke University Press, 1997). Warhol will return to this theme in his *Reigning Queens* series (exhibited in 1985), which features portraits of the queens of England, Denmark, the Netherlands, and Swaziland.

44. Scherman and Dalton, *Pop*, 271.

45. Margot Canaday, *The Straight State: Sexuality and Citizenship in Twentieth-Century America* (Princeton, NJ: Princeton University Press, 2009), 241; Lee Dode, *A History of Homosexuality* (Victoria, BC: Trafford, 2003), 87.

46. Michael Moon, *A Small Boy and Others: Imitation and Initiation in American Culture from Henry James to Andy Warhol* (Durham, NC: Duke University Press, 1998), 121.

47. Moon, *Small Boy and Others*, 123.

48. This sexless reading follows Juan Suárez in seeing "the film revolv[ing] around the commodity status of the hustler-protagonist," but where Suárez understands the film to confirm his commodity status in terms of use value, I see the film largely in terms of exchange value and the ensuing social relations created and transfigured through exchange. Juan A. Suárez, *Bike Boys, Drag Queens, and Superstars: Avant-Garde, Mass Culture, and Gay Identities in the 1960s Underground Cinema* (Bloomington: Indiana University Press, 1996), 241–242.

49. Eve Kosofsky Sedgwick, *Between Men: English Literature and Male Homosocial Desire* (New York: Columbia University Press, 1985), 49.

50. In *Chelsea Girls* (1966), Eric offers a Warholian example of this more familiar

autoerotic celibacy: "I don't have anything to say so I'll just sit and groove on myself. . . . Do you ever just groove on your body?"

51. Sholom Asch's *The God of Vengeance* further suggests the difficulty of reading chastity in relation to queer sexuality. When asked by her father whether she is "still a chaste Jewish daughter" after (possibly) engaging in lesbian acts, Rifkele responds, "I don't know . . ." Sholom Asch, *The God of Vengeance* (Charleston: Bibliolife, 2009), 94.

52. Warhol, *Philosophy*, 45.

53. Quoted in Breanne Fahs, "The Radical Possibilities of Valerie Solanas," *Feminist Studies* 34, no. 3 (2008): 601.

54. Avital Ronell, "Deviant Payback: The Aims of Valerie Solanas," in Valerie Solanas, scum *Manifesto* (New York: Verso, 2004), 8n7. Another critical tradition sees Warhol and Solanas as sharing a great deal: "When Andy Warhol looked into the eyes of Valerie Solanas, he would have seen much more of himself than when he looked in the eyes of a beautiful debutante like Edie Sedgwick or of one of the gorgeous male hustlers who decorated the Factory." Mary Harron, "Introduction: On Valerie Solanas," in *I Shot Andy Warhol* (New York: Grove, 1995), xix.

55. While Emma Goldman did marry, it was an ironic marriage of convenience (rather than love) and occurred after a lifetime of philosophical opposition to marriage. Similarly, Beauvoir famously turned down Sartre's marriage proposal, choosing to remain unmarried all her life.

56. Ronell, "Deviant Payback," 8.

57. Valerie Solanas, scum *Manifesto* (New York: Verso, 2004), 72, 74.

58. Quoted in Fahs, "Radical Possibilities of Valerie Solanas," 591.

59. Fahs, "Radical Possibilities of Valerie Solanas," 591.

60. Warhol and Hackett, *POPism*, 16.

61. Ronell, "Deviant Payback," 6, 11; Fahs, "Radical Possibilities of Valerie Solanas," 604.

62. A Southern Women's Writing Collective, "Sex Resistance in Heterosexual Arrangements," in *The Sexual Liberals and the Attack on Feminism*, ed. Dorchen Leidholdt and Janice G. Raymond (New York: Pergamon, 1990), 140–147.

63. Solanas, scum *Manifesto*, 35. This interest in the destruction of masculinity is echoed in another 1968 text: Gore Vidal's *Myra Breckinridge*. Gore Vidal, *Myra Breckinridge / Myron* (New York: Penguin Books, 1997).

64. Solanas, scum *Manifesto*, 69.

65. Solanas, scum *Manifesto*, 65.

66. Solanas, scum *Manifesto*, 69.

67. Solanas, scum *Manifesto*, 60.

68. See, for example, the interview I quoted from earlier in which Warhol says to George Gruskin, "I don't have any [sex life]." Gruskin follows up with "That's strange. Are you devoted so much to your art and movie-making that you have no time?," to which Warhol replies, "That is right." Warhol, *I'll Be Your Mirror*, 218.

69. Fahs, "Radical Possibilities of Valerie Solanas," 595; Ronell, "Deviant Payback," 9.

70. Solanas, scum *Manifesto*, 69.

71. Solanas, scum *Manifesto*, 71.

72. Solanas, scum Manifesto, 76.

73. A Walk into the sea: Danny Williams and the Warhol Factory, directed by Esther Robinson (2007), dvd.

74. Quoted in Marcie Frank, "Popping Off Warhol: From the Gutter to the Underground and Beyond," in Pop Out, ed. Jennifer Doyle, Jonathan Flatley, and José Esteban Muñoz (Durham, NC: Duke University Press, 1996), 210.

75. After getting an editing job, Warhol's sometime boyfriend Danny Williams says, "'I finally have an identity of my own. Up until now, I was just a groupie with no real reason to exist.'" Warhol and Hackett, POPism, 154.

76. On Warhol's relationship to his coterie, see Koestenbaum, Andy Warhol, 2–5; and Warhol and Hackett, POPism, 73.

77. Joseph Cornell's Duchamp Dossier might suggest another example of this kind of collaborative work. See Joseph Cornell and Marcel Duchamp, Joseph Cornell/Marcel Duchamp . . . in resonance (Ostfildern-Ruit, Germany: Hatje, 1998).

78. Warhol, Philosophy, 13–14.

79. Warhol, Philosophy, 14.

80. Wilcock, Autobiography and Sex Life of Andy Warhol, n.p. [Charles Henri Ford, p. 3].

81. Queen Ed and Solanas would do better to direct without seeming "capable of giving the slightest direction." While here Paul Morrissey self-servingly accuses Warhol of incompetence in order to claim that he is the "real" direction behind Warhol's films, this passive direction seems at the heart of Warhol's style of governance. Warhol's "Hello Again" music video for the Cars (1984) furnishes another example of this passive control. Koestenbaum, Andy Warhol, 138.

82. Warhol and Hackett, POPism, 108.

83. Stephen Koch, Stargazer: Andy Warhol's World and His Films (New York: Marion Boyars, 1985), 121.

84. Warhol, Philosophy, 96. Fred Hughes might be thought of as fulfilling this desire for a boss for the later Warhol.

85. Warhol, Philosophy, 96.

86. My reading here owes much to Jennifer L. Fleissner, "Dictation Anxiety: The Stenographer's Stake in Dracula," in Literary Secretaries/Secretarial Culture, ed. Leah Price and Pamela Thurschwell (Burlington, VT: Ashgate, 2005), 63.

87. In Warhol's Blood for Dracula, directed by Paul Morrissey (Italy, 1974), the vampire is in search of virgin blood—but is himself a figure of celibate sexuality in the sense that he never engages in normative sexual acts. The vampire's inadequate masculinity and pale color also suggest him as a figure for Warhol. For a discussion of Dracula's celibacy, see Elizabeth Miller, "Coitus Interruptus: Sex, Bram Stoker, and Dracula," Romanticism on the Net 44 (2006). See also Franco Moretti, Signs Taken for Wonder: Essays in the Sociology of Literary Forms, trans. Susan Fischer, David Forgacs, and David Miller (London: Verso, 1983), 90–91.

88. Warhol, Philosophy, 15.

89. Warhol, Philosophy, 15.

90. Solanas, scum Manifesto, 47.

91. Solanas, SCUM Manifesto, 52.

92. Steven Shaviro, "Warhol before the Mirror," in *Who Is Andy Warhol?*, ed. Colin MacCabe with Mark Francis and Peter Wollen (London: British Film Institute, 1997), 93.

93. Margreta de Grazia, Maureen Quilligan, and Peter Stallybrass, "Introduction," in *Subject and Object in Renaissance Culture*, ed. Margreta de Grazia, Maureen Quilligan, and Peter Stallybrass (Cambridge: Cambridge University Press, 1996), 4.

94. Warhol, *I'll Be Your Mirror*, 16. My understanding of Warhol's escape from the iron cage dovetails with Jonathan Flatley's reading of Warhol's proliferation of likenesses as "an escape from the binary opposition between the same and the different . . . [that] displaces the primary organizing logic of capitalism (in which everything must be at once universally exchangeable - the same - and qualitatively specific - the different)." Jonathan Flatley, "Like: Collecting and Collectivity in the Work of Andy Warhol" (paper presented at the American Studies Association, October 13, 2006). See also Jonathan Flatley, "Like: Collecting and Collectivity," *October* 132 (spring 2010): 71–98.

95. Dilip Parameshwar Gaonkar, "On Alternative Modernities," in *Alternative Modernities*, ed. Dilip Parameshwar Gaonkar (Durham, NC: Duke University Press, 2001), 9, 7. Scott Herring's excellent work on hoarding provides another way of understanding Warhol's consumption. Scott Herring, "Pathological Collectibles" (unpublished manuscript).

96. Wilcock, *Autobiography and Sex Life of Andy Warhol*, n.p. [Charles Henri Ford, p. 3].

Conclusion

1. Lauren Berlant, "Starved," *South Atlantic Quarterly* 106, no. 3 (2007): 433.

2. For information on the history of abstinence education, see Michelle Goldberg, "AIDS Is Not the Enemy: Sin, Redemption, and the Abstinence Industry," in *Kingdom Coming: The Rise of Christian Nationalism* (New York: Norton, 2006), 134–153. On the (in)effectiveness of abstinence-first and abstinence-based education, see John B. Jemmott III and Dana Fry, "The Abstinence Strategy for Reducing Sexual Risk Behavior," in *Beyond Condoms: Alternative Approaches to HIV Prevention*, ed. Ann O'Leary (New York: Kluwer Academic/Plenum, 2002), 109–137.

3. Ian McEwan, *On Chesil Beach* (New York: Doubleday, 2007); Tom Perrotta, *The Abstinence Teacher* (New York: St. Martin's, 2007); Stephen MacCauley, *Alternatives to Sex* (New York: Simon and Schuster, 2006); Janice Eidus, *The Celibacy Club: Stories* (San Francisco: City Lights, 1997); Walter Keady, *Celibates and Other Lovers* (Denver: MacMurray and Beck, 1997); Michael Arditti, *The Celibate* (New York: Soho Press, 1997). David Lodge's *Author, Author* (New York: Penguin, 2004) is exceptional for being one of the few novels that depicts celibacy differently.

4. Cynthia Dailard, "The Other Shoe Drops: Federal Abstinence Education Program Becomes More Restrictive," *Guttmacher Policy Review* 9, no. 1 (2006): 19.

5. The punk subculture "straight edge" provides another example of leftist energy around the nonsexual. Straight edge is a movement that emerged in the early 1980s out

of the band Minor Threat's song of the same name. While what constitutes a straight edge lifestyle, known as sXe (pronounced "sexy"), has been heavily debated, some of its core values include abstaining from alcohol, drugs, smoking, and promiscuous sex. Many straight edge punks also practice celibacy, vegetarianism, or veganism and refrain from drinking caffeine or working mainstream jobs. What is striking about the sXe stance on celibacy is that sex is not pathologized as dirty or wrong as it is by many faith-based virginity movements. Rather, sXe understands sex as entailing power and requiring a thoughtful, considered choice. The sXe practice of celibacy is an effort to resist sexual commodification, excess, and meaningless damage to others through disease or emotional harm. Here, the individualized leftist choice of celibacy and other aspects of the sXe lifestyle are attempts to change an aggregate culture. Ross Haenfler, *Straight Edge: Clean-Living Youth, Hard Core Punk, and Social Change* (New Brunswick, NJ: Rutgers University Press, 2006), 44, 111.

6. AVEN, "Asexual Visibility and Education Network," www.asexuality.org.

7. Nancy Cott, "Passionlessness: An Interpretation of Victorian Sexual Ideology, 1790–1850," *Signs* 4, no. 2 (1978): 221.

8. Ralph Werther (Earl Lind, pseud.), *The Female-Impersonators* (New York: Arno, 1975), 13.

9. Werther, *The Female-Impersonators*, 14, his emphasis.

10. Werther, *The Female-Impersonators*, 14.

11. Alfred C. Kinsey, *Sexual Behavior in the Human Male* (Bloomington: Indiana University Press, 1998), 658.

12. Boston marriage and frigidity might provide two other possible avenues for excavating the history of asexuality. While my history of Boston marriage in chapter 1 would certainly not see it as part of the history of asexuality, Esther D. Rothblum and Kathleen A. Brehony might provide a fruitful point of departure for a different position. Esther D. Rothblum and Kathleen A. Brehony, eds., *Boston Marriages* (Amherst: University of Massachusetts Press, 1993). The literature on frigidity (with its heavy emphasis on women) might provide an archive for further charting asexuality as a gender identity and also for developing intersections between asexuality and hetero-sexuality. Wilhelm Stekel, *Frigidity in Woman in Relation to Her Love Life*, trans. James S. van Teslaar (New York: Boni and Liveright, 1926); Eduard Hitschmann, *Frigidity in Women: Its Characteristics and Treatment* (Washington, DC: Nervous and Mental Disease Publishing, 1936); Otto Adler, "The Frigid Woman: Deficiency in Woman's Sexual Sensibility," *Medico-pharmaceutical Critic and Guide* 18 (1915): 329–336.

13. Personal correspondence with Karli June Cerankowski.

14. Werther's cold anaphrodites are similarly associated with cessation: "They neither progress nor regress." Werther, *The Female-Impersonators*, 13.

15. Roland Barthes, *The Neutral*, trans. Rosalind E. Krauss and Denis Hollier (New York: Columbia University Press, 2005), 211.

16. Barthes, *The Neutral*, 11, xvi, 27.

17. Barthes, *The Neutral*, xiv.

18. Barthes, *The Neutral*, 8.

19. The extent to which the theorization of homoromantic and heteroromantic

asexuals is coterminous with the theorization of homosexuality and heterosexuality, respectively, is a topic for further inquiry.

20. Samuel R. Delany, *Times Square Red, Times Square Blue* (New York: New York University Press, 2001), 123.

21. Delany, *Times Square Red, Times Square Blue*, 168.

22. Delany, *Times Square Red, Times Square Blue*, 167, 121.

23. For an alternative genealogy of the relationship between aesthetics and sexuality, see Christopher Looby, "Sexuality's Aesthetic Dimension: Kant and the *Autobiography of an Androgyne*," in *American Literature's Aesthetic Dimensions*, ed. Cindy Weinstein and Christopher Looby (New York: Columbia University, 2012), 156–177.

24. Leo Bersani, "Father Knows Best," *Raritan* 29, no. 4 (2010): 102.

25. Bersani, "Father Knows Best," 102.

26. Barthes, *The Neutral*, 13.

27. Sarah Dowling, "'And through its naming became owner': Translation in James Thomas Stevens's *Tokinish*," GLQ: *A Journal of Lesbian and Gay Studies* 16, nos. 1–2 (2010): 195.

28. Samuel R. Delany, "Aye, and Gomorrah . . . ," in *Aye, and Gomorrah and Other Stories* (New York: Vintage, 2003), 98.

29. Delany, "Aye, and Gomorrah . . . ," 97.

30. Delany, "Aye, and Gomorrah . . . ," 97.

31. This dynamic is further highlighted by the text's repeated conflation and mis-identification of spacers for frelks and frelks for spacers. The spacer/frelk binary is less a binary than a similitude (much as the text also participates in the long tradition of understanding homosexuality as a mirror).

32. Barthes, *The Neutral*, 32, 211.

33. Barthes, *The Neutral*, 26. For example, the distinction between romantic and aromantic asexuals marks a reinscription of asexuality into binary constructions of meaning that Barthes's Neutral can only momentarily arrest.

34. Delany, "Aye, and Gomorrah . . . ," 98.

35. Delany, "Aye, and Gomorrah . . . ," 101, 99.

36. Delany, "Aye, and Gomorrah . . . ," 99.

37. Eunjung Kim, "Asexualities and Disabilities in Constructing Sexual Normalcy," in *Asexualities: Feminist and Queer Perspectives*, ed. Karli June Cerankowski and Megan Milks (Routledge, forthcoming).

38. AVEN, "Asexual Visibility and Education Network."

39. Karli June Cerankowski and Megan Milks, "New Orientations: Asexuality and Its Implications for Theory and Practice," *Feminist Studies* 36, no. 3 (2010): 659, their emphasis.

40. Leo Bersani, "Is the Rectum a Grave?," *October* 43 (1987): 205.

41. Adrienne Rich, "Compulsory Heterosexuality and Lesbian Existence," *Signs* 5, no. 4 (1980): 648.

Bibliography

Abbott, Elizabeth. *A History of Celibacy: From Athena to Elizabeth I, Leonardo da Vinci, Florence Nightingale, Gandhi, and Cher*. New York: Scribner, 2000.

Abbott, Mary. *Family Affairs: A History of the Family in 20th Century Britain*. New York: Routledge, 2003.

Abelove, Henry. *Deep Gossip*. Minneapolis: University of Minnesota Press, 2003.

Adams, Henry. "The Education of Henry Adams." In *Henry Adams*, edited by Ernest Samuels and Jayne N. Samuels, 715–1192. New York: Library of America, 1983.

Adams, Kimberly VanEsveld. *Our Lady of Victorian Feminism: The Madonna in the Works of Anna Jameson, Margaret Fuller, and George Eliot*. Athens: Ohio University Press, 2001.

Adler, Otto. "The Frigid Woman: Deficiency in Woman's Sexual Sensibility." *Medico-pharmaceutical Critic and Guide* 18 (1915): 329–336.

Agulhon, Maurice. *Marianne into Battle: Republican Imagery and Symbolism in France, 1789–1880*. Translated by Janet Lloyd. Cambridge: Cambridge University Press, 1981.

Anderson, Charles. "Introduction." In Henry James, *The Bostonians*. New York: Penguin, 1974.

Anderson, Mary M. *Hidden Power: The Palace Eunuchs of Imperial China*. Buffalo, NY: Prometheus, 1990.

Anderson, Sherwood. *Winesburgh, Ohio: A Group of Tales of Ohio Small-Town Life*. Wickford, RI: North Books, 1998.

Ansen, Alan. "Atlantis." Berg Collection at New York Public Library. Call No. (Auden).

———. "Crisis and Festival: A Study of W. H. Auden's *The Sea and the Mirror*." Berg Collection at New York Public Library. Call No. (Auden).

Appleton, Thomas Gold. *A Sheaf of Papers*. Boston: Roberts Brothers, 1875.

Arditti, Michael. *The Celibate*. New York: Soho Press, 1997.

Asch, Sholom. *The God of Vengeance*. Charleston: Bibliolife, 2009.

Ashbery, John. "Jerboas, Pelicans, and Peewee Reese: Marianne Moore." In John Ashbery, *Selected Prose*, edited by Eugene Richie, 83–88. Ann Arbor: University of Michigan Press, 2004.

Auden, W. H. *The Complete Works of W. H. Auden: Prose*. Vol. 2, *1939–1948*. Edited by Edward Mendelson. Princeton, NJ: Princeton University Press, 1996.

———. *Double Man*. New York: Random House, 1941.

———. *The English Auden: Poems, Essays, and Dramatic Writings 1927–1939*. Edited by Edward Mendelson. London: Faber, 1977.

———. *Lectures on Shakespeare*. Edited by Arthur C. Kirsch. Princeton, NJ: Princeton University Press, 2000.

———. *The Sea and the Mirror: A Commentary on Shakespeare's "The Tempest."* Edited by Arthur Kirsch. Princeton, NJ: Princeton University Press, 2003.

Auden, W. H., to E. R. Dodds, March 11, 1940. In W. H. Auden, *The Map of All My Youth: Early Works, Friends, and Influences*, edited by Katherine Bucknell and Nicholas Jenkins, 113–115. Oxford: Oxford University Press, 1990.

Auden, W. H., to John Auden, n.d. [1926 or 1927?]. Uncataloged letters in the Berg Collection at New York Public Library.

Ayalon, David. *Eunuchs, Caliphs and Sultans: A Study of Power Relations*. Jerusalem: Magnes Press, Hebrew University, 1999.

Baldwin, James. "Dark Days." In *The Price of the Ticket: Collected Nonfiction, 1948–1985*, 657–66. New York: St. Martin's, 1985.

———. "East River, Downtown." In *Nobody Knows My Name: More Notes of a Native Son*, 72–82. New York: Dial, 1961.

———. *Just above My Head*. New York: Dial, 1979.

———. "Stagolee." In *A Lonely Rage: The Autobiography of Bobby Seale*, ix–x. New York: Times Books, 1978.

Banta, Martha. *Imaging American Women: Idea and Ideals in Cultural History*. New York: Columbia University Press, 1987.

Barker, David J. "Where Is Ireland in *The Tempest*?" In *Shakespeare and Ireland: History, Politics, Culture*, edited by Mark Thornton Burnett and Ramona Wray, 68–88. London: Macmillan, 1997.

Barry, Kathleen M. *Femininity in Flight: A History of Flight Attendants*. Durham, NC: Duke University Press, 2007.

Bartels, Emily C. *Speaking of the Moor: From "Alcazar" to "Othello."* Philadelphia: University of Pennsylvania Press, 2008.

Barthes, Roland. *The Neutral*. Translated by Rosalind E. Krauss and Denis Hollier. New York: Columbia University Press, 2005.

———. *Writing Degree Zero*. Translated by Annette Lavers and Colin Smith. New York: Hill and Wang, 1968.

Basch, Norma. *In the Eyes of the Law: Women, Marriage, and Property in Nineteenth-Century New York*. Ithaca, NY: Cornell University Press, 1982.

Baudelaire, Charles. *Intimate Journals*. Translated by Christopher Isherwood. Hollywood: Marcel Rodd, 1947.

Beauvoir, Simone de. *The Second Sex*. New York: Vintage, 1989.

Bedell, Madelon. *The Alcotts: Biography of a Family*. New York: Clarkson N. Potter, 1980.

Beecher, Catherine, to Sister Sarah Buckingham Beecher. August 20, 1843. In *The Limits of Sisterhood: The Beecher Sisters on Women's Rights and Woman's Sphere*, edited by Jeanne Boydston, Mary Kelley, and Anne Margolis, 239. Chapel Hill: University of North Carolina Press, 1988.

Behling, Laura L. *The Masculine Woman in America 1890–1935*. Urbana: University of Illinois Press, 2001.

Bell, David, and Jon Binnie. *The Sexual Citizen: Queer Politics and Beyond*. Cambridge: Polity, 2000.

Berend, Zsuzsa. "'The Best or None!': Spinsterhood in Nineteenth-Century New England." *Journal of Social History* 33, no. 4 (2000): 935–957.

———. "Cultural and Social Sources of Spinsterhood in Nineteenth-Century New England." PhD diss., Columbia University, 1994.

———. "'Written All Over with Money': Earning, Spending, and Emotion in the Alcott Family." *Journal of Historical Sociology* 16, no. 2 (2003): 209–236.

Berlant, Lauren. *The Queen of America Goes to Washington City: Essays on Sex and Citizenship*. Durham, NC: Duke University Press, 1997.

———. "Starved." *South Atlantic Quarterly* 106, no. 3 (2007): 433–444.

Bernard, Emily. "The Renaissance and the Vogue." In *The Cambridge Companion to the Harlem Renaissance*, edited by George Hutchinson, 28–40. Cambridge: Cambridge University Press, 2007.

Bersani, Leo. "Ardent Masturbation." *Critical Inquiry* 38, no. 1 (2011): 1–16.

———. "Father Knows Best." *Raritan* 29, no. 4 (2010): 92–104.

———. "Genital Chastity." In *Homosexuality and Psychoanalysis*, edited by Tim Dean and Christopher Lane, 351–366. Chicago: University of Chicago Press, 2001.

———. *Homos*. Cambridge, MA: Harvard University Press, 1995.

———. "Is the Rectum a Grave?" *October* 43 (1987): 197–222.

Bertolini, Vincent J. "Fireside Chastity: The Erotics of Sentimental Bachelorhood in the 1850s." In *Sentimental Men: Masculinity and the Politics of Affect in American Culture*, edited by Mary Chapman and Glenn Hendler, 19–42. Berkeley: University of California Press, 1999.

Besant, Walter. *Autobiography of Sir Walter Besant*. New York: Dodd, Mead, 1902.

Best, Stephen, and Sharon Marcus. "Surface Reading: An Introduction." *Representations* 109, no. 1 (2010): 1–21.

Bishop, Elizabeth. "A Brief Reminiscence and a Brief Tribute: Marianne Moore, W. H. Auden." In *Elizabeth Bishop: Poems, Prose, and Letters*, edited by Robert Giroux and Lloyd Schwartz, 728–731. New York: Library of America, 2008.

———. "Efforts of Affection: A Memoir of Marianne Moore." In *The Collected Prose*, edited by Robert Giroux, 121–156. New York: Farrar, Straus and Giroux, 1984.

Blair, Sara. "Realism, Culture, and the Place of the Literary: Henry James and *The Bostonians*." In *The Cambridge Companion to Henry James*, edited by Jonathan Freeman, 151–168. Cambridge: Cambridge University Press, 1998.

Blood for Dracula. Directed by Paul Morrissey. Italy, 1974. DVD.

Blow Job. Directed by Andy Warhol. New York, 1963. Film.

Bockris, Victor. *Warhol: The Biography*. Cambridge, MA: Da Capo, 2003.

Bogan, Louise. "Verse." Review of *For the Time Being*, W. H. Auden, *New Yorker*, September 23–30, 1944, 77–78.

Boone, Joseph A. "Modernist Re-orientations: Imagining Homoerotic Desire in the 'Nearly' Middle East." *Modernism/Modernity* 17, no. 3 (2010): 561–605.

Boroff, Marie. *Language and the Poet: Verbal Artistry in Frost, Stevens, and Moore*. Chicago: University of Chicago Press, 1979.

Boswell, John. *Christianity, Social Tolerance, and Homosexuality: Gay People in Western Europe from the Beginning of the Christian Era to the Fourteenth Century*. Chicago: University of Chicago Press, 2005.

Bourdieu, Pierre. *The Bachelors' Ball: The Crisis in Peasant Society in Béarn*. Translated by Richard Nice. Chicago: University of Chicago Press, 2008.

Bozorth, Richard R. *Auden's Games of Knowledge: Poetry and the Meanings of Homosexuality*. New York: Columbia University Press, 2001.

Braniff Airlines. "If You've Got It, Flaunt It" campaign. Advertisement. 1969.

Bray, Alan. *The Friend*. Chicago: University of Chicago Press, 2003.

Brown, Sterling. Letter to Gorham Munson, January 9, 1940, National Archives, Record Group 69, Records of the Works Projects Administration, PI-57, Entry 27, Records of the Federal Writers' Project, Records of the Central Office, Reports and Miscellaneous Records Pertaining to Negro Studies, Box 2, Folder: Negro Studies.

———. *Sterling A. Brown's A Negro Looks South*. Edited by John Edgar Tidwell and Mark A. Sanders. Oxford: Oxford University Press, 2007.

Brown, Wendy. *Edgework: Critical Essays on Knowledge and Politics*. Princeton, NJ: Princeton University Press, 2005.

Burgett, Bruce. "Sex, Panic, Nation." *American Literary History* 21, no. 1 (2009): 67–86.

Burke, Carolyn. "The New Poetry and the New Woman: Mina Loy." In *Coming to Light: American Women Poets in the Twentieth Century*, edited by Diane Wood Middlebrook and Marilyn Yalom, 37–57. Ann Arbor: University of Michigan Press, 1985.

Burnham, Kenneth E. *God Comes to America: Father Divine and the Peace Mission Movement*. Boston: Lambeth, 1979.

Burstein, Jessica. *Cold Modernism: Literature, Fashion, Art*. University Park: Pennsylvania State University Press, 2012.

Butler, Judith. *Gender Trouble: Feminism and the Subversion of Identity*. 1990. Reprint, New York: Routledge, 1999.

Canaday, Margot. *The Straight State: Sexuality and Citizenship in Twentieth-Century America*. Princeton, NJ: Princeton University Press, 2009.

———. "Who Is Homosexual? The Consolidation of Sexual Identities in Mid-Twentieth-Century American Immigration Law." *Law and Social Inquiry* 28, no. 2 (2003): 351–386.

Carby, Hazel V. *Reconstructing Womanhood: The Emergence of the Afro-American Woman Novelist*. New York: Oxford University Press, 1987.

Carpenter, Humphrey. *W. H. Auden: A Biography*. Boston: George Allen and Unwin, 1981.

Cars, the. "Hello Again." Directed by Andy Warhol. 1984. Music video.

Carter, Christine Jacobson. *Southern Single Blessedness: Unmarried Women in the Urban South, 1800–1865.* Urbana: University of Illinois Press, 2006.

Casal, Mary [Ruth Fuller Field, pseud.]. *The Stone Wall: An Autobiography.* Chicago: Eyncourt, 1930.

Caserio, Robert L. "Auden's New Citizenship." *Raritan* 17, no. 2 (1997): 90–103.

Castle, Terry. *The Apparitional Lesbian: Female Homosexuality and Modern Culture.* New York: Columbia University Press, 1993.

Cerankowski, Karli June, and Megan Milks. "New Orientations: Asexuality and Its Implications for Theory and Practice." *Feminist Studies* 36, no. 3 (2010): 650–664.

Chambers-Schiller, Lee Virginia. *Liberty, a Better Husband: Single Women in America: The Generations of 1780–1840.* New Haven, CT: Yale University Press, 1984.

Chauncey, George. *Gay New York: Gender, Urban Culture, and the Making of the Gay Male World, 1890–1940.* New York: Basic Books, 1994.

Chelsea Girls. Directed by Paul Morrissey and Andy Warhol. 1966. DVD.

Cheney, Ednah D. "Correspondence." *Open Court, a Quarterly Magazine,* January 5, 1893.

———. *Reminiscences of Ednah Dow Cheney.* Boston: Lee and Shepard, 1902.

"Child Lost through Hypnotism." *Chicago Tribune,* December 22, 1892, 4.

Christie, Stuart. "Disorientations: Canon without Context in Auden's 'Sonnets from China.'" PMLA 120, no. 5 (2005): 1576–1587.

Chudacoff, Howard P. *The Age of the Bachelor: Creating an American Subculture.* Princeton, NJ: Princeton University Press, 1999.

Clarke, Eric O. *Virtuous Vice: Homoeroticism and the Public Sphere.* Durham, NC: Duke University Press, 2000.

Cobb, Michael. "Lonely." *South Atlantic Quarterly* 106, no. 3 (2007): 445–457.

Coburn, Carol K., and Martha Smith. *Spirited Lives: How Nuns Shaped Catholic Culture and American Life, 1836–1920.* Chapel Hill: University of North Carolina Press, 1999.

Cohen, Matt. "Walt Whitman, the Bachelor, and Sexual Poetics." *Walt Whitman Quarterly Review* 16, nos. 3–4 (1999): 145–152.

Cook, Blanche Wiesen. "Female Support Networks and Political Activism: Lillian Wald, Crystal Eastman, Emma Goldman." In *A Heritage of Her Own: Toward a New Social History of American Women,* edited by Nancy F. Cott and Elizabeth H. Pleck, 412–455. New York: Simon and Schuster, 1977.

Cooper, John Xiros. "'The Crow on the Crematorium Chimney': Germany, Summer 1945." *English Studies in Canada* 30, no. 3 (2004): 129–144.

Corbould, Clare. *Becoming African Americans: Black Public Life in Harlem, 1919–1939.* Cambridge, MA: Harvard University Press, 2009.

Cornell, Joseph, and Marcel Duchamp. *Joseph Cornell/Marcel Duchamp . . . in resonance.* Ostfildern-Ruit, Germany: Hatje, 1998.

Costello, Bonnie. *Marianne Moore: Imaginary Possessions.* Cambridge, MA: Harvard University Press, 1981.

Cott, Nancy. "Passionlessness: An Interpretation of Victorian Sexual Ideology, 1790–1850." *Signs* 4, no. 2 (1978): 219–236.

Crain, Caleb. *American Sympathy: Men, Friendship, and Literature in the New Nation.* New Haven, CT: Yale University Press, 2001.

Cresap, Kelly. *Pop, Trickster, Fool: Warhol Performs Naivete.* Urbana: University of Illinois Press, 2004.

Crimp, Douglas. "How to Have Promiscuity in an Epidemic." In AIDS: *Cultural Activism, Cultural Analysis,* edited by Douglas Crimp, 237–271. Cambridge, MA: MIT Press, 1988.

Crisp, Quentin. *The Naked Civil Servant.* New York: Holt, Rinehart, and Winston, 1977.

Dailard, Cynthia. "The Other Shoe Drops: Federal Abstinence Education Program Becomes More Restrictive." *Guttmacher Policy Review* 9, no. 1 (2006): 19.

Daniels, Elam J. *"Father Divine": The World's Chief False Christ.* Winter Garden, FL: Biblical Echo, 1937.

Danto, Arthur C. "Andy Warhol: Brillo Box." *Artforum International* 32, no. 1 (1993): 128–129.

———. *Beyond the Brillo Box: The Visual Arts in Post-historical Perspective.* New York: Farrar, Straus and Giroux, 1992.

Davenport-Hines, Richard. *Auden.* New York: Pantheon, 1995.

Davidson, Arnold I. *The Emergence of Sexuality: Historical Epistemology and the Formation of Concepts.* Cambridge, MA: Harvard University Press, 2001.

Davidson, Cathy N., and Jessamyn Hatcher, eds. *No More Separate Spheres!* Durham, NC: Duke University Press, 2002.

Davis, Adrienne D. "Regulating Polygamy: Intimacy, Default Rules, and Bargaining for Equality." 110 *Columbia Law Review* 110 (2010): 1955–2046.

Davis, Katharine B. *Factors in the Sex Life of Twenty-Two Hundred Women.* New York: Harper, 1929.

Dean, Tim. *Beyond Sexuality.* Chicago: University of Chicago Press, 2000.

DeCosta, Dr. B. F. *The White Cross: Its Origin and Progress.* Chicago: Sanitary Publishing, 1887.

———. *The White Cross Society Christian Union.* January 29, 1885.

———. *The White Cross Society Christian Union.* March 3, 1887.

Deggs, Sister Mary Bernard. *No Cross, No Crown: Black Nuns in Nineteenth Century New Orleans.* Edited by Virginia Meacham Gould and Charles E. Nolan. Bloomington: Indiana University Press, 2001.

Degler, Carl N. *At Odds: Women and the Family in America from the Revolution to the Present.* New York: Oxford University Press, 1980.

de Gourmont, Remy. *The Natural Philosophy of Love.* Translated by Ezra Pound. New York: Liveright, 1932.

de Grazia, Margreta, Maureen Quilligan, and Peter Stallybrass. "Introduction." In *Subject and Object in Renaissance Culture,* edited by Margreta de Grazia, Maureen Quilligan, and Peter Stallybrass, 1–13. Cambridge: Cambridge University Press, 1996.

Delany, Samuel R. *Aye, and Gomorrah and Other Stories.* New York: Vintage, 2003.

———. *Times Square Red, Times Square Blue.* New York: New York University Press, 2001.

Dell, Floyd. *Love in the Machine Age: A Psychological Study of the Transition from Patriarchal Society.* New York: Octagon Books, 1973.

del Punta, Lawler Francesco. "The Genre of Commentaries in the Middle Ages and Its Relation to the Nature and Originality of Medieval Thought." In *Was ist Philosophie im Mittelalter? / Qu'est-ce que la philosophie au Moyen Âge? / What Is Philosophy in the Middle Ages*, edited by Jan Aertsen and Andreas Speer, 138–151. Berlin: Walter de Gruyter, 1998.

D'Emilio, John. "Capitalism and Gay Identity." In *The Lesbian and Gay Studies Reader*, edited by Henry Abelove, Michèle Aina Barale, and David M. Halperin, 467–476. New York: Routledge, 1993.

D'Emilio, John, and Estelle B. Freedman. *Intimate Matters: A History of Sexuality in America*. New York: Harper and Row, 1988.

Derrida, Jacques. "Living on—Border Lines." In *Deconstruction and Criticism*, edited by Harold Bloom, Paul de Man, Jacques Derrida, Geoffrey Hartman, and J. Hillis Miller, 62–152. New York: Seabury, 1979.

De Villiers, Nicholas. *Opacity and the Closet: Queer Tactics in Foucault, Barthes, and Warhol*. Minneapolis: University of Minnesota Press, 2012.

di Leonardo, Micaela. "Warrior Virgins and Boston Marriages: Spinsterhood in History and Culture." In *Que(e)ry Religion: A Critical Anthology*, edited by Gary David Comstock and Susan E. Henking, 138–155. New York: Continuum, 1997.

Diner, Hasia R. *Erin's Daughters in America: Irish Immigrant Women in the Nineteenth Century*. Baltimore: Johns Hopkins University Press, 1983.

Dode, Lee. *A History of Homosexuality*. Victoria, BC: Trafford, 2003.

Dodson, Jualynne E., and Cheryl Townsend Gilkes. "'There's Nothing Like Church Food': Food and the U.S. Afro-Christian Tradition: Re-membering Community and Feeding the Embodied S/spirit(s)." *Journal of the American Academy of Religion* 63, no. 3 (1995): 519–538.

Dowling, Sarah. "'And through its naming became owner': Translation in James Thomas Stevens's *Tokinish*." *GLQ: A Journal of Lesbian and Gay Studies* 16, nos. 1–2 (2010): 191–206.

Doyle, Jennifer, Jonathan Flatley, and José Esteban Muñoz. "Introduction." In *Pop Out*, edited by Jennifer Doyle, Jonathan Flatley, and José Esteban Muñoz, 1–19. Durham, NC: Duke University Press, 1996.

DuBois, Ellen Carol. *Feminism and Suffrage: The Emergence of an Independent Women's Movement in America, 1848–1869*. Ithaca, NY: Cornell University Press, 1980.

Duggan, Lisa. "Censorship in the Name of Feminism." In *Sex Wars: Sexual Dissent and Political Culture*, edited by Lisa Duggan and Nan D. Hunter, 29–39. New York: Routledge, 2006.

———. *Sapphic Slashers: Sex, Violence, and American Modernity*. Durham, NC: Duke University Press, 2000.

———. *The Twilight of Equality: Neoliberalism, Cultural Politics, and the Attack on Democracy*. Boston: Beacon, 2003.

Dunbar-Ortiz, Roxanne. *Outlaw Woman: A Memoir of the War Years, 1960–1975*. San Francisco: City Lights, 2001.

Edel, Leon. *Henry James: A Life*. New York: Harper and Row, 1985.

Edelman, Lee. "Tearooms and Sympathy; or, the Epistemology of the Water Closet."

In *Homographesis: Essays in Gay Literary and Cultural Theory*, 148–170. New York: Routledge, 1994.

Edwards, Brent Hayes. *The Practice of Diaspora: Literature, Translation, and the Rise of Black Internationalism*. Cambridge, MA: Harvard University Press, 2003.

Eidus, Janice. *The Celibacy Club: Stories*. San Francisco: City Lights, 1997.

Elbert, Monika M., ed. *Separate Spheres No More: Gender Convergence in American Literature, 1830–1930*. Tuscaloosa: University of Alabama Press, 2000.

Eliot, T. S. "The Idea of a Christian Society." In *Selected Prose of T. S. Eliot*, edited by Frank Kermode, 285–291. New York: Harvest, 1975.

Eng, David. *The Feeling of Kinship: Queer Liberalism and the Racialization of Intimacy*. Durham, NC: Duke University Press, 2010.

———. *Racial Castration: Managing Masculinity in Asian America*. Durham, NC: Duke University Press, 2001.

Erasmus, Desiderius. *Erasmus on Women*. Edited by Erika Rummel. Toronto: University of Toronto Press, 1996.

Erenberg, Lewis A. *Greatest Fight of Our Generation: Louis vs. Schmeling*. New York: Oxford University Press, 2006.

Esteve, Mary. "Anerotic Excursions: Memory, Celibacy, and Desire in *The American Scene*." In *Questioning the Master: Gender and Sexuality in Henry James's Writings*, edited by Peggy McCormack, 196–216. Cranbury, NJ: Associated University Presses, 2000.

Evans, Kasey. "How Temperance Becomes 'Blood Guiltie' in *The Fairie Queen*." SEL: *Studies in English Literature, 1500–1900* 49, no. 1 (2009): 35–66.

Faderman, Lillian. "Nineteenth-Century Boston Marriage as a Possible Lesson for Today." In *Boston Marriages*, edited by Esther D. Rothblum and Kathleen A. Brehony, 29–42. Amherst: University of Massachusetts Press, 1993.

———. "Romantic Friendship and Boston Marriage." In *Encyclopedia of Lesbian, Gay, Bisexual, and Transgender History in America*, edited by Marc Stein, 3:47. New York: Scribner, 2004.

———. *Surpassing the Love of Men: Romantic Friendship and Love between Women from the Renaissance to the Present*. 1981. Reprint, New York: Perennial, 2001.

Faderman, Lillian, and Stuart Timmons. *Gay L.A.: A History of Sexual Outlaws, Power Politics, and Lipstick Lesbians*. New York: Basic Books, 2006.

Fahs, Breanne. "The Radical Possibilities of Valerie Solanas." *Feminist Studies* 34, no. 3 (2008): 591–617.

Farnan, Dorothy J. *Auden in Love*. New York: Simon and Schuster, 1984.

Faulkner, William. *The Sound and the Fury*. New York: Vintage, 1984.

Fauset, Jessie Redmon. *Plum Bun: A Novel without a Moral*. Boston: Beacon, 1990.

Fialka, John J. *Sisters: Catholic Nuns and the Making of America*. New York: St. Martin's, 2004.

Fiedler, Leslie A. *Love and Death in the American Novel*. Champaign, IL: Dalkey Archive Press, 2003.

Fitzgerald, Maureen. *Habits of Compassion: Irish Catholic Nuns and the Origins of New York's Welfare System, 1830–1920*. Urbana: University of Illinois Press, 2006.

Flatley, Jonathan. "Like: Collecting and Collectivity." *October* 132 (spring 2010): 71–98.

———. "Like: Collecting and Collectivity in the Work of Andy Warhol." Paper presented at the American Studies Association, Oakland, CA, October 13, 2006.

Flaubert, Gustave. *Correspondance*. Vol. 1. Paris: Gallimard, 1973.

———. *Selected Letters*. Translated by Geoffrey Wall. New York: Penguin, 1997.

Fleissner, Jennifer L. "Dictation Anxiety: The Stenographer's Stake in *Dracula*." In *Literary Secretaries / Secretarial Culture*, edited by Leah Price and Pamela Thurschwell, 63–90. Burlington, VT: Ashgate, 2005.

———. *Women, Compulsion, Modernity: The Moment of American Naturalism*. Chicago: University of Chicago Press, 2004.

Foley, Barbara. *Radical Representations: Politics and Form in U.S. Proletarian Fiction, 1929–1941*. Durham, NC: Duke University Press, 1993.

———. *Spectres of 1919: Class and Nation in the Making of the New Negro*. Urbana: University of Illinois Press, 2003.

Foote, Stephanie. "The Little Brothers of the Rich: Queer Families in the Late Nineteenth Century." *American Literature* 79, no. 4 (2007): 701–724.

Foucault, Michel. "The Battle for Chastity." In *Ethics: Subjectivity and Truth. The Essential Works of Michel Foucault, 1954–1984*, edited by Paul Rabinow, 1:185–197. New York: New Press, 1994.

———. *The History of Sexuality*. Vol. 1, *An Introduction*. Translated by Robert Hurley. New York: Vintage, 1990.

Frank, Marcie. "Popping Off Warhol: From the Gutter to the Underground and Beyond." In *Pop Out*, edited by Jennifer Doyle, Jonathan Flatley, and José Esteban Muñoz, 210–223. Durham, NC: Duke University Press, 1996.

Franzen, Trisha. *Spinsters and Lesbians*. New York: New York University Press, 1996.

Fraser, George. "Auden in Midstream." In *Essays on Twentieth Century Poets*, 140–141. Totowa, NJ: Rowman and Littlefield, 1977.

Freccero, Carla. *Queer/Early/Modern*. Durham, NC: Duke University Press, 2006.

Freeman, Elizabeth. "Packing History, Count(er)ing Generations." *New Literary History* 31, no. 4 (2000): 727–744.

———. *The Wedding Complex: Forms of Belonging in Modern American Culture*. Durham, NC: Duke University Press, 2002.

Freud, Sigmund. *Totem and Taboo: Some Points of Agreement between the Mental Lives of Savages and Neurotics*. Translated by James Strachey. New York: Norton, 1989.

Froide, Amy M. *Never Married: Singlewomen in Early Modern England*. Oxford: Oxford University Press, 2005.

Fuller, Margaret. "The Great Lawsuit: Man *Versus* Men. Woman *Versus* Women." In *Transcendentalism: A Reader*, edited by Joel Myerson, 383–427. Oxford: Oxford University Press, 2000.

———. *Woman in the Nineteenth Century*. Edited by Larry J. Reynolds. New York: Norton, 1998.

Furbank, P. N. *E. M. Forster: A Life*. New York: Harcourt Brace, 1978.

Gabbin, Joanna V. *Sterling A. Brown: Building the Black Aesthetic Tradition*. Westport, CT: Greenwood Press, 1985.

Gaines, Kevin K. *Uplifting the Race: Black Leadership, Politics, and Culture in the Twenti-eth Century*. Chapel Hill: University of North Carolina Press, 1996.

Gaonkar, Dilip Parameshwar. "On Alternative Modernities." In *Alternative Modernities*, edited by Dilip Parameshwar Gaonkar, 1–23. Durham, NC: Duke University Press, 2001.

Gilbert, Sandra. "Marianne Moore as Female Female Impersonator." In *Marianne Moore: The Art of a Modernist*, edited by Joseph Parisi, 27–46. Ann Arbor: University of Michigan Press, 1990.

Girard, René. *Deceit, Desire, and the Novel: Self and Other in Literary Structure*. Translated by Yvonne Freccero. Baltimore: Johns Hopkins University Press, 1976.

Gleckner, Robert F. *Gray Agonistes: Thomas Gray and Masculine Friendship*. Baltimore: Johns Hopkins University Press, 1997.

Glick, Elisa. *Materializing Queer Desire: Oscar Wilde to Andy Warhol*. Albany: SUNY Press, 2009.

Goldberg, Jonathan. *Tempest in the Caribbean*. Minneapolis: University of Minnesota Press, 2004.

———. "Under the Covers with Caliban." In *Shakespeare's Hand*, 286–308. Minneapolis: University of Minnesota Press, 2003.

Goldberg, Michelle. "AIDS Is Not the Enemy: Sin, Redemption, and the Abstinence Industry." In *Kingdom Coming: The Rise of Christian Nationalism*, 134–153. New York: Norton, 2006.

Gollin, Rita K. *Annie Adams Fields: Woman of Letters*. Amherst: University of Massachusetts Press, 2002.

Gottlieb, Susannah Young-ah. "'With Conscious Artifice': Auden's Defense of Marriage." *diacritics* 35, no. 4 (2005): 23–41.

Graham, Wendy. *Henry James's Thwarted Love*. Stanford, CA: Stanford University Press, 1999.

Gray, Thomas. *The Works of Thomas Gray in Prose and Verse*. Vol. 3. Edited by Edmund Gosse. New York: AMS Press, 1968.

Gregory, Elizabeth. *Quotation and Modern American Poetry: "Imaginary Gardens with Real Toads."* Houston: Rice University Press, 1996.

———. "Stamps, Money, Pop Culture, and Marianne Moore." *Discourse* 17, no. 1 (1994): 123–146.

Griffith, R. Marie. "Body Salvation: New Thought, Father Divine, and the Feast of Material Pleasures." *Religion and American Culture* 11, no. 2 (2001): 119–153.

Guillory, John. "The Bachelor State: Philosophy and Sovereignty in Bacon's *New Atlantis*." In *Politics and the Passions, 1500–1800*, edited by Victoria Kahn, Neil Saccamano, and Daniela Coli, 49–74. Princeton, NJ: Princeton University Press, 2006.

Haenfler, Ross. *Straight Edge: Clean-Living Youth, Hard Core Punk, and Social Change*. New Brunswick, NJ: Rutgers University Press, 2006.

Haggerty, George E. *Men in Love: Masculinity and Sexuality in the Eighteenth Century*. New York: Columbia University Press, 1999.

Haller, John S., and Robin M. Haller. *The Physician and Sexuality in Victorian America*. Carbondale: Southern Illinois University Press, 1995.

Halperin, David M. *How to Do the History of Homosexuality*. Chicago: University of Chicago Press, 2002.

Harron, Mary. "Introduction: On Valerie Solanas." In *I Shot Andy Warhol*, vii–xxxi. New York: Grove, 1995.

Hartmann, Charles O. *Free Verse: An Essay on Prosody*. Princeton, NJ: Princeton University Press, 1980.

Hayden, Robert. "An Interview with Dennis Gendron." In *Robert Hayden: Essays on the Poetry*, edited by Laurence Goldstein and Robert Chrisman, 15–29. Ann Arbor: University of Michigan Press, 2001.

———. "Witch-Doctor." In *Collected Poems*, edited by Frederick Glaysher, 35–37. New York: Liveright, 1997.

Hayes, Kevin J., ed. *Henry James: The Contemporary Reviews*. Cambridge: Cambridge University Press, 1996.

Hayot, Eric. *The Hypothetical Mandarin: Sympathy, Modernity, and Chinese Pain*. Oxford: Oxford University Press, 2009.

Heath, Stephen. *The Sexual Fix*. New York: Schocken Books, 1984.

Herring, Scott. "Pathological Collectibles." Unpublished manuscript.

Herzog, Dagmar. *Sex in Crisis: The New Sexual Revolution and the Future of American Politics*. New York: Basic Books, 2008.

Heuving, Jeanne. *Omissions Are Not Accidents: Gender in the Art of Marianne Moore*. Detroit: Wayne State University Press, 1992.

Higginbotham, Evelyn Brook. *Righteous Discontent: The Women's Movement in the Black Baptist Church, 1880–1920*. Cambridge, MA: Harvard University Press, 1993.

Hill, Bridget. *Women Alone: Spinsters in England, 1660–1850*. New Haven, CT: Yale University Press, 2001.

Himes, Chester. *A Rage in Harlem*. New York: Vintage, 1991.

Hitschmann, Eduard. *Frigidity in Women: Its Characteristics and Treatment*. Washington, DC: Nervous and Mental Disease Publishing, 1936.

Holden, Katherine. *The Shadow of Marriage: Singleness in England, 1914–60*. Manchester: Manchester University Press, 2007.

Holley, Margaret. *The Poetry of Marianne Moore: A Study in Voice and Value*. Cambridge: Cambridge University Press, 1987.

Hopkins, Pauline. "Higher Education of Colored Women in White Schools and Colleges." In *Daughter of the Revolution*, edited by Ira Dworkin, 193–198. New Brunswick, NJ: Rutgers University Press, 2007.

———. *Of One Blood or, The Hidden Self*. New York: Washington Square, 2004.

Horowitz, Helen Lefkowitz. *The Power and Passion of M. Carey Thomas*. New York: Knopf, 1994.

Howe, Helen. *The Gentle Americans, 1864–1960: Biography of a Breed*. New York: Harper and Row, 1965.

Howe, Nicholas. "Praise and Lament: The Afterlife of Old English Poetry in Auden, Hill, and Gunn." In *Words and Works: Studies in Medieval English Language and Literature in Honour of Fred C. Robinson*, edited by Peter S. Baker and Nicholas Howe, 293–310. Toronto: University of Toronto Press, 1998.

Howie, Cary. *Claustrophilia: The Erotics of Enclosure in Medieval Literature*. New York: Palgrave, 2007.

Hughes, Langston. *The Big Sea*. New York: Thunder's Mouth, 1986.

———. *The Collected Poems of Langston Hughes*. Edited by Arnold Rampersad. New York: Vintage, 1995.

Humphreys, Laud. *Tearoom Trade: Impersonal Sex in Public Places*. Chicago: Aldine, 1975.

Hutchinson, George. *The Harlem Renaissance in Black and White*. Cambridge, MA: Belknap, 1995.

Irvine, Martin. Review of "*Medieval Literary Criticism and Theory, c. 1100–c. 1375: The Commentary-Tradition*." *Speculum* 66, no. 2 (1991): 451–453.

Isherwood, Christopher, and Edward Upward. *The Mortmere Stories*. London: Enitharmon, 1995.

Isherwood, Lisa. *The Power of Erotic Celibacy: Queering Heteropatriarchy*. New York: T. and T. Clark, 2006.

Jagose, Annamarie. *Inconsequence: Lesbian Representation and the Logic of Sexual Sequence*. Ithaca, NY: Cornell University Press, 2002.

James, Alan G. "A Memorable Naturalization: How Henry James Became a British Subject and Lost His United States Citizenship." *Henry James Review* 12, no. 1 (1991): 55–68.

James, Henry. "The Art of Fiction." In *Henry James: Literary Criticism: Essays on Literature, American Writers, and English Writers*, edited by Leon Edel, 1:44–65. New York: Library of America, 1984.

———. *Autobiography*. New York: Criterion Books, 1956.

———. *The Bostonians*. Edited by Pierre A. Walker. New York: Modern Library, 2003.

———. *The Complete Notebooks of Henry James*. Edited by Leon Edel and Lyall H. Powers. Oxford: Oxford University Press, 1987.

———. "The Future of the Novel." In *Henry James: Literary Criticism: Essays on Literature, American Writers, and English Writers*, edited by Leon Edel, 1:100–110. New York: Library of America, 1984.

———. *Henry James Letters*. Vol. 4, *1895–1916*. Edited by Leon Edel. Boston: Belknap, 1984.

———. "Introduction to *The Tempest*." In *Henry James: Literary Criticism: Essays on Literature, American Writers, and English Writers*, edited by Leon Edel, 1:1205–1220. New York: Library of America, 1984.

James, Winston. *Holding Aloft the Banner of Ethiopia: Caribbean Radicalism in Early Twentieth-Century America*. New York: Verso, 1998.

Jankowski, Theodora. *Pure Resistance: Queer Virginity in Early Modern English Drama*. Philadelphia: University of Pennsylvania Press, 2000.

Jemmott, John B., III, and Dana Fry. "The Abstinence Strategy for Reducing Sexual Risk Behavior." In *Beyond Condoms: Alternative Approaches to HIV Prevention*, edited by Ann O'Leary, 109–137. New York: Kluwer Academic/Plenum, 2002.

Jenkins, Nicholas. "Auden in America." In *The Cambridge Companion to W. H. Auden*, edited by Stan Smith, 39–54. Cambridge: Cambridge University Press, 2004.

Jennings, Rebecca. *Tomboys and Bachelor Girls: A Lesbian History of Postwar Britain, 1945–1971.* New York: Manchester University Press, 2007.

Johnson, John W. *Griswold v. Connecticut: Birth Control and the Constitutional Right of Privacy.* Lawrence: University Press of Kansas, 2005.

Johnson, Penelope Delafield. *Equal in Monastic Profession: Religious Women in Medieval France.* Chicago: University of Chicago Press, 1994.

Jones, James H. *Alfred C. Kinsey.* New York: Norton, 1997.

Jones, William H. *Recreation and Amusement among Negroes in Washington, D.C.* Washington, DC: Howard University Press, 1927.

Joyce, James. *Finnegans Wake.* New York: Penguin, 1999.

Kann, Mark E. *A Republic of Men: The American Founders, Gendered Language, and Patriarchal Politics.* New York: New York University Press, 1998.

Kaplan, Fred. *Henry James: The Imagination of a Genius: A Biography.* New York: Morrow, 1992.

Kaye, Richard. *The Flirt's Tragedy: Desire without End in Victorian and Edwardian Fiction.* Charlottesville: University of Virginia Press, 2002.

Keady, Walter. *Celibates and Other Lovers.* Denver: MacMurray and Beck, 1997.

Kellman, Steven G. "Raising Muscovite Ducks and Government Suspicions: Henry Roth and the FBI." In *Modernism on File: Writers, Artists, and the FBI, 1920–1950,* edited by Claire A. Culleton and Karen Leick, 39–52. New York: Palgrave, 2008.

Kelly, Kathleen Coyne, and Marina Leslie. "Introduction: The Epistemology of Virginity." In *Menacing Virgins: Representing Virginity in the Middle Ages and Renaissance,* edited by Kathleen Coyne Kelly and Marina Leslie, 15–25. Newark: University of Delaware Press, 1999.

———. *Menacing Virgins: Representing Virginity in the Middle Ages and Renaissance.* Newark: University of Delaware Press, 1999.

Kent, Kathryn R. *Making Girls into Women: American Women's Writing and the Rise of Lesbian Identity.* Durham, NC: Duke University Press, 2003.

Kern, Louis J. *An Ordered Love: Sex Roles and Sexuality in Victorian Utopias—The Shakers, the Mormons, and the Oneida Community.* Chapel Hill: University of North Carolina Press, 1981.

Kim, Eunjung. "Asexualities and Disabilities in Constructing Sexual Normalcy." In *Asexualities: Feminist and Queer Perspectives,* edited by Karli June Cerankowski and Megan Milks. Routledge, forthcoming.

Kinsey, Alfred C. *Sexual Behavior in the Human Male.* Bloomington: Indiana University Press, 1998.

Kitch, Sally L. *Chaste Liberation: Celibacy and Female Cultural Status.* Urbana: University of Illinois Press, 1989.

Koch, Stephen. *Stargazer: Andy Warhol's World and His Films.* New York: Marion Boyars, 1985.

Koestenbaum, Wayne. *Andy Warhol.* New York: Viking, 2001.

———. *Double Talk: The Erotics of Male Literary Collaboration.* New York: Routledge, 1989.

Korobkin, Laura Hanft. *Criminal Conversations: Sentimentality and Nineteenth-Century Legal Stories of Adultery.* New York: Columbia University Press, 1998.

Kracauer, Siegfried. *Soziologie als Wissenschaft; Der Detektiv-Roman; Die Angestellten.* Frankfurt: Suhrkamp, 2006.

Kramer, Hilton. "Freezing the Blood and Making One Laugh." *New York Times*, March 15, 1981.

Kranidis, Rita S. *The Victorian Spinster and Colonial Emigration: Contested Subjects.* New York: St. Martin's, 1999.

Krauss, Rosalind. *Bachelors.* Cambridge, MA: MIT Press, 1999.

Kuefler, Matthew. *The Manly Eunuch: Masculinity, Gender Ambiguity, and Christian Ideology in Late Antiquity.* Chicago: University of Chicago Press, 2001.

Kurnick, David. "An Erotics of Detachment: *Middlemarch* and Novel-Reading as Critical Practice." ELH 74, no. 3 (2007): 583–608.

Kutzer, M. Daphne. *Beatrix Potter: Writing in Code.* New York: Routledge, 2003.

Laipson, Peter. "'I Have No Genius for Marriage': Bachelorhood in Urban America, 1870–1930." PhD diss., University of Michigan, 2000.

Lanser, Susan S. "'Queer to Queer': The Sapphic Body as Transgressive Text." In *Lewd and Notorious: Female Transgression in the Eighteenth Century*, edited by Katharine Kittredge, 21–46. Ann Arbor: University of Michigan Press, 2003.

Laplanche, Jean. "Sublimation and/or Inspiration." *Formations: A Journal of Culture/Theory/Politics* 48 (2002–2003): 30–50.

Larsen, Nella. *The Complete Fiction of Nella Larsen: Passing, Quicksand, and the Stories.* Norwell, MA: Anchor, 2001.

Launderville, Dale. *Celibacy in the Ancient World: Its Ideal and Practice in Pre-Hellenistic Israel, Mesopotamia, and Greece.* Collegeville, MN: Liturgical Press, 2010.

Lawrence, D. H. *Studies in Classic American Literature.* New York: T. Seltzer, 1923.

Lea, Henry C. *History of Sacerdotal Celibacy in the Christian Church.* London: Watts, 1932.

Leavell, Linda. "'Frightening Disinterestedness': The Personal Circumstances of Marianne Moore's 'Marriage.'" *Journal of Modern Literature* 31, no. 1 (2007): 64–79.

———. "Marianne Moore, the James Family, and the Politics of Celibacy." *Twentieth Century Literature* 49 (2003): 219–245.

Lehr, Elizabeth Drexel. *"King Lehr" and the Gilded Age.* Philadelphia: Lippincott, 1935.

Leonard, Amy. *Nails in the Wall: Catholic Nuns in Reformation Germany.* Chicago: University of Chicago Press, 2005.

Levy, Ellen. *Criminal Ingenuity: Moore, Cornell, Ashbery, and the Struggle between the Arts.* New York: Oxford University Press, 2011.

Lewis, David Levering. *When Harlem Was in Vogue.* New York: Knopf, 1981.

Liggins, Emma. "'The Life of a Bachelor Girl in the Big City': Selling the Single Lifestyle to Readers of *Woman* and the *Young Woman* in the 1890s." *Victorian Periodicals Review* 40, no. 3 (2007): 216–238.

Lindsey, Ben Barr, and Wainwright Evans. *The Companionate Marriage.* New York: Boni and Liveright, 1927.

Lodge, David. *Author, Author.* New York: Penguin, 2004.

Lois, George. $ellebrity. New York: Phaidon, 2003.

Looby, Christopher. "Innocent Homosexuality: The Fiedler Thesis in Retrospect." In

Mark Twain: "The Adventures of Huckleberry Finn"; A Case Study in Critical Controversy, ed. Gerald Graff and James Phelan, 535–550. New York: Bedford Books, 1995.

———. "Sexuality's Aesthetic Dimension: Kant and the Autobiography of an Androgyne." In American Literature's Aesthetic Dimensions, edited by Cindy Weinstein and Christopher Looby, 156–177. New York: Columbia University Press, 2012.

Love, Heather. Feeling Backward: Loss and the Politics of Queer History. Cambridge, MA: Harvard University Press, 2007.

———. "Gyn/Apology: Sarah Orne Jewett's Spinster Aesthetics." ESQ: A Journal of the American Renaissance 55, nos. 3–4 (2009): 305–334.

Loy, Mina. The Lost Lunar Baedeker. New York: Farrar, Straus and Giroux, 1996.

Lucas, John. "Auden's Politics: Power, Authority, and the Individual." In The Cambridge Companion to W. H. Auden, edited by Stan Smith, 152–164. Cambridge: Cambridge University Press, 2004.

MacCauley, Stephen. Alternatives to Sex. New York: Simon and Schuster, 2006.

Mack, Thomas L. Thomas Gray: A Life. New Haven, CT: Yale University Press, 2000.

Marcus, Sharon. Between Women: Friendship, Desire, and Marriage in Victorian England. Princeton, NJ: Princeton University Press, 2007.

Margolick, David. Beyond Glory: Joe Louis vs Max Schmeling, and a World on the Brink. New York: Knopf, 2005.

Martin, Tony. Literary Garveyism: Garvey, Black Arts, and the Harlem Renaissance. Dover, MA: Majority, 1983.

Maxwell, William J. "F.B. Eyes: The Bureau Reads Claude McKay." In Left of the Color Line: Race, Radicalism, and Twentieth-Century Literature of the United States, edited by Bill V. Mullen and James Smethurst, 39–65. Chapel Hill: University of North Carolina Press, 2003.

———. "Ghostreaders and Diaspora-Writers: Four Theses on the FBI and African American Modernism." In Modernism on File: Writers, Artists, and the FBI, 1920–1950, edited by Claire A. Culleton and Karen Leick, 23–38. New York: Palgrave, 2008.

———. New Negro, Old Left: African-American Writing and Communism between the Wars. New York: Columbia University Press, 1999.

McCullough, Kate. "The Boston Marriage as the Future of the Nation: Queerly Regional Sexuality in Diana Victrix." American Literature 69, no. 1 (1997): 67–103.

McCurdy, John Gilbert. Citizen Bachelors: Manhood and the Creation of the United States. Ithaca, NY: Cornell University Press, 2009.

McDiarmid, Lucy S., and John McDiarmid. "Artifice and Self-Consciousness in The Sea and the Mirror." In W. H. Auden: Modern Critical Views, edited by Harold Bloom, 69–90. New York: Chelsea House, 1986.

McEwan, Ian. On Chesil Beach. New York: Doubleday, 2007.

McFadden, Margaret. "Boston Teenagers Debate the Woman Question, 1837–1838." Signs 15, no. 4 (1990): 841–847.

McGuinness, Margaret M. Called to Serve: A History of Nuns in America. New York: New York University Press, 2013.

McKay, Claude. Amiable with Big Teeth: A Novel of the Love Affair between the Commu-

nists and the Poor Black Sheep of Harlem. Columbia University Library, Samuel Roth Papers, Box 29, Folder 7.

———. "14." In Claude McKay, *Complete Poems*, edited by William J. Maxwell, 248. Urbana: University of Illinois Press, 2004.

———. *Harlem: Negro Metropolis*. New York: Harcourt Brace Jovanovich, 1968.

Mead, Rebecca. *How the Vote Was Won: Woman Suffrage in the Western United States, 1868–1914*. New York: New York University Press, 2004.

Mendelson, Edward. *Later Auden*. New York: Farrar, Straus and Giroux, 1999.

Meyerowitz, Joanne. "Thinking Sex with an Androgyne." *GLQ: A Journal of Lesbian and Gay Studies* 17, no. 1 (2011): 97–105.

———. *Women Adrift: Independent Wage Earners in Chicago, 1880–1930*. Chicago: University of Chicago Press, 1988.

Mezei, Kathy. "Spinster, Surveillance, and Speech: The Case of Miss Marple, Miss Mole, and Miss Jekyll." *Journal of Modern Literature* 30, no. 2 (2007): 103–120.

Miller, Cristanne. "Rhythms of Embodiment." Paper presented at the Modernist Studies Association, Vancouver, BC, October 22, 2004.

Miller, D. A. *Jane Austen, or the Secret of Style*. Princeton, NJ: Princeton University Press, 2003.

Miller, Elizabeth. "Coitus Interruptus: Sex, Bram Stoker, and Dracula." *Romanticism on the Net* 44 (2006).

Miller, Monica L. *Slaves to Fashion: Black Dandyism and the Styling of Black Diasporic Identity*. Durham, NC: Duke University Press, 2009.

Molesworth, Charles. *Marianne Moore: A Literary Life*. New York: Atheneum, 1990.

Monk, Ray. *Ludwig Wittgenstein: The Duty of Genius*. New York: Free Press, 1990.

Moon, Michael. *A Small Boy and Others: Imitation and Initiation in American Culture from Henry James to Andy Warhol*. Durham, NC: Duke University Press, 1998.

Moore, John Warner, to Marianne Moore. February 22, 1941. Rosenbach Museum and Library Marianne Moore Collection, VI:36:03.

Moore, Katherine. *Cordial Relations: The Maiden Aunt in Fact and Fiction*. London: Heinemann, 1966.

Moore, Marianne. *The Complete Prose of Marianne Moore*. Edited by Patricia C. Willis. New York: Viking, 1986.

———. Letter to Viking Press, May 2, 1966, Rosenbach Museum and Library Marianne Moore Collection, V:67:19.

———. *Selected Letters*. Edited by Bonnie Costello, Celeste Goodridge, and Cristanne Miller. New York: Penguin, 1997.

———. *Tell Me, Tell Me: Granite, Steel, and Other Topics*. New York: Viking, 1966.

Moran, Rachel F. "How Second-Wave Feminism Forgot the Single Woman." *Hofstra Law Review* 33, no. 1 (2004): 226.

Moretti, Franco. *Signs Taken for Wonder: Essays in the Sociology of Literary Forms*. Translated by Susan Fischer, David Forgacs, and David Miller. London: Verso, 1983.

Morgan, Ted. *Literary Outlaw: The Life and Times of William S. Burroughs*. New York: Holt, 1988.

Morrow, Diane Batts. *Persons of Color and Religious at the Same Time: The Oblate*

Sisters of Providence, 1828–1860. Chapel Hill: University of North Carolina Press, 2002.

Mosher, Clelia Duel. *The Mosher Survey: Sexual Attitudes of 45 Victorian Women*. Edited by James MaHood and Kristine Wenburg. New York: Arno, 1980.

Muñoz, José Esteban. *Cruising Utopia: The Then and There of Queer Futurity*. New York: New York University Press, 2009.

Murphy, Kevin P. *Political Manhood: Red Bloods, Mollycoddles, and the Politics of Progressive Era Reform*. New York: Columbia University Press, 2008.

Myler, Patrick. *Ring of Hate: Joe Louis vs Max Schmeling: The Fight of the Century*. New York: Arcade, 2005.

Ngai, Mae M. *Impossible Subjects: Illegal Aliens and the Making of Modern America*. Princeton, NJ: Princeton University Press, 2005.

Nietzsche, Friedrich. *Beyond Good and Evil*. Translated by Judith Norman. Cambridge: Cambridge University Press, 2002.

Nightingale, Florence. *Notes on Nursing*. New York: Dover, 1969.

North, Michael. *Machine-Age Comedy*. Oxford: Oxford University Press, 2009.

Nugent, Richard Bruce. *Gentleman Jigger*. Cambridge, MA: Da Capo, 2008.

Ochs, Stephen J. *Desegregating the Altar: The Josephites and the Struggle for Black Priests, 1871–1960*. Baton Rouge: Louisiana State University Press, 1990.

O'Hara, Frank. "Why I Paint as I Do" (interview with Larry Rivers). *Horizon* 2, no. 1 (1959): 98.

Okrent, Daniel. *Last Call: The Rise and Fall of Prohibition*. New York: Scribner, 2010.

Ong, Aihwa. *Flexible Citizenship: The Cultural Logics of Transnationality*. Durham, NC: Duke University Press, 1999.

O'Shea, Edward. "Modernist Versions of *The Tempest*: Auden, Woolf, Tippett." In *The Tempest: Critical Essays*, edited by Patrick M. Murphy, 543–559. New York: Routledge, 2001.

Pagliarini, Marie Anne. "The Pure American Woman and the Wicked Catholic Priest: An Analysis of Anti-Catholic Literature in Antebellum America." *Religion and American Culture* 9, no. 1 (winter 1999): 97–128.

Payne, Robert. "On Mariamna De Maura." In *Festschrift for Marianne Moore's Seventy-Seventh Birthday*, edited by Tambimuttu, 21–27. New York: Tambimuttu and Mass, 1964.

Penthouse Forum: The International Journal of Human Relations 10, no. 4 (1981).

Perlmann, Joel, and Robert A. Margo. *Women's Work? American Schoolteachers, 1650–1920*. Chicago: University of Chicago Press, 2001.

Perrotta, Tom. *The Abstinence Teacher*. New York: St. Martin's, 2007.

Petty, Leslie. *Romancing the Vote: Feminist Activism in American Fiction, 1870–1920*. Athens: University of Georgia Press, 2006.

Phelan, Shane. *Sexual Strangers: Gays, Lesbians, and Dilemmas of Citizenship*. Philadelphia: Temple University Press, 2001.

Pines, Davida. *The Marriage Paradox: Modernist Narratives and the Cultural Imperative to Marry*. Gainesville: University Press of Florida, 2006.

Pivar, David J. *Purity Crusade: Sexual Morality and Social Control, 1868–1900*. Westport, CT: Greenwood Press, 1973.

Pollak, Vivian R. "Moore, Plath, Hughes, and 'The Literary Life.'" *American Literary History* 17, no. 1 (2005): 95–117.

Poole, Mary. *The Segregated Origins of Social Security: African-Americans and the Welfare State*. Chapel Hill: University of North Carolina Press, 2006.

Potter, Beatrix. *The Tailor of Gloucester*. New York: Frederick Warne, 1981.

Primiano, Leonard Norman. "'Bringing Perfection in These Different Places': Father Divine's Vernacular Architecture of Intention." *Folklore* 115 (2004): 3–26.

Puar, Jasbir. *Terrorist Assemblages: Homonationalism in Queer Times*. Durham, NC: Duke University Press, 2007.

Puchner, Martin. *Stage Fright: Modernism, Anti-theatricality, and Drama*. Baltimore: Johns Hopkins University Press, 2002.

Putney, Clifford. *Muscular Christianity*. Cambridge, MA: Harvard University Press, 2001.

Rackin, Donald. "Mind over Matter: Sexuality and Where the 'Body Happens to Be' in the *Alice* Books." In *Textual Bodies: Changing Boundaries of Literary Representations*, 161–183. Albany: SUNY Press, 1997.

Rambuss, Richard. "After Male Sex." *South Atlantic Quarterly* 106, no. 3 (2007): 577–588.

Rampersad, Arnold. *The Life of Langston Hughes*. Vol. 2. Oxford: Oxford University Press, 2002.

Reverby, Susan M. *Ordered to Care: The Dilemma of American Nursing, 1850–1945*. Cambridge: Cambridge University Press, 1987.

Rich, Adrienne. "Compulsory Heterosexuality and Lesbian Existence." *Signs* 5, no. 4 (1980): 631–660.

Riley, Denise. "The Right to Be Lonely." In *Impersonal Passion: Language as Affect*, 49–58. Durham, NC: Duke University Press, 2005.

Ringrose, Kathryn M. *The Perfect Servant: Eunuchs and the Social Construction of Gender in Byzantium*. Chicago: University of Chicago Press, 2003.

Riss, Arthur. *Race, Slavery, and Liberalism in Nineteenth-Century American Literature*. Cambridge: Cambridge University Press, 2006.

Rohy, Valerie. *Anachronism and Its Others: Sexuality, Race, Temporality*. Albany: SUNY Press, 2009.

Ronell, Avital. "Deviant Payback: The Aims of Valerie Solanas." In Valerie Solanas, *SCUM Manifesto*, 1–31. New York: Verso, 2004.

Roosevelt, Theodore. "On American Motherhood." In Theodore Roosevelt, *Addresses and Papers*, edited by Willis Fletcher Johnson, 242. New York: Sun Dial Classics, 1909.

Rorem, Ned. *Settling the Score: Essays on Music*. New York: Anchor, 1989.

Rosenberg, Rosalind. *Beyond Separate Spheres: Intellectual Roots of Modern Feminism*. New Haven, CT: Yale University Press, 1982.

Rothblum, Esther D., and Kathleen A. Brehony, eds. *Boston Marriages*. Amherst: University of Massachusetts Press, 1993.

Said, Edward W. *Beginnings: Intention and Method*. New York: Columbia University Press, 1985.

Salvato, Nick. *Uncloseting Drama: American Modernism and Queer Performance.* New Haven, CT: Yale University Press, 2010.

Salzman, Neil V. *Reform and Revolution: The Life and Times of Raymond Robins.* Kent, OH: Kent State University Press, 1991.

Santayana, George. *The Last Puritan: A Memoir in the Form of a Novel.* Edited by William G. Holzberger and Herman J. Saatkamp Jr. Cambridge, MA: MIT Press, 1986.

———. *The Sense of Beauty: Being the Outline of Aesthetic Theory.* New York: Scribner's, 1896. Reprint, Dover, 1955.

Satter, Beryl. "Marcus Garvey, Father Divine and the Gender Politics of Race Difference and Race Neutrality." *American Quarterly* 48, no. 1 (1996): 43–76.

Scherman, Tony, and David Dalton. *Pop: The Genius of Andy Warhol.* New York: Harper-Collins, 2009.

Screen Test # 1. Directed by Ronald Tavel and Andy Warhol. New York, 1965. Film.

Sedgwick, Eve Kosofsky. *Between Men: English Literature and Male Homosocial Desire.* New York: Columbia University Press, 1985.

———. *Epistemology of the Closet.* Berkeley: University of California Press, 1990.

———. *Touching Feeling: Affect, Pedagogy, Performativity.* Durham, NC: Duke University Press, 2003.

Seifer, Marc. *Wizard: The Life and Times of Nikola Tesla: Biography of a Genius.* Secaucus, NJ: Birch Lane Press, 1996.

Shakespeare, William. *The Tempest.* Edited by Stephen Orgel. Oxford: Oxford University Press, 1998.

Shaviro, Steven. "Warhol before the Mirror." In *Who Is Andy Warhol?*, edited by Colin MacCabe with Mark Francis and Peter Wollen, 89–95. London: British Film Institute, 1997.

Shaw, George Bernard. "Preface to Androcles and the Lion: On the Prospects of Christianity." In *Androcles and the Lion; Overruled; Pygmalion.* New York: Dodd, Mead, 1916.

Shaw, Robert Burns. *Blank Verse: A Guide to Its History and Use.* Athens: Ohio University Press, 2007.

Shoptaw, John. *On the Outside Looking Out: John Ashbery's Poetry.* Cambridge, MA: Harvard University Press, 1994.

Showalter, Elaine. *Sexual Anarchy: Gender and Culture at the Fin de Siècle.* New York: Viking, 1990.

Sielke, Sabine. *Fashioning the Female Subject: The Intertextual Networking of Dickinson, Moore, and Rich.* Ann Arbor: University of Michigan Press, 1997.

Single Blessedness; Or, Single Ladies and Gentlemen against the Slanders of the Pulpit, the Press, and the Lecture Room. New York: C. S. Francis, 1852.

Smethurst, James. *The New Red Negro: The Literary Left and African American Poetry, 1930–1946.* New York: Oxford University Press, 1999.

Smith, Henry Nash. *Virgin Land: The American West as Symbol and Myth.* Cambridge, MA: Harvard University Press, 2005.

Snyder, Katherine V. *Bachelors, Manhood, and the Novel, 1850–1925.* Cambridge: Cambridge University Press, 1999.

Solanas, Valerie. SCUM *Manifesto*. New York: Verso, 2004.

Somerville, Siobhan. *Queering the Color Line: Race and the Invention of Homosexuality in American Culture*. Durham, NC: Duke University Press, 2000.

———. "Sexual Aliens and the Racialized State: A Queer Reading of the 1952 U.S. Immigration and Nationality Act." In *Queer Migrations: Sexuality, U. S. Citizenship, and Border Crossings*, edited by Eithne Luibhéid and Lionel Cantú Jr., 75–91. Minneapolis: University of Minnesota Press, 2005.

A Southern Women's Writing Collective. "Sex Resistance in Heterosexual Arrangements." In *The Sexual Liberals and the Attack on Feminism*, edited by Dorchen Leidholdt and Janice G. Raymond, 140–147. New York: Pergamon, 1990.

Spears, Monroe K. *The Poetry of W. H. Auden: The Disenchanted Island*. New York: Oxford University Press, 1963.

Spender, Stephen. "Stephen Spender on Argument or Experience, Auden." Review of *For the Time Being*, W. H. Auden, *Time and Tide*, August 25, 1945, 711–712.

———. *The Temple*. New York: Grove, 1988.

Spring, Justin. *Secret Historian: The Life and Times of Samuel Steward, Professor, Tattoo Artist, and Sexual Renegade*. New York: Farrar, Straus and Giroux, 2010.

Spurlock, John C. *Free Love: Marriage and Middle-Class Radicalism in America, 1825–1860*. New York: New York University Press, 1988.

Stanley, Amy Dru. "Conjugal Bonds and Wage Labor: Rights of Contract in the Age of Emancipation." In *Women and the American Legal Order*, edited by Karen J. Maschke, 149–178. New York: Garland, 1997.

Stein, Gertrude. *Selected Writings*. Edited by Carl Van Vechten. New York: Vintage, 1972.

Stein, Jean. *Edie: American Girl*. New York: Grove, 1994.

Stein, Robert. "Girls' Coöperative Boarding Homes." *Arena* 19 (March 1898): 397–417.

Stekel, Wilhelm. *Frigidity in Woman in Relation to Her Love Life*. Translated by James S. van Teslaar. New York: Boni and Liveright, 1926.

Stephens, Michelle Ann. *Black Empire: The Masculine Global Imaginary of Caribbean Intellectuals in the United States, 1914–1962*. Durham, NC: Duke University Press, 2005.

Stevens, Hugh. *Henry James and Sexuality*. New York: Cambridge University Press, 1998.

Stockton, Kathryn Bond. "Growing Sideways, or Versions of the Queer Child: The Ghost, the Homosexual, the Freudian, the Innocent, and the Interval of Animal." In *Curiouser: On the Queerness of Children*, edited by Steven Bruhm and Natasha Hurley, 277–315. Minneapolis: University of Minnesota Press, 2004.

Strocchia, Sharon T. *Nuns and Nunneries in Renaissance Florence*. Baltimore: Johns Hopkins University Press, 2009.

Strom, Sharon Hartman. *Beyond the Typewriter: Gender, Class, and the Origins of Modern American Office Work, 1900–1930*. Urbana: University of Illinois Press, 1992.

Suárez, Juan A. *Bike Boys, Drag Queens, and Superstars: Avant-Garde, Mass Culture, and Gay Identities in the 1960s Underground Cinema*. Bloomington: Indiana University Press, 1996.

Sundquist, Eric J. *Faulkner: A House Divided*. Baltimore: Johns Hopkins University Press, 1985.

Symons, A. J. A. *The Quest for Corvo: An Experimental Biography*. New York: NYRB Classics, 2001.

Terada, Rei. *Feeling in Theory: Emotion after the "Death of the Subject."* Cambridge, MA: Harvard University Press, 2001.

Terry, Jennifer. "Loving Objects." *Trans-humanities* 2, no. 1 (2010): 33–75.

Thomas, Brook. *American Literary Realism and the Failed Promise of Contract*. Berkeley: University of California Press, 1997.

Thomas, Katie-Louise. "A Queer Job for a Girl: Women Postal Workers, Civic Duty and Sexuality 1870–80." In *In a Queer Place: Sexuality and Belonging in British and European Contexts*, edited by Kate Chedgzoy, Emma Francis, and Murray Pratt, 50–70. Burlington, VT: Ashgate, 2002.

Thoreau, Henry David. *Walden and Civil Disobedience*. Edited by Sherman Paul. Boston: Houghton Mifflin, 1960.

Thrasher, Frederic M. *The Gang: A Study of 1,313 Gangs in Chicago*. Chicago: University of Chicago Press, 1927.

Thurman, Wallace. *The Blacker the Berry*. New York: Arno, 1969.

———. *Infants of the Spring*. Boston: Northeastern University Press, 1992.

Thurschwell, Pamela. *Literature, Technology, and Magical Thinking, 1880–1920*. Cambridge: Cambridge University Press, 2001.

———. "'That Imperial Stomach Is No Seat for Ladies': Henry James, the First World War and the Politics of Identification." In *Modernist Sexualities*, edited by Hugh Stevens and Caroline Howlett, 167–183. New York: Manchester University Press, 2000.

Tippins, Sherill. *February House: The Story of W. H. Auden, Carson McCullers, Jane and Paul Bowles, Benjamin Britten, and Gypsy Rose Lee, under One Roof in Wartime America*. New York: Houghton Mifflin, 2005.

Traister, Bryce. "The Wandering Bachelor: Irving, Masculinity, and Authorship." *American Literature* 74, no. 1 (2002): 111–137.

Traub, Valerie. "Making Sexual Knowledge." *Early Modern Women* 5 (2010): 251–259.

———. "The Present Future of Lesbian Historiography." In *A Companion to Lesbian, Gay, Bisexual, Transgender, and Queer Studies*, edited by George Haggerty and Molly McGarry, 124–145. Oxford: Blackwell, 2007.

———. *The Renaissance of Lesbianism in Early Modern England*. Cambridge: Cambridge University Press, 2002.

Trilling, Lionel. *The Opposing Self: Nine Essays in Criticism*. New York: Viking, 1955.

Trinkaus, John, Alvin Puryear, and Joseph A. Giacaone. "Father Divine and the Development of African-American Small Business." *Journal of Developmental Entrepreneurship* 5, no. 3 (2000): 221–234.

Ullman, Sharon R. *Sex Seen: The Emergence of Modern Sexuality in America*. Berkeley: University of California Press, 1997.

U.S. National Archives and Records Administration, Record Group INS, File 51787/11, Box 228.

United States v. Ginzburg. 224 F. Supp. 129 (E.D. Pa. 1963), aff'd, 338 F.2d 12 (3d Cir. 1964), aff'd, 383 U.S. 463 (1964).

United States v. Schneiderman. 33 F. Supp. 510, 1940.

United States v. West Coast News Co. 228 F. Supp. 171 (W.D. Mich. 1964), *aff'd*, 357 F.2d 855 (6th Cir. 1966).

Vicinus, Martha. *Intimate Friends: Women Who Loved Women, 1778–1928.* Chicago: University of Chicago Press, 2004.

Vidal, Gore. *Myra Breckinridge / Myron.* New York: Penguin, 1997.

Vincent, John Emil. *Queer Lyrics.* New York: Palgrave Macmillan, 2002.

Violet, Ultra. *Famous for 15 Minutes: My Years with Andy Warhol.* London: Backinprint, 2004.

Vogel, Shane. *The Scene of the Harlem Cabaret: Race, Sexuality, Performance.* Chicago: University of Chicago Press, 2009.

A Walk into the SEA*: Danny Williams and the Warhol Factory.* Directed by Esther Robinson. 2007. DVD.

Wall, Barbara Mann. *Unlikely Entrepreneurs: Catholic Sisters and the Hospital Marketplace, 1865–1925.* Columbus: Ohio State University Press, 2005.

Ward, Geoff. *Statutes of Liberty: The New York School of Poets.* New York: Palgrave Macmillan, 2001.

Wardley, Lynn. "Bachelors in Paradise: The State of a Theme." In *The Return of Thematic Criticism*, edited by Werner Sollors, 217–241. Cambridge, MA: Harvard University Press, 1993.

Warhol, Andy. *The Andy Warhol Diaries.* Edited by Pat Hackett. New York: Warner Books, 1989.

———. *I'll Be Your Mirror: The Selected Andy Warhol Interviews.* Edited by Kenneth Goldsmith. New York: Carroll and Graf, 2004.

———. *The Philosophy of Andy Warhol (From A to B and Back Again).* New York: Harcourt Brace Jovanovich, 1975.

Warhol, Andy, and Pat Hackett. *POPism: The Warhol Sixties.* New York: Mariner Books, 1990.

Warner, Michael. "Irving's Posterity." ELH 67, no. 3 (2000): 773–799.

———. *Publics and Counterpublics.* New York: Zone Books, 2002.

———. "Thoreau's Bottom." *Raritan* 11, no. 3 (1992): 53–79.

———. "Thoreau's Erotic Economy." In *Comparative American Identities: Race, Sex, and Nationality in the Modern Text*, edited by Hortense Spillers, 157–174. New York: Routledge, 1991.

———. "Uncritical Reading." In *Polemic: Critical or Uncritical*, ed. Jane Gallop, 13–38. New York: Routledge, 2004.

Wasley, Aidan. "Auden and Poetic Inheritance." *Raritan* 19, no. 2 (1999): 128–157.

Watts, Jill. *God, Harlem U.S.A.: The Father Divine Story.* Berkeley: University of California Press, 1992.

Weisbrot, Robert. *Father Divine and the Struggle for Racial Equality.* Urbana: University of Illinois Press, 1983.

Werther, Ralph. *Autobiography of an Androgyne.* Edited by Scott Herring. New Brunswick, NJ: Rutgers University Press, 2008.

———[Earl Lind, pseud.]. *The Female-Impersonators*. New York: Arno, 1975.

Wilcock, John, and a cast of thousands. *The Autobiography and Sex Life of Andy Warhol*. New York: Other Scenes, 1971.

Willis, Patricia C. "Notes." *Marianne Moore Newsletter* 7, nos. 1–2 (1983): 13–14.

Wilson, James F. *Bulldaggers, Pansies, and Chocolate Babies: Performance, Race, and Sexuality in the Harlem Renaissance*. Ann Arbor: University of Michigan Press, 2010.

Wilson, Jeremiah Moses. *Black Messiah and Uncle Toms: Social and Literary Manipulations of a Religious Myth*. University Park: Pennsylvania State University Press, 1982.

Wintz, Cary D., and Paul Finkelman. *Encyclopedia of the Harlem Renaissance*. New York: Routledge, 2004.

Woolf, Virginia. *Granite and Rainbow*. London: Hogarth Press, 1956.

———. *Orlando: A Biography*. San Diego: Harcourt, 1956.

———. *To the Lighthouse*. San Diego: Harcourt, 1981.

Woolston, Florence Guy. "Marriage Customs and Taboo among the Early Heterodites." Reprinted in Judith Schwarz, *Radical Feminists of Heterodoxy: Greenwich Village, 1912–1940*, 95–96. Lebanon, NH: New Victoria, 1982.

Wright, Richard. "Fire and Cloud." In *Uncle Tom's Children: Four Novellas*, 221–317. New York: Harper, 1938.

Zangwill, Israel. *The Celibates' Club: Being the United Stories of the Bachelors' Club and the Old Maids' Club*. New York: Macmillan, 1905.

Zapperi, Giovanna. "Marcel Duchamp's *Tonsure*: Towards an Alternate Masculinity." *Oxford Art Journal* 30, no. 2 (2007): 289–303.

Zwarg, Christina. *Feminist Conversation: Fuller, Emerson, and the Play of Reading*. Ithaca, NY: Cornell University Press, 1995.

Index

Browning, Elizabeth Barrett, 46

Bryn Mawr College: lesbianism and, 68; in Moore's work, 62–63, 66–68, 79, 174n37; singleness of graduates from, 21

Buchanan, James, 138, 164n132

Burgett, Bruce, 12

"A Burning Desire to Be Explicit" (Moore), 67–68, 73–77

Burroughs, William, 101–102

Burstein, Jessica, 157n29

Bush, George W., 142

Butler, Judith, 77, 135, 152, 173n24, 186n37

Byzantine eunuchs, prehomosexual discourse and, 34

Cabaret School, Vogel's concept of, 86

Caliban: Auden and, 112–119, 189n54, 189n57; Shakespeare and, 112

The Cambridge Companion to the Harlem Renaissance, 84

Canaday, Margot, 22, 100

career, 7, 22, 34–36, 42–43, 165n4, 171n63

Caribbean radicalism, Harlem Renaissance and, 85

Carroll, Lewis, 64–65, 127

Caserio, Robert, 190n74

Castle, Terry, 41, 169n48

Cather, Willa, 9

Catholicism: African Americans and, 95–98; roots of celibate reform and, 13–22

celebrity: Moore and, 56, 59, 66, 77–79; Solanas and, 134; Warhol and, 137; W. H. Auden and, 113

celibacy: asexuality and, 143–153; Catholicism and, 13–22, 95–97; definitions of, 1–3, 10–13; desire and, 3, 6, 13, 21, 28–29, 31, 50–52, 56, 67–70, 105, 122, 129, 132–134, 137, 141, 143, 152; Father Divine's promotion of, 86–98; gender and, 2, 8, 10–12, 16, 19, 22, 31, 37, 92, 171n63; as imprisonment of women, 7; intelligibility of, 1–6, 60; modernism and, 1, 6–9; objections to, 1, 6–9; as a phase, 2, 31, 69, 104–108, 186n38; plot in *The Bostonians* of, 48–52; as political identity, 2, 8, 10, 13–15, 17, 19–29, 31, 44–45, 52, 61, 76, 80, 92, 151–153, 169n41; as public topic, 142; as sexual identity, 2–6, 8, 22, 25, 27, 66, 69, 79, 95,

97, 157n30; as social identity, 8, 10, 17, 22, 41, 59

The Celibacy Club (Eidus), 142

The Celibate (Arditti), 142

celibate modernity: Solanas and, 134–141; Warhol and, 30, 121–141

Celibates and Other Lovers (Keady), 142

The Celibates' Club: Being the United Stories of the Bachelors' Club and the Old Maids' Club (Zangwill), 11

celibate temporality, 27–28, 57, 59, 60–66, 80, 127–128, 175n50

Cell 16, 27, 136

censorship, 2, 4–6

"Censorship in the Name of Feminism" (Duggan), 4

Chambers-Schiller, Lee Virginia, 17–18

The Changing Light of Sandover (Merrill), 102

chastity: celibacy and, 11–12, 69, 77, 156n20; gender and, 7–8, 21–23; homosexuality and, 36–37, 194n51; Moore and, 60, 65; and politics, 24–25, 85; race and, 97

Chauncey, George, 10, 23, 98, 103

cheating, 104–108

Cheney, Ednah Dow Littlehale, 39–41, 43, 47, 168n35

Cheney, Seth, 168n35

Chesnutt, Charles, 93–94

Chewed Water (Rahman), 83

childhood, celibacy and, 12, 35, 55, 58, 66, 160n62

childlessness, 8, 16, 21–23, 51–54, 64, 127–129, 158n38, 170n61, 177n72

choice, sexual discourse of, 2, 17, 30–31, 53, 69, 100, 106, 127–129, 151–153, 197n5

Christie, Stuart, 190n73

Chudacoff, Howard, 23

citizenship, celibacy and, 16, 20, 27, 78, 94, 99–120

City Reform Club, 24

Civil War, 21

class: celibacy and, 10, 14–15, 21, 29, 85–88, 158n39; Harlem Renaissance and role of, 84–85

Clements, Lemuel, 96

Cleveland, Grover, 24–25

Cloistered Order of the Conclaved Knights of Sophisticracy, 26

love, concept of, 17, 117, 119, 144, 146, 151, 168n35, 170n61; ambition and, 35, 111; Auden and, 104; disappointment and, 16; Flaubert and, 105–107; free love and, 9, 26, 162n106; homosexuality and, 34; preterition and, 3; reform and, 43; rivalry and, 48–50; Warhol and, 125, 141; writing and, 69

Love, Heather, 6, 31, 37, 54

Love in the Machine Age (Dell), 22

Loy, Mina, 7–9, 26

lynching, 29, 86, 93, 97–98, 180n30

MacCauley, Stephen, 142

MacDermott, John, 130–131

Malanga, Gerard, 126, 130, 134

Mann, Erika, 104

Mann, Thomas, 104

Marcus, Sharon, 156n17, 157n37

marriage: in *The Bostonians*, 42–48; celibacy as alternative to, 14–17, 158n43; demographics and, 13, 20–21, 41–42; gayness and, 31; racial patterns in, 94–95, 182n67; sexuality and, 20; Warhol's discussion of, 31, 128–129, 193n37

"Marriage" (Moore), 66, 175n44

marriage bars: Boston marriage and, 42–48; employment barriers and, 15

Married Women's Property Acts, 14–15

Marshall, Paule, 83

Martin, Tony, 84

Martinez, José, 99–101, 103

Marvel, Ik, 11, 23

Marxism: Auden's engagement with, 109–110; Harlem Renaissance and, 85

masochism, 12

masturbation, celibacy and, 6, 12, 23–24, 31, 133, 193n50

Mattachine Society, 26

Maxwell, William, 84, 114

McCarran-Walter Act, 100–101, 188n46

McEwan, Ian, 142

McKay, Claude: career of, 181n37; citizenship problems for, 114–115; Father Divine and, 29, 83, 87–98, 179n10; moorishness and, 178n81

Melville, Herman, 11, 23, 170n61

"Memorial Day 1950" (O'Hara), 103

Mendelson, Edward, 189n57

Meriwether, Louise, 83

Merrill, James, 102

Merton, Thomas, 31

mesmerism, 167n29

Meyerowitz, Joanne, 91, 170n63

Miller, Cristanne, 71, 175n46

Miller, D. A., 161n87, 176n59, 182n66

Miller, Monica, 181n42

Minor Threat, 196n5

miscegenation, 97–98

modernism: celibacy and, 1, 6–9, 12, 16, 26, 79, 84; childhood and, 12; literature and, 6; modernity and, 9, 30–31, 65, 127, 140–141; queer theory and, 13; transgression and, 7–8

Modernism and the Harlem Renaissance (Baker), 83

Moe, Henry Allen, 64

Molesworth, Charles, 66

monasticism: asceticism and, 140; homosexuality and, 34–35, 171n63

Monk, Ray, 192n26

Monroe, Harriet, 70–71

Montherlant, Henry de, 9

Moon, Bucklin, 83

Moon, Michael, 131–132

Moore, George, 9

Moore, John Warner, 76–77, 177n71

Moore, Marianne, 11, 12, 26, 28–29, 54, 134; Braniff airlines and, 56–60, 172n6; celibate engagement in work of, 75–80; celibate temporality of, 60–66; depathologization of spinsterhood by, 70–75; literary legacy of, 59; living arrangements of, 73–74, 160n62; poetics of, 70–80; sexuality of, 66–70; television appearances by, 77

Moran, Rachel, 164n143

Morrissey, Paul, 126, 131, 195n81, 195n87

Morrow, Diane Batts, 95

Mosher Survey, 20

motherhood, celibacy vs., 7–8, 13, 16, 27

Mugwumps, 24

Murphy, Kevin, 24

muscular Christianity, 76–77, 177n71

"My Crow, Pluto—a Fantasy" (Moore), 79

My Hustler (Warhol), 130–134